The Use of

Marihuana

A Psychological and Physiological Inquiry

Contributors

Thomas F. Babor Associate in Psychiatry (Psychology), Harvard Medical School and Assistant Psychologist, McLean Hospital.

David J. Becker Assistant Clinical Professor of Medicine, Harvard Medical School.

Jerrold G. Bernstein Assistant Clinical Professor of Psychiatry, Harvard Medical School, Assistant Medical Director, Human Resource Institute of Boston, and Assistant Psychiatrist, McLean Hospital.

Gerald E. Kochansky Assistant Professor of Psychology in the Department of Psychiatry, Harvard Medical School.

Jack H. Mendelson Professor of Psychiatry, Harvard Medical School and Director, Alcohol and Drug Abuse Research Center, McLean Hospital.

Roger E. Meyer Associate Professor of Psychiatry, Harvard Medical School and Associate Director, Alcohol and Drug Abuse Research Center, McLean Hospital.

John O'Brien Staff Psychologist, Department of Psychiatry, St. Elizabeth's Hospital.

Vernon D. Patch Associate Professor of Psychiatry, Harvard Medical School and Director, City of Boston Drug Treatment Program.

Linda Porrino Formerly a Research Assistant in the Psychopharmacology Research Laboratory, Massachusetts Mental Health Center; presently a Graduate Student in the Department of Psychology, New York University.

Homer B. C. Reed, Jr. Associate Professor of Pediatrics (Psychology), Tufts-New England Medical Center.

A. Michael Rossi Formerly Associate Professor of Psychology in the Department of Psychiatry, Harvard Medical School; presently Lecturer on Psychology in the Department of Psychiatry, Harvard Medical School, Associate Attending Psychologist, McLean Hospital, and Associate Professor, Department of Psychology, Southeastern Massachusetts University.

Gerald Sagotsky Formerly Research Associate, Department of Psychiatry, Boston University Medical School; presently a Graduate Student in the Department of Psychology (Child Development), Stanford University.

Carl Salzman Assistant Professor of Psychiatry, Harvard Medical School and Co-Director, Psychopharmacology Research Laboratory, Massachusetts Mental Health Center.

The Use of

Marihuana

A Psychological and Physiological Inquiry

Edited by

Jack H. Mendelson

A. Michael Rossi

and Roger E. Meyer

PLENUM PRESS · NEW YORK AND LONDON

615.782
m52u

Library of Congress Cataloging in Publication Data

Mendelson, Jack Harold, 1929-
  The use of marihuana.

  Bibliography: p.
  1. Marihuana—Psychological aspects. 2. Marihuana—Physiological aspects.
I. Rossi, A. Michael, 1926-   joint author. II. Meyer, Roger E., joint author.
III. Title. [DNLM: 1. Cannabis. WM276 M537u]
BF209.M3M46   615'.782   74-17169
ISBN 0-306-30805-3

First Printing – October 1974
Second Printing – October 1975

© 1974 Plenum Press, New York
A Division of Plenum Publishing Corporation
227 West 17th Street, New York, N.Y. 10011

United Kingdom edition published by Plenum Press, London
A Division of Plenum Publishing Company, Ltd.
4a Lower John Street, London W1R 3PD, England

Contents

Chapter 7
GROUP BEHAVIOR: PROBLEM SOLVING EFFICIENCY .. 81
*Thomas F. Babor, A. Michael Rossi, Gerald Sagotsky, and
   Roger E. Meyer*

Chapter 8
MEMORY AND TIME ESTIMATION 89
A. Michael Rossi and John O'Brien

Chapter 12
PHYSIOLOGICAL ASSESSMENTS: CARDIOPULMONARY
   FUNCTION
Jerrold G. Bernstein, David Becker, Thomas F. Babor, and
   Jack H. Mendelson

Chapter 13
SLEEP-WAKEFULNESS BEHAVIOR
A. Michael Rossi, Jerrold G. Bernstein, and Jack H. Mendelson

1
Background and Experimental Design

Jack H. Mendelson, A. Michael Rossi, and Roger E. Meyer

Although marihuana has been used extensively as a drug in many parts of the world for over 1000 years (Walton 1938), objective data dealing with the pharmacology of this substance have, until recently, been scant. During the past four years there has been a striking increase in research activities in the United States as a consequence of the growing prevalence of marihuana use among the young and the need to define the public health implications of this phenomenon. Currently, casual or experimental use of marihuana is extensive within the community of young adults in the United States (King 1969; Manheimer *et al.* 1969). However, recent comprehensive and critical reviews of marihuana research revealed that all but three of the experimental studies of the effect of marihuana on human behavior have focused only upon the effects of acute doses of the drug (Hollister 1971; Synder 1971; Grinspoon 1971). While information about acute dose effects is essential, knowledge of effects of chronic use is probably more relevant to the questions posed by social and health agencies concerned with consequences of the increasing use of marihuana.

The situation appears to be analogous to the chronic use of alcohol and tobacco, wherein it is impossible to ascertain medical risk on the basis of acute administration of the substances in naive or infrequent users. Rather, the consequences of habitual and chronic use can only be observed in populations of heavy users over time, and by careful observation of the effects of repeat dose administration on persons who habitually use these substances. The analogy becomes more important with the rising number of marihuana smokers who indulge every day and who generally also experiment with a range of other substances.

Most studies of acute marihuana administration have reported relatively benign findings (Weil *et al.* 1968; Clark and Nakashima 1968; Melges *et al.* 1970*a*, 1970*b*; Hollister and Gillespie 1970; Clark *et al.* 1970; Waskow *et al.* 1970). However, some data some indicated that serious effects may occur in chronic users (Dally 1967). Moreover, consideration of the natural history of other forms of drug abuse (e.g., alcohol) suggests that when a large number of people use a drug, it is only among the heaviest users that one would expect to find severe psychopathology, adverse medical effects, and evidence (if any) of tolerance and physical dependence.

In the reported experimental studies of the effects of repeat dose administration (Williams *et al.* 1946; Mayor's Committee on Marihuana 1944; Siler *et al.* 1933), limitations in the design relative to dose control and precision of task measurements seriously compromised both the interpretation and generality of the research findings. One recent study of acute laboratory administration of marihuana cigarettes attempted to differentiate the smoking experiences of heavy and casual marihuana users. Meyer *et al.* (1971) found that casual users showed a greater degree of impairment on perceptual and psychomotor tasks than did heavy users. Heavy users experienced more profound subjective effects within 30 minutes of smoking, but were less intoxicated than casual users one hour later. The study of acute marihuana administration suggested that behavioral tolerance to the effects of marihuana may occur in man. Alternately, there may be a predominance of stimulant effects in the group of heavy users and depressant effects in the group of casual users which could be explained by tolerance to the depressant effects of the drug in habitual users.[1]

The present study focused on physiological, mood, and behavioral effects of repeat dose administration of marihuana under controlled ward conditions. Utilizing an experimental paradigm which has been used previously in self-administration studies with alcoholics (Mello and Mendelson 1970*a*; 1970*b*; 1972), the present research design compared the free choice

---

[1] Obviously, in the absence of measured blood levels of active principle (THC), such speculations cannot be confirmed or refuted. However, support for the possibility of tolerance to marihuana gains credibility from recently reported animal studies using tetrahydrocannabinol (McMillan *et al.* 1970).

marihuana consumption patterns of casual and heavy marihuana users in two separate but identical studies.

The following objectives of the research were to provide data concerning the following questions.

1. *Does chronic use of marihuana systematically affect motivation to engage in a variety of social and goal-directed activities?*

(A) Are there discernible differences in type, frequency, and intensity of specific activities (e.g. studying, initiating social contacts, personal grooming, etc.) when subjects chronically smoke marihuana? (B) Does work at an operant task for money reinforcement decline with repeated doses of marihuana? (C) Is the period of relaxation and passivity reported to follow marihuana intake associated with increased or decreased work output, i.e., are relaxation and passivity transient and reconstituting, or are they persistent?

2. *Are there consistent relationships between free-choice marihuana intake and antecedent and consequent mood states?*

(A) Are there characteristic mood states that precede marihuana intake (tenseness, boredom, etc.)? (B) Are there stable relationships between antecedent and consequent mood states (i.e., does marihuana intensify existing mood states or does it change them)? (C) Are there differences in such antecedent or consequent mood states between casual and heavy users of the drug?

3. *What are the relationships between free-choice marihuana intake and patterns of verbal interaction?*

(A) Are frequency and timing of marihuana smoking related to social structure within a group? (B) Do patterns and types of verbal interaction differ during periods when marihuana is and is not available? (C) Are there differences in verbal interaction patterns between casual and heavy users of the drug?

4. *What are the relationships between free-choice chronic marihuana intake and performance on psychological tasks which assess functions such as problem solving and risk taking, memory, time estimation, and cognitive function?*

(A) Does free-choice marihuana intake lead to an improvement or impairment of performance? (B) Do subjects consistently smoke marihuana before engaging in skilled tests or do they avoid marihuana at those times? (C) Are there differences between casual and heavy users either in their use of marihuana in relation to task performance or in the effect of marihuana on performance?

5. *Are there characteristic differences in marihuana smoking patterns between casual and heavy users, and are there identifiable parameters related to the different patterns?*

(A) Are individual patterns of use (temporal spacing, frequency, mode of use) stable or fluctuating? (B) Are there differences in these patterns between casual and heavy users beyond frequency of intake alone? (C) Do any initial differences that may exist between casual and heavy users change with self-determined repeat dose administration?

6. *Are physiological and biochemical changes associated with repeated doses of marihuana?*

(A) Do casual users differ from heavy users with respect to cardiovascular and pulmonary function? (B) Are there dose and dose–time relationships between marihuana intake and physiological effects? (C) Is there any adaptation of physiological and biochemical factors altered by marihuana intake which would reflect acute or chronic tolerance? (D) Are there any body functions uniquely sensitive to the acute and/or chronic effects of marihuana?

1. SETTING

The research was carried out in the Department of Psychiatry at Boston City Hospital. Subjects lived on a closed hospital research ward for 31 days, under living conditions that were made as comfortable as possible, consistent with security and experimental requirements.

The research ward consisted of ten individual subject bedrooms, a nursing station, kitchen, lavatory, shower room, dining room, lounge, recreation room, examination room, and staff offices. The ward was comfortably furnished and contained a television set, radio, phonograph, ping pong table, card table, and an assortment of recreational materials. A large open lawn area was available to subjects for outdoor recreational activities, including volleyball, touch football, and soccer. Subjects were not allowed visitors or to receive incoming telephone calls, but they were allowed to write and receive letters and to make telephone calls under restricted conditions.

2. RESEARCH PARADIGM

Two separate but identical studies were conducted with two groups of subjects. One group of ten subjects, defined as casual users, had at least a one-year history of marihuana use, and were currently averaging eight smoking sessions per month. The other group of ten subjects, defined as heavy users, had a two-to-nine-year history of marihuana use and were currently averaging 33 smoking sessions per month. Two groups of subjects with quantitatively distinct prior marihuana use histories were employed in order to evaluate the influence of past use on the acute and short-term cumulative effects of repeat dose marihuana administration. A full description of subjects is presented in Chapter 2.

Both studies were divided into three periods: A five-day *pre-drug* period in which subjects did not have access to marihuana; a 21-day drug period, from the sixth to the twenty-sixth day of each study, when subjects were permitted to purchase and smoke marihuana cigarettes on a free choice basis; and a five-day *post-drug* period without access to marihuana. On the last day of the drug period (study day 26) subjects were required to smoke one marihuana cigarette before a series of assessments of cognitive function were made. The method by which subjects could purchase marihuana and the amount and temporal distribution of their marihuana consumption are described in Chapter 3.

The assessments carried out during the study included the following: (1) Work contingent operant acquisition and free-choice marihuana consumption patterns; (2) mood states; (3) individual and group behavior; (4) clinical psychiatric evaluations; (5) psychomotor skills;[2] (6) physiological functions; (7) psychological functions. Figures 1.1–1.3 present the scheduled assessments. Times of assessments for vital signs, vital capacity, weight, memory function, time estimation, psychomotor performance, mood assessment, task-oriented group discussion, sleep-wakefulness observations, electrocardiograms, and recording of operant data are shown in Figure 1.1. Special assessments related to marihuana smoking which were made during the drug period are shown in Figure 1.2. Figure 1.3 presents a series of tests and assessments which were carried out at varying periods during the study.

A detailed description of the procedures and techniques employed for each assessment is included along with the discussion of results presented in following chapters.

All assessments, as far as possible, were scheduled so as not to interfere with the operant task or free choice marihuana smoking. Certain specific evaluations (Figure 1.2) were made in close temporal contiguity with marihuana use. This technique permitted differentiation of acute and repeat dose effects of the drug.

Subjects had an operant manipulandum available at all times (see Chapter 3) with which they could earn reinforcement points. The points

---

[2] An enclosed, photoelectric shooting gallery was used in assessments of psychomotor skills. Analyses of data obtained in these assessments failed to disclose consistent trends in either intra- or interindividual scores. The large amount of variability in the data indicated that the scoring procedures were unreliable, so further discussion of results of this assessment is omitted in this book.

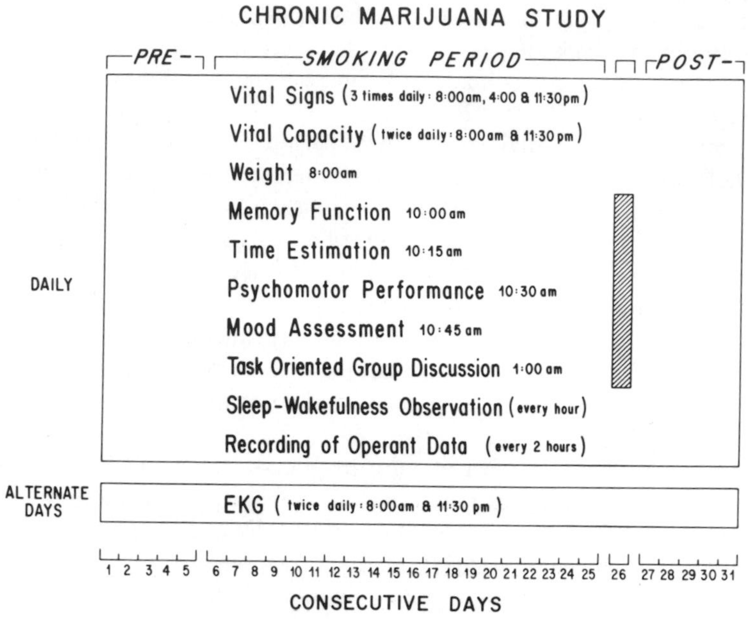

CHRONIC MARIJUANA STUDY

Figure 1.1. Regular assessments made daily throughout study.

could be used to purchase tobacco cigarettes during all periods of the study, or marihuana cigarettes during the 21-day smoking period. Points could also be accumulated for conversion into money at the end of the study. In addition to being paid for cumulative reinforcement points, subjects also received payment for accurate performance on certain tasks, and for cooperation during other assessments. Individual subject assessments required about three and one-half hours per day. During the remaining hours of the day, subjects were free to do as they wished within the research ward and adjacent outdoor lawn area.

Subjects were fully informed of the nature and conditions of the study at the outset. They had the option to terminate their participation at any time, with the understanding that they could then not be paid for their participation. This condition was decided upon in order to motivate subjects to remain throughout the study period.

Marihuana is the common name applied to the weed *Cannabis sativa.* This weed grows wild or can be readily cultivated in most climates. The potency of the various cannabis preparations in use varies in relation to climate and soil conditions where the plant is grown. Potency is also determined by the portion of the plant utilized in making a given preparation,

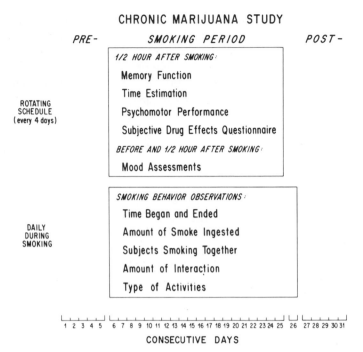

Figure 1.2. Special assessments made only during smoking period.

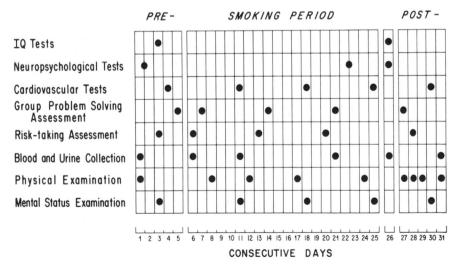

Figure 1.3. Tests and assessments made at various periods during study.

as well as by the presence of various inert substances that are commonly mixed with marihuana. Several biologically active substances termed *cannabinoids* are synthesized by the growing cannabis plant. These substances include cannabinol, cannabidiol, cannavionic acid, and several isomers of tetrahydrocannabinol. The isomer which appears to be responsible for the characteristic psychological and behavioral effect of marihuana is delta 9 tetrahydrocannabinol (delta 9 THC).

Marihuana cigarettes which could be purchased and smoked during the 21-day drug period were obtained from the National Institute of Mental Health in a lot standard dosage form. The cigarettes were machine-rolled in order to ensure maximal standardization and equivalent dosage and "draw" characteristics. Each cigarette contained approximately one gram of marihuana with a delta 9 THC content of 1.8–2.3% and less than 0.1% delta 8 THC, 0.1% cannabinol, and 0.1% cannabidiol (as assayed by the National Institute of Mental Health). This contrasts with the quality of marihuana usually available on the street, which is generally acknowledged to contain less than 1.0% delta 9 THC.

Subjects were permitted to purchase and smoke marihuana cigarettes whenever they chose during the drug period, with two conditions: (1) All smoking of marihuana was to be done under the observation of a staff member; (2) the unsmoked portion of the cigarette was to be returned to the staff upon completion of smoking. These conditions were established both to ensure security and to permit accurate recording of observations relating to smoking behavior.[3]

In the chapters which follow, detailed descriptions are presented for the findings of the biological, behavioral, and social studies which were carried out within the general context of this experiment. A discussion of the significance of these findings in relation to the work of other investigators is also presented. In the final chapter, we have summarized these data and have attempted to answer the questions which were posed at the beginning of this report.

---

[3] During the latter part of the second study, some subjects devised a technique that enabled them to occasionally "snip" a small portion of marihuana from the cigarettes they were smoking. The intent was to save this pilfered marihuana for smoking during the five-day post-drug period. The technique was discovered and counteracted during the drug period, and a search conducted on the unit during the second day of the post-drug period uncovered a total of approximately two grams of marihuana in subjects' possession.

The search also uncovered a small portion of hashish that one subject had brought into the unit at the start of the study. During an interview conducted at the end of the study, it was determined that most heavy user subjects had smoked some marihuana during the post-drug period, but the amounts smoked averaged less than one gram per subject. The subject with the hashish stated that he had smoked it four times during the drug period, and two or three times during the post-drug period. The amounts smoked surreptitiously are considered to be too minor to affect any of the results of this research.

2
The Subjects

Roger E. Meyer, Vernon D. Patch,
Jerrold G. Bernstein, and A. Michael Rossi

In the past fifty years, American society and those who interpret it have changed their view of marihuana use concurrent with changes in the social patterns of use and in the law. The use of alcohol was more generally popular than the use of marihuana, even during Prohibition. Prior to the passage of the Marihuana Tax Act of 1937, cannabis smoking was not universal, but was prevalent among lower socioeconomic groups in particular geographic and cultural enclaves. From the enactment of the federal law against possession of marihuana (1937) until the middle of the last decade, marihuana use was limited primarily to persons on the lower socioeconomic fringes of this society, and to musicians.

Since the mid-sixties, a number of surveys (Manheimer *et al.* 1969; McGlothlin *et al.* 1970; Walters *et al.* 1972; American Institute of Public Opinion 1972) document the spread of marihuana use to youth of all social classes, with the most dramatic increase occurring among young people in college. The early surveys documenting this phenomenon compared the social and psychological characteristics of users and nonusers. As the incidence of use increased, however, and the surveys became more sophisticated, it became clear that marihuana smoking in itself could no longer be considered a measure of deviance. As the behavior became common in certain age groups, the *extent* of use was found to correlate with the degree of manifest psychopathology among the users. The problem for survey research investigation has now focused upon defining the *extent* of use which will differentiate the "problem marihuana smoker" from the "social user."

The Marihuana Commission (Shafer Commission) recently defined four discrete categories which are appropriate to the problem (National Commission on Marihuana and Drug Abuse 1972*a,b*):

1. *"Frequency of use"* refers to the total number of marihuana experiences.
2. *"Intensity of use"* refers to the frequency of use within a given time period.
3. *"Amount of use"* refers to the amount of marihuana (THC content or number of cigarettes) used during a given time period or at a single sitting.
4. *"Duration of use"* refers to the length of time one has used the drug since the first experience.

In the Shafer Commission review of surveys conducted through 1971, no single investigation adequately accounted for the use patterns of respondents in all four categories. Moreover, even when smoking patterns are reasonably well quantified, there is little data which would differentiate social use from problem smoking. This is of no small importance. Quantification without some differentiation of associated consequences would be of methodological significance, but *would be of little practical importance in the definition of public health or social implications.*

McGlothlin (1972) recently compared usage patterns in the West with traditional and current practices in Eastern countries. He observed that the *maximum* daily consumption of ten cigarettes, or 50 mg of THC, for current heavy smokers in the United States is equivalent to the *average* intake of daily users in other countries, and only 25% (or less) of the *maximum* consumed in these other countries.

It is McGlothlin's contention that the usage pattern in the United States is characterized by a disproportionate percentage of infrequent users of small amounts of cannabis (because of the recency and popularity of the fad). He has also predicted that many of these experimenters and casual users will discontinue the use of marihuana; and that the percentage and actual number of daily users will increase. Moreover, the average daily consumption of marihuana by daily users in the United States may approach the heavy users' pattern in other countries, as a function of pharmacological tolerance.

The findings of a number of surveys (McGlothlin *et al.* 1970; Mizner *et al.* 1970; Lipp 1971) tend to support the notion that most persons who experiment with marihuana do not indulge beyond the initial period of experimentation. Changes in the intensity and amount of use among frequent users over time (in the United States) have not been examined because of the relative recency of the phenomenon. Experience in the area of alcohol research suggests that there are different biological, psychological, and social concomitants and consequences of alcohol use in problem drinkers which differentiates them from social drinkers (Mendelson and Stein 1966). While the characteristics of the problem marihuana user have not yet been defined, it may be possible to identify potentially harmful patterns of smoking among those who use it daily and to differentiate these from persons who smoke on a more casual basis.

In previous work (Mirin *et al.* 1971), one of the authors (Meyer) was involved in a study comparing 12 heavy and 12 casual users of marihuana. These subjects were selected from questionnaire data relative to the frequency, duration, and current intensity of marihuana use in a volunteer population of 66 subjects.

The heavy users (persons smoking 20–30 times a month) demonstrated poor social and work adjustment and a history of multiple drug use that was not characteristic of casual users (persons using the drug one to four times a month). The correlation of polydrug use with the intensity and frequency of marihuana smoking has been confirmed by other observers (Goldstein *et al.* 1970; G. M. Smith 1970). In the previous work (Mirin *et al.* 1971) heavy and casual users did not differ significantly in their duration of use. There were no data on the amount of use at a single smoking session. Because the laboratory administration of marihuana to these subjects occurred at weekly intervals on three separate occasions (generally on a week night or Saturday), the participants could continue to work or remain at school in their usual manner.

In the present study, attempts were made to recruit subjects whose questionnaire data approximated the characteristics of heavy and casual users defined in the earlier work. It was expected that the conditions of the research, requiring hospitalization for a period of 31 days, could be met without interfering with the requirements of school or work by recruiting subjects on summer holiday. However, the process of contract negotiations (necessary to support the project) delayed the start of the research until mid-September. Thus, the subject population was drawn largely from unemployed, itinerant young men whose smoking and drug use patterns did not replicate those of the heavy and casual users in the earlier study. The present group of subjects may also represent a skewed population, relative to the total population of marihuana smokers in their age group.

1.   RECRUITMENT OF SUBJECTS

Volunteers were located by placing classified advertisements on two occasions in Boston's two "underground" newspapers, *The Phoenix* and *Boston*

After Dark. Approximately 380 telephone call inquiries were received in response to these advertisements, and 228 persons followed up the telephone inquiry and came to the Department of Psychiatry at Boston City Hospital to complete a Drug Use Questionnaire.

The 58 subjects who most closely met the criteria of casual and heavy users were asked to have an interview with a psychiatrist. Heavy users were defined as males with a two-to-nine-year history of marihuana use, who smoked daily for at least one year prior to the study. Casual users were defined as males with a current smoking pattern of at least one year's duration of one to four smoking sessions per month. The amount of use per session was not documented.

In the selection of subjects, preference was given in both groups to those subjects with minimal additional experience with other drugs of abuse, although it was recognized that a history of multiple drug use might be found for many subjects. On the basis of drug use information, 27 heavy users and 31 casual users were selected for interviewing by the project psychiatrist. Persons with a history of neurological disease (including seizure disorders), hepatic, renal, pulmonary, cardiac, gastrointestinal, genitourinary, and nutritional disorders were excluded from the study, and persons with a past history of psychotic illness were also excluded from the sample.[1]

Ten heavy users and ten casual users whose availability for the study period was confirmed were selected. The ten casual users were studied in an initial 31-day period; the ten heavy users were studied in a second 31-day period.

As confirmation of the residential mobility of the population, few of the heavy users recruited prior to the commencement of the research with the casual users remained in the area long enough to begin their participation in the second study. Selection of additional subjects for the heavy user group thus continued up to the day research begun with this group.

2. CHARACTERISTICS OF THE SUBJECT GROUPS

The characteristics of both groups of subjects are described in Tables 2.1–2.6. As described above, the conditions of the research design, including a 31-day period of hospitalization without outside contact (except for correspondence), discouraged potential volunteers who were married or involved in full-time work or school. Thus, subjects described as casual

---

[1] One volunteer with a history of epilepsy, three with a history of serious emotional disorder, and one who was borderline retarded were excluded during the selection process.

users in the present study more closely approximate the heavy users studied previously with regard to frequency of marihuana use, tendency toward multiple drug use, and being unmarried and unemployed. In contrast to the earlier study in which casual and heavy users differed along several parameters, the groups in the present study appeared to differ primarily in quantitative patterns of marihuana and other drug use.

Personal data and family histories of casual users are described in Table 2.1. The subjects in this group had a mean age of 24, with a mean I.Q. of 122.2, nearly 2.6 years of completed college work, and a rather erratic job history, consistent with an itinerant life style. The usual employment of all subjects, with the exception of subjects 6C and 10C, was considerably below expected levels of ability, based upon I.Q. Subjects shared a preference for brief periods of employment at unskilled jobs. All casual users came from intact families, with the exception of subject 6C, whose mother died when he was 14 years old. Families' socioeconomic status was generally middle to upper middle class. Five of the subjects reported some family history of alcohol or drug abuse.

Personal data and family histories of the heavy user group are described in Table 2.2. The mean age of this group was 22, with a mean I.Q. of 117.4, and 2.3 years of completed college. Here again the work pattern was that of underachievement.[2] When Table 2.1 and Table 2.2 are compared, the two groups of subjects appear to be more alike than different. Heavy users, however, generally came from lower middle class families, and four of the subjects came from broken homes. Of special interest is a significant family history of drug or alcohol abuse for eight of the ten heavy users, with several family members involved in many cases. Several surveys (Smart 1970; Lavenhar 1971) have demonstrated a correlation between parental drug use and the use of marihuana among their offspring. The data here suggest that heavy users of marihuana may come from families in which alcohol or drug abuse has been a problem for some family members.

How do the background data obtained on these subjects compare with background data obtained on marihuana users in other studies? Most recent surveys (Abelson et al. 1972; Bogg et al. 1969; Josephson et al. 1971) have suggested that youthful users of marihuana tend to come from middle, upper middle, and upper class families, with a disproportionately large number of Jewish youth involved in marihuana smoking. Our subjects do not constitute a representative sample of the total youth adult male popu-

---

[2] With the information obtained in this study it is not possible to either attribute or refute an etiological role or marihuana use in the apparent underachievement suggested by the work histories in both groups. It was mentioned above that the 31-day hospitalization required for participation tended to select out potential subjects who were either employed or in school.

Table 2.1

Personal Data and Family History: *Casual Users*

	Subject number										Mean
	1C	2C	3Cᵃ	4C	5C	6C	7C	8C	9C	10C	
Age	28	22	31	21	22	27	24	21	21	23	24
I.Q.	139	121	112	125	118	120	127	113	119	128	122.2
Years of college	4	3	0	1½	3	4	4	1	1	4 (grad)	2.55
Usual employment	Odd jobs	Newspaper writer	Actor, postal employee	Lab asst.	Newspaper layout	Financial analyst	Carpenter's apprentice	Taxi driver	Newspaper hawker	Office work (Publ. co.)	—
Number of jobs in past 3 years	3	3	4	5	4	1	3	7	5	4	3.9
Longest period on one job, months	—	4	48	6	4	18	12	3	3	3	10.4
Military status	1-Yᵇ	2-S deferment	Refused induction	Has not been drafted	2-S deferment	Army 2 yr, sgt., hon. dis.	2-S deferment	1-Yᵇ	Has not been drafted	2-S deferment	—

	Family socio-economic status	Religious background	Parents' marital status	Number of siblings[b,c]	Position in sibship	Family members' problem substance use[c,d]
	II	Jewish	Married	None	—	None
	I	Catholic	Married	1 Br; 1 Si	Youngest	None
	IV	Protestant (Episcopalian)	Married	4 Si	2nd Youngest	GF-A; 2 Si-M
	II	Catholic	Married	1 Si	Oldest	None
	II	Catholic	Married	4 Br; 1 Si	2nd Oldest	2 Br-M
	II	Catholic	Mother died when subject age 14	3 Br; 2 Si; 3 StepBr	Youngest	Fa-A
	II	Catholic	Married	2 Si	Oldest	None
	II	Protestant	Married	1 Br	Youngest	Br(22)-M
	II	Catholic	Married	4 Br; 1 Si	2nd Oldest	None
	III	Catholic	Married	1 Br	Youngest	Br(25)-M, H
Total	I: 1; II: 7 III: 1, IV: 1	1 Jewish, 7 Catholic, 2 Protestant	All married	2.6 ± 1.95 (not counting stepBr)	4 youngest, 1 2nd youngest, 2 2nd oldest, 2 oldest, 1 only child	—

[a] Subject 3C was the only Black subject in the study.
[b] Letter from psychiatrist.
[c] Fa = father; Mo = mother; Br = brother; Si = sister; GF = grandfather; M = marihuana; H = hallucinogens; A = alcohol.
[d] Number in parentheses indicates age of sibling.

Table 2.2

Personal Data and Family History: Heavy Users

					Subject number						
	1H	2H	3H	4H	5H	6H	7H	8H	9H	10H	Mean
Age	23	22	22	23	22	22	21	23	21	21	22
I.Q.	118	130	117	120	111	110	111	108	121	128	117.4
Years of college	4	4 (grad)	2	4 (grad)	½	0	0	4	1½	3	2.3
Usual employment	House-painter; student	Parking lot attendant	Factory worker; carpenter	Radio announcer	Auditing clerk	Garment factory worker	Truck driver	Musician	Shoe salesman Flagpole installer	Park ranger student	—
Number of jobs in past 3 years	1	3	6	5	4	2	3	4	5	2	3.5
Longest period on one job, months	48 part-time	13	12	6	18	11	30	24	24	3	18.9
Military status	1-Yᵃ	1-Yᵃ	Refused induction	C.O.	Army 2 yr, hon. dis.	1-Y	1-Y	Army 2 yr, hon. dis.	Lottery no. exemption	2-S	—

Family socio-economic status	III	III	IV	III	III	IV	V	II	III	IV	II: 1, III: 5 IV: 3, V: 1
Religious background	Protestant (Baptist)	Jewish	Mormon	Catholic	Greek Orthodox	Catholic	Protestant (Methodist)	Jewish	Catholic	Catholic	2 Jewish, 4 Catholic, 4 Other
Parents' marital status	Married	Divorced when subject age 12	Divorced when subject age 10	Married	Married	Divorced when subject age 10	Married	Married	Separated when subject age 18	Married	6 married, 3 divorced, 1 separated
Number of siblings[b]	2 Br; 2 Si	2 Si	1 Br; 3 Si	2 Br; 3 Si	2 Br	2 Br; 1 Si	1 Si	None	3 Br; 5 Si	1 Br; 1 Si	3.1
Position in sibship[b]	2nd Oldest	Middle	Youngest	2nd Youngest	Middle	2nd Oldest	Oldest	—	2nd Oldest	Middle	1 youngest 1 2nd youngest 2 middle 3 2nd oldest 1 oldest 1 only child
Family members' problem substance use[b,c]	Fa-A; Br(21)	Si(23)-M, H Si(16)-M	None	Br(20) + Si(28, 25)-M; Br(18) + Si(27)-M	Br(24)-M, H; Br(17)-M	2 Un-A; Br(21, 16)-M	Si(16)-M, B	—	Fa-A; Si(19, 15, 14)-M; Br(18, 12)-M	Mo, Fa-Heavy A; Br(17)-M	—

[a] Letter from psychiatrist.
[b] Fa = father; Mo = mother; Br = brother; Si = sister; Un = uncle; M = marihuana; B = barbiturates; H = hallucinogens; A = alcohol.
[c] Number in parentheses indicates age of sibling.

lation of Boston, so that correlations of marihuana use with specific demographic characteristics (as social class, religion, etc.) would not be meaningful. Nevertheless, the data in our heavy user group suggest that some of the sons of the blue collar working class appear to be involved in the current behavioral epidemic of cannabis smoking.

Table 2.3 describes patterns of substance use for casual users of marihuana. The first substance used was generally alcohol, with the mean starting age at 16.6 years, followed by marihuana at 18.5 amphetamines at 19.7, and hallucinogens at 21.3. Alcohol and illicit drug use tended to be sparse and nonhabitual. Six of the subjects had used hallucinogens less than ten times, and only four subjects used more than ten times.

Table 2.4 presents the substance use patterns of the heavy users. Alcohol use began at a mean age of 15.3, marihuana at 17.0, hallucinogens at 18.4, and amphetamines at 19.0. Comparison of data from Tables 2.3 and 2.4 shows that alcohol use was similar in the two groups, but the use of hallucinogens was significantly higher among the heavy marihuana users. Only one of the ten heavy user subjects had used hallucinogens less than ten times; four used them more than ten times; two more than 50 times; and three greater than 100 times. One subject also reported a history of heroin addiction, but was currently in remission. Six of the heavy users reported a history of intermittent cocaine use, but only three of the casual users had a similar history. The multiple and heavy drug use patterns among the heavy users is consistent with data obtained in studies by other investigators (Mirin *et al.* 1971; Goldstein *et al.* 1970; Smith 1970).

The sequence of substance use, where alcohol antedates marihuana use, is consistent with surveys of high school students (Bogg *et al.* 1969) and college students (Blum *et al.* 1969), where tobacco smoking and alcohol drinking correlated with and antedated marihuana use. It appears that the earlier involvement with hallucinogens by the heavy users may be consistent with a rapid progression into a pattern of heavy marihuana and multiple drug use for these subjects.

The marihuana use histories of the casual users are presented in Table 2.5; that of the heavy users in Table 2.6. Of interest is the fact that only one heavy user reported that his response to marihuana was extremely pleasant on the first occasion. Seven heavy users reported that their most recent smoking session was extremely pleasant. This is in contrast to four casual users, who reported that marihuana use was extremely pleasant on the first occasion, with only three finding it extremely pleasant on the most recent one. These data are remarkably similar to data which are available in the literature on alcohol. It has been found that the initial drinking experience of the alcohol does not necessarily correspond with the subsequent ingestions that produce a very pleasant response to alcohol. Also of interest is the finding that nine of the ten heavy users report feeling relaxed when smoking marihuana, while only three of the casual users report feeling relaxed, and one reported feeling more anxious with marihuana.[3]

Tart (1971) has emphasized changes in sense perception, understanding positive emotion, and sense of identity as the principal subjective effects of the marihuana experience. While both groups of subjects in the present study reported altered perception and euphoria as part of the subjective state, the retrospectively perceived "relaxation" reported by nine out of ten heavy users suggests that this effect may be more important in differentiating motivation for heavy versus casual use.

The mean frequency of cannabis use per month clearly differentiates between the two groups: 33 times per month among the heavy users and 7.7 times per month among the casual users. However, there is a wide variation in the intensity of smoking in the two groups. The similarity in duration of smoking in the two groups suggests that the greater intensity of use among the heavy users was not a function of exposure for a longer period of time. The patterns suggest daily use by the heavy users and weekend use by the casual users. Both frequencies exceed the norm as defined in various high school and college surveys. The Shafer Commission reported that 75–85% of high school and 50% of college youth smoke less than once per week. Among the college groups, less than 10% use marihuana as often as once per day. Moreover, Goode is quoted in this report that "progression . . . culminating in daily use, particularly use which involves being high all one's working hours is extremely atypical . . . casual and episodic use is the rule" (National Commission on Marihuana and Drug Abuse 1972*b*, p. 327).

Neither group of subjects evinced a set of personality characteristics which could be related to the pattern or frequency of marihuana smoking. Data were obtained on the MMPI and the Edwards Personal Preference Scale but these data did not differentiate between the groups, nor did it suggest a common uniqueness to our subject population. Personality factors do not appear to account for marihuana use or the extent of use in any characteristic way. In comparison to casual users, the past histories of heavy users included more frequent and intensive use of marihuana (as a function of our selection process), a greater degree of involvement with other illicit substances (particularly hallucinogenic drugs), and a greater likelihood of emerging from a broken family and/or a family with a history of substance abuse.

[3] It is of interest that of the three casual users who retrospectively reported relaxation while smoking marihuana, two were the heaviest users of marihuana (among the casual users) during the study (see Chapter 3). Their marihuana use patterns during the study were similar to that of the heavy users.

Table 2.3

Substance Use: Casual Users

Subject number	Alcohol		Hallucinogens		Amphetamines		Other drug use, number of times
	Age first used	Subsequent use	Age first used	Subsequent use, number of times	Age first used	Subsequent use, number of times	
1C	21	Rare–light	25	<10	—	—	—
2C	14	Rare–light	19	<10	20	<10	—
3C	12	Occasional–light	28	<10	—	—	Cocaine, 3
4C	16	Rare–light	18	>50	19	<10	Barbiturates, 2–3
5C	16	Rare–light	20	<10	20	<10	—
6C	21	Occasional–light	24	<10	—	—	—
7C	16	Occasional–light	21	<10	20	<10	Opium smoked, 1
8C	16	Rare–light	18	<50	18	>10	Cocaine, 1; barbiturates, 2–3
9C	13	Rare–light	19	>10	20	<10	Heroin snorted, cocaine, 2–3
10C	21	Occasional–light	21	>10	21	<10	—
Mean	16.6	Rare–light: 6 Occasional–light: 4	21.3	<10: 6 >10: 2 >50: 2	19.7	0: 3 <10: 6 >10: 1	
S.D.	3.34		3.33		0.95		

Table 2.4
Substance Use: Heavy Users

Subject number	Alcohol		Hallucinogens		Amphetamines		Other drug use, number of times
	Age first used	Subsequent use	Age first used	Subsequent use, number of times	Age first used	Subsequent use, number of times	
1H	16	Frequent–moderate	20	>100	20	>50	Cocaine, 1–2
2H	17	Rare–light	18	>10	19	>10	Cocaine, 2; barbiturates, 3
3H	15	Rare–light	18	>50	17	>10	Cocaine, 2
4H	16	Rare–light	—	<10	—	>10	Barbiturates, 1
5H	14	Rare–light	21	>10	—	—	—
6H	14	Occasional–moderate	18	>50	—	—	Cocaine, 4; barbiturates, 6; heroin i.v. (3 bags/day for 8 mo); no heroin for past 13 mo
7H	16	Rare–light	18	>100	18	>100	Cocaine, 2
8H	15	Rare–light	16	>100	21	>25	—
9H	15	Rare–light	18	>10	—	1	Cocaine, 5; barbiturates, 4; heroin snorted, 1
10H	15	Rare–light	19	>10	—	2–3	Opium smoked, 2
Mean	15.3	Rare–light: 8 Frequent–moderate: 1 Occasional–moderate: 1	18.44	<10: 1 >10: 4 >50: 2 >100: 3	19.0	0: 2 <10: 2 >10: 3 >25: 1 >50: 1 >100: 1	
S.D.	0.95		1.42		1.58		

Table 2.5

Marihuana Use: Casual Users

Subject number	Age first used	Reaction to first use	Total years of use	Current smoking sessions, no./mo.	Usual affective response to smoking marihuana[a]		Altered perception	When last smoked	Reaction to last smoking session
					Euphoria	Anxiety			
1C	22	Mildly pleasant	6	5	E	R	Increase	5 days	Mildly pleasant
2C	16	Extremely pleasant	6	5	E	0	Increase	1 day	Extremely pleasant
3C	14	Mildly pleasant	17	15	0	R	None	7 days	Extremely pleasant
4C	18	Neutral	3	5	0	0	Increase + decrease	1 day	Mildly pleasant
5C	18	Mildly pleasant	4	5	E + D	0	Increase	1 day	Mildly pleasant
6C	22	Extremely pleasant	5	12	E	0	Increase	5 days	Mildly pleasant
7C	21	Mildly pleasant	3	3	E	0	Decrease	7 days	Extremely pleasant
8C	18	Extremely pleasant	3	10	E	0	Decrease	1 day	Mildly pleasant
9C	17	Neutral	4	10	0	R	Decrease + increase	1 day	Mildly pleasant
10C	19	Extremely pleasant	4	7	E	A	Decrease	10 days	Neutral
Mean	18.5		5.5	7.7			Increase 3.9		
S.D.	2.59		4.20	3.86			Decrease 3.35		

[a] E = Euphoria; D = dysphoria; R = relaxation; A = anxiety.

Table 2.6

Marihuana Use: Heavy Users

Subject number	Age first used	Reaction to first use	Total years of use	Current smoking sessions, no./mo.	Usual affective response to smoking marihuana		Altered perception	When last smoked	Reaction to last smoking session
					Euphoria	Anxiety			
1H	19	Mildly pleasant	4	30	E	R	Increase	1 day	Extremely pleasant
2H	18	Neutral	4	25	0	R	Increase	2 days	Mildly pleasant
3H	17	Mildly pleasant	5	50	E	R	Increase	3 days	Mildly pleasant
4H	18	Neutral	5	30	E	R	None	3 days	Mildly pleasant
5H	17	Extremely pleasant	5	75	E	R	None	0 days	Extremely pleasant
6H	17	Mildly pleasant	5	10	E	R	Increase + decrease	5 days	Extremely pleasant
7H	17	Mildly pleasant	4	40	0	R	Increase + decrease	3 days	Extremely pleasant
8H	12	Mildly pleasant	9	25	E	R	Increase + decrease	0 days	Extremely pleasant
9H	16	Neutral	5	25	E	R	Increase	0 days	Extremely pleasant
10H	19	Mildly pleasant	2	20	0	—	Increase	0 days	Extremely pleasant
Mean	17.0		4.8	33.0				1.7	
S.D.	2		1.75	18.29				1.77	

[a] E = Euphoria; R = relaxation.

On admission to the research ward, the heavy users (as a group) appeared to be more depressed in mood that the casual users, according to the clinical impression of the admitting psychiatrist. During the clinical interview, two of the heavy users showed some deficit in abstracting ability, but no overt psychotic symptomatology. These two subjects had frequent "blank stares" suggestive of lapses in attention. Two of the three casual users who smoked most heavily during the study were initially felt to be the most neurotic subjects in the group; while the third subject was felt to be very well adjusted (and turned out to be one of the best liked subjects in the group).

Many readers may wonder about the apparent "underachievement" suggested by the work histories in both groups of users in the present study. It is not possible to attribute or refute an etiological role for marihuana use in this adjustment, based upon the information reported by the subjects. Motivation is obviously a complex phenomenon related to early life experiences, peer and adult approval, and stability of identity and role models. It is always tempting to place great stock in retrospective accounts of subjects' experiences (including intoxications), and to build hypothetical relationships from these accounts. However, the unique advantage of the design used in the present study is that it allows one to explore the intoxication first hand. By the same token, background information described in the present chapter is useful in placing the experimental data into an appropriate context. The best formulation should emerge from a mixture of the two.

3

Experimental Analysis of Marihuana Acquisition and Use

A. Michael Rossi, Jack H. Mendelson, and Roger E. Meyer

The National Commission on Marihuana and Drug Abuse (1972) noted that one of the primary concerns of society regarding marihuana use is its alleged effect in reducing both motivation for achievement and interest in conventional goals. Previous researchers have described the severity of this effect as ranging from a transient, mild reduction in motivation during acute intoxication to a chronic condition that has been termed the "amotivational syndrome." This syndrome has been defined as a loss of interest in all activities (except marihuana acquisition and use), lethargy, amorality, instability, and social and personal deterioration (McGlothlin and West 1968; Allen and West 1968). Demonstration of such a chronic effect occurring as a sequelae to habitual marihuana use is a legitimate source of public concern, since impaired motivation may prove a serious handicap in our achievement-oriented, competitive society.

Evidence of marihuana-induced motivational change has been incon-
clusive, and the existence of such an effect has yet to be widely accepted
within the scientific community. Belief in this effect is apparently based
upon the fact that the highest incidence of cannabis use occurs in groups
that are among the least economically productive (National Commission
on Marihuana and Drug Abuse 1972; Grinspoon 1971). The prohibitions
against interpreting a statistical correlation as confirmation of a cause–effect relationship are too well known to belabor here. However, the finding
of some correlation is often the first indication that a cause–effect relationship may exist and stimulates controlled laboratory research designed to
investigate the relationship more fully.

Reliable research evidence of a motivational change associated with
marihuana use is difficult to obtain, partly because of the few controlled
studies that have been attempted in this area, and partly because of the
inherent problems in assessing motivational changes. Most of the research
has focused on the acute effects of the drug on general motivational indices,
such as spontaneous or goal-directed activity levels. The results of these
studies have been inconsistent when extrapolated and applied to the
question of motivational change as a sequelae to repeated use of the drug.
For example, some authors have reported hypermotility to follow
marihuana use (Allentuck and Bowman 1942; Walton 1938); other authors
have reported hypomotility to occur (Oursler 1968); and still others have
reported both hypo and hypermotility to occur as a function of dose (Barry
and Kubena 1969). Research employing natural or synthetic tetrahydrocannabinols with animal subjects have produced similarly equivocal results regarding the effects of these compounds on spontaneous or goal-directed
activity (Valle *et al.* 1966; Dagirmanjian and Boyd 1962, Garriott *et al.*
1967; Boyd *et al.* 1963; Garattini 1965).

Grinspoon (1971) suggests that differences in research results may be
related to differences in experimental settings. He also suggests that the hypomotility of marihuana-intoxicated subjects may be more indicative of
the effect of the drug on the motor system than on motivation. That is,
while the *inclination* toward activity may remain unaffected, "the typical
incoordination and clumsiness of which the user is in most cases aware,
prevent him from attempting many activities" (p. 127).

Haines and Green (1970) invoke the difference between spontaneous
and planned activity in their explanation of the inconsistent effects of
marihuana on motivated activity. The respondents in their questionnaire
survey were about equally divided between those who become stimulated
and others who become lethargic following marihuana use. However, the
respondents were almost unanimous in reporting that they completed
planned activities. Thus, Haines and Green conclude: "It seems that

marihuana only depresses spontaneous action, and has little effect on scheduled plans" (p. 358).

In two of the three previous studies of the effects of repeated use of marihuana, it was reported that a lowering of subjects' motivation occurred during the studies. The authors of the LaGuardia report stated that during the four to six weeks of their study, subjects demonstrated a lessening of the need to accomplish particular tasks, even those that had seemed worth doing before taking marihuana, and that typical changes included a "lowering of drive or incentive" (Mayor's Committee on Marihuana 1944). In describing the results of clinical observations in the 53-day Lexington Hospital study, Williams states:

"After (an) initial period of increase in activity all subjects showed decreased activity which persisted throughout the period of smoking. They were indolent, nonproductive, and showed neglect of personal hygiene. During periods of exhilaration they showed evidence of a mildly confused type of lassitude and their conversation was voluble and somewhat circumstantial at times. There was no gross interference with coordination; they all played ball in the yard, threw the ball hard and accurately, and caught it consistently. There was no hangover on awakening in the morning. One patient, who was given a work assignment in order to determine the effect of smoking marihuana on his work, lost interest and stopped work early in the experiment. Another, who styled himself as a painter in oils, brought with him some work which he said he would complete while undergoing the study. After the first day he abandoned his painting. Another patient, the musician, had stated that during the study he intended to do a great deal of practicing, but did practically none for the entire period of the study and stopped playing in the institution orchestra" (Williams *et al.* 1946, p. 1069).

The latter results are reported here in detail in order to facilitate comparison with the results of the present study, which also included assessments of the effects of repeated use of marihuana on motivational behavior.

1. METHOD

The general design of this study and subject selection have been described in Chapters 1 and 2. Two groups of experienced marihuana users were employed as subjects in two separate but identical studies. One group of ten subjects, defined as casual users, had at least a one-year history of marihuana use and were currently averaging approximately eight smoking sessions per month. The other group of ten subjects, defined as heavy users, had a two-to-nine-year history of marihuana use and were currently averaging approximately 33 smoking sessions per month. Each group of subjects lived on a closed hospital research ward for 31 days, under living conditions made as comfortable as possible, consistent with security and experimental requirements.

From the sixth through the twenth-sixth day of each study subjects were permitted to purchase and smoke *ad lib* one-gram marihuana cigarettes with approximately 2.0% delta 9 THC content. Subjects were permitted to smoke marihuana where they chose within the confines of the research ward, with the requirement that a research observer be present. The observer recorded a number of events, including the times that smoking began and ended. These latter data provided records of quantitative and temporal patterns of marihuana use during the study.

Subjects had operant manipulanda available at all times with which they could earn reinforcement points. The operant manipulanda consisted of four-digit hand counters in the first study, and five-digit hand counters in the second study. The operant task consisted simply of accumulating points on the counter. This relatively uncomplicated and easy task was chosen because results obtained in previous alcohol-related research indicated that motor impairments in performance did not occur even at high drug levels (Mello and Mendelson 1972).

A fixed ratio reinforcement schedule was utilized and one response (one button press) produced one reinforcement point on the counter. The reinforcement points could be used to purchase either marihuana or tobacco cigarettes during the study, or they could be accumulated for monetary conversion at the end of the study. The monetary conversion value for reinforcement points was fixed at one cent for 60 points. This exchange rate was based, in part, on data obtained in previous alcohol-related research which indicated that an average work output of 30 minutes was required to produce 6000 reinforcement points with apparatus similar to that employed in the present research (Mello and Mendelson 1972). The cost of the cigarettes was set to correspond to current prices in the Boston area, i.e., 3000 points ($0.50) for a package of tobacco cigarettes and 6000 points ($1.00) for one marihuana cigarette.

Subjects had access to their hand counters at all times. However, they were allowed to earn no more than 60,000 points (an equivalent of $10.00) within a 24-hour period.[1] This restriction was imposed primarily for budgetary reasons, but even with this restriction each subject could potentially earn up to $310.00 for performance on the operant task. Accumulated reinforcement points were recorded every two hours to provide a temporal record of work output.

An operant task was included in this study to permit an objective, quantitative, and reliable measurement of the reinforcement values of money and marihuana cigarettes. Data relating to operant performance in

[1] The restriction was not in effect on the first day of the first study. The high rates of work output that occurred during that day made it imperative to impose a daily limit.

this research is relevant to determining whether marihuana has a differentiating effect on motivation for either of the two reinforcers.

During the study a shift-log was maintained in which the research staff recorded general descriptions of subjects' behavior before, during, and after marihuana smoking. After the study, every member of the research staff was interviewed regarding subjects' recreational, social, and personal interest behavior while on the research unit. Both the shift-log and interview data were examined to determine whether repeated marihuana use affects motivation to engage in a variety of social and goal-directed activities.

2. RESULTS

2.1. Operant Data

During the early days of both studies, subjects discovered that the digit wheels on their hand counters would rotate if the counter levers were given a hard, sharp jolt. The rotation of the digit wheels was erratic, so that, after a jolt, the reading on the counter could be more or less than it was before the jolt. Nevertheless, practically all subjects chose to use this method in accumulating points because, in balance, points could be accumulated much faster even though there may not have been any savings in total work-energy output. That is, rather than a simple, quickly habituated, painless thumb twitch requiring very little thought or attention, the method they chose to use required attention, involvement of large muscle groups, the possibility of a small amount of pain while giving the lever a sharp jolt, and some decision making as to whether they should give the counter another jolt (and possibly lose more points than they can gain). The latter decision was particularly important when the counter reading was near maximum (9999) because subjects had to show this reading to a member of the research staff before they were credited with the points. Thus, if the counter reading went beyond this point before being shown to the staff, it would revert back to 0000 and subjects would not be credited with the points. Another decision was added to the task because counter readings were recorded every two hours. Since subjects believed that the staff was not aware of the method they were using to accumulate points, subjects were careful not to accumulate more points in a two-hour period than they could have accumulated by simply button pressing.

No attempt was made to interfere with subjects preferred method of accumulating points once it had been discovered. There were three reasons for this decision: (1) Their preferred method required at least as much (and

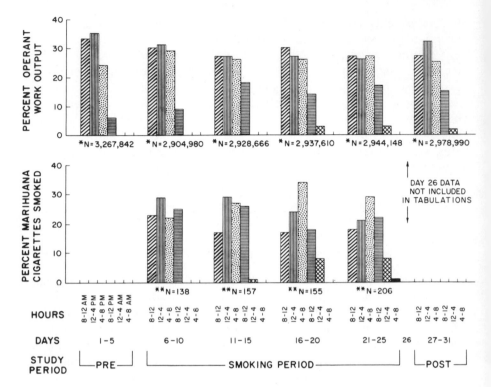

Figure 3.1. Casual users: Temporal distribution of daily operant work output and marihuana cigarettes smoked.

possibly more) total work-energy output as the regular method; (2) a change in method in mid-study would interfere with making comparisons of work output during different phases of the study (and interfere with comparisons between the first and second study); (3) there would be no basic differences in interpretations of temporal patterns of work output since subjects felt the two-hour readings compelled them to distribute their work throughout the day.

Daily work outputs were examined for the appearance of patterns relating to quantity, temporal distribution, and temporal relationship to marihuana smoking. Work patterns relating to quantity of daily work output were similar for all subjects. With very minor exceptions, every subject earned the maximum number of reinforcement points (60,000) every day of both studies. Quantity of daily work output remained constant and unchanged before, during, and after the extended marihuana smoking period. These results are in marked contrast to results obtained in alcohol-related research, in which subjects demonstrated pronounced variations in quantity of work output (including complete cessation) during drinking periods (Mendelson and Mello 1966; Nathan *et al*. 1970).

While total daily work output remained constant, there appeared to be a slight shift in the temporal distribution of this work toward the later hours of the day for both groups of subjects (Figures 3.1 and 3.2). The shifts began during the smoking period, but it is difficult to discern whether the shifts were or were not related to the marihuana smoking. The shifts appeared earlier in the smoking period among heavy users than among casual users. Furthermore, the heavy users smoked approximately twice as

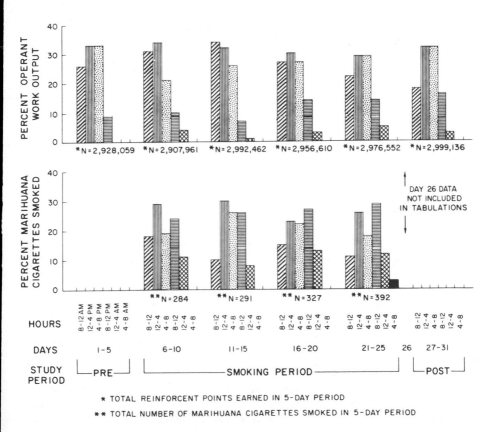

Figure 3.2.   Heavy users: Temporal distribution of daily operant work output and marihuana cigarettes smoked.

Table 3.1

Casual Users' Responses to Question: Why Did You Volunteer to Participate in This Study?

Subject	Response
1C	Wanted grass and money. Thought it would be a cool job.
2C	I needed money and a temporary place to live, plus I'm always interested in saving myself from working. Also, I enjoy smoking.
3C	I was interested in the study of marihuana and I was also interested in how I would react to being confined 30 days with 10 or more people that I didn't know.
4C	Mostly monetary reasons. Also an interest in marihuana research. I could have smoked just as much or more on the outside.
5C	I felt that there was an opportunity to earn money while still having the freedom to be with my own thoughts.
6C	Money, free grass, and a *strong* belief that grass is harmless. A desire to leave the day to day life and take stock of myself (in relation to nine other "antiestablishment" types) for 30 days.
7C	To personally see what effect marihuana had and for the "experience" itself.
8C	In order of importance: (1) money, (2) search my own head, (3) the dope, (4) it was an interesting prospect.
9C	For the money.
10C	I was broke and the only way to make some money and thus stay in Boston was this study. I also felt this could be a hell of an experience and a time to reflect on the changes which might occur in this kind of a drug study in long confinement. It was just exotic enough to be irresistible.

much marihuana as the casual users, and were smoking a larger percentage of it later in the day during the early phases of the smoking period. This may suggest that the shift toward distribution of work over more hours of the day was related to the marihuana smoking. Thus, although there was no overt decrement in subjects' total work output, there may have been a trend toward a marihuana-related procrastination in performing the work.

However, in comparing the temporal distributions of both marihuana smoking and work output for either group of subjects (Figures 3.1 and 3.2), there are no indications of an inverse relationship between the two distributions. That is, there are no indications that subjects' work output decreased during the hours of the day their marihuana smoking increased. For example, the casual users smoked a larger percentage of marihuana cigarettes between the hours of 4:00 p.m. and 8:00 p.m. during the third quarter (study days 16–20) of the drug period than during similar hours in other drug period quarters, and yet their work output during this time

Table 3.2

Heavy Users' Responses to Question: Why Did You Volunteer to Participate in This Study?

Subject	Response
1H	I volunteered to participate in this study for a variety of reasons: One obviously was to smoke grass, the other almost equally as important was to make approximately $200.00. Besides these two major reasons, there are many minor ones: the uniqueness of the situation, the chance to interact with ten new people, and it seemed a pleasant retreat for a month.
2H	I volunteered because (a) I needed the money; (b) it is something of a status thing to be included in this program; (c) I am fascinated with all aspects of drug culture and was very curious about government weed.
3H	I volunteered (1) to mark time and make money while I figured out where to travel to next; (2) to experience clinical tests, i.e., psychological evaluation of my personality; (3) to smoke government dope and have tall tales for my friends.
4H	I volunteered for the study because I am a heavy pot smoker and the chance of smoking grass for what I originally thought was 25 days appealed to me along with the money which I needed. Also I was curious about what the study of pot habits involved.
5H	For the novelty in general; interaction between ten new people and myself; how I would relate to them; want to know physical aspect related to grass.
6H	I had one main reason which I think I've kept secret from most of the people concerned with the study. The reason is that I was starting to get back into the heroin scene which I've had many frustrating battles with. The morning that I was contacted by the people from the study, I didn't know which I wanted to do most, a hit of heroin or try to stay away from it for 30 days. . .So I'm here and it's been a real help to me as I really don't have any urge at the time which I feel will stick with me as long as I keep my mind open and free. There was also the obvious reasons for wanting to enter a marihuana study. I knew it had to have something that I would be interested in by offering $200 and grass. Even though it was a bummer having to pay for the weed. I feel it would have been a nicer and freer high. I feel much better smoking grass that's been laid on me because of the fact that something that is shared with good feeling has more meaning (real life meaning) not a project trip. So to help you set your and my data straight I'll inform you of use of heroin in the last year. Last winter I did dope on and off until March when I split to Florida and started to get back into grass for the same reason as doing the study (I can't explain how the grass helps me except that it makes me see the path in which I am heading. Grass may be a temporary thing but it's the best thing I've found. . . .)
7H	I signed up because it was a once in a lifetime opportunity and I think grass should at least have a more lenient penalty, if any! If I had my way it would be legal and cheap. And I don't think it leads to harder drugs, that is to the individual to decide.

Table 3.2 (Continued)

Subject	Response
8H	I volunteered for this study for many reasons; I thought the regular food would be good for me, however, it wasn't very good at all. When I applied, my lease was coming to an end and I was getting ready to leave Boston and I was going to need a place to live before I moved. Also, I thought I would make a good study subject because I was concerned about the results of the study and I had lived under similar conditions before and it didn't especially bother me to be confined, this was as long as I had a lot of work to do. Another reason is that I was curious—I thought it would be a fascinating thing to do and profitable at the same time.
9H	I volunteered (1) out of curiosity; (2) the study coincided with plans for employment in December; (3) needed money.
10H	Because I had been looking for a job that interested me since June and this was the first opportunity I saw that I liked. I also wanted to find out any information possible about the effects of marihuana and the fact that I could save about $450 through money I made here plus money I saved on the outside (example: no rent, no food, or expenses, etc.).

remained unchanged (Figure 3.1). The lack of a direct relationship between marihuana and work output was also suggested by the observation that subjects often performed very high work outputs both while they were smoking marihuana and when they were experiencing the maximum subjective effects of the drug.

In a post-study interview subjects were asked why they had volunteered to participate in the study, and their written responses are presented in Tables 3.1 and 3.2. It is apparent from their responses that both marihuana and monetary conversion were especially strong reinforcements for the subjects. This may be one of the reasons (coupled with the fact that the operant task was relatively simple) why no decrement occurred in total work output. Different results in operant work performance might be obtained with more complex tasks and different reinforcers. Nevertheless, the results of the present study stand in sharp contrast to the effects of acute and chronic consumption of alcohol on similar operant assessments of work output (Mello and Mendelson 1972; Nathan *et al.* 1970).

2.2.   Marihuana Consumption

Results presented here are confined to data relating to quantity and temporal distribution of marihuana consumption. Findings related to other aspects of smoking patterns and behavior are discussed in other chapters of this book.

The amounts of marihuana cigarettes smoked by subjects during each quarter of the drug period are presented in Table 3.3. Marihuana consumption during the last day of the drug period (study day 26) were clearly so atypical that data from this day are treated separately and are not included in averaged data. The number of marihuana cigarettes smoked on the last smoking day ranged from one to 13 among the casual users and from nine to a phenomenal 20 among the heavy users. It is noteworthy that although

Table 3.3

Mean Daily Number of One-Gram Marihuana Cigarettes Started and Mean Daily Gram Amount of Marihuana Returned Unsmoked (in Parentheses)

	Marihuana smoking period					
	1st 5 days	2nd 5 days	3rd 5 days	4th 5 days	Last (21st) day of smoking	First 20 days of smoking
Casual users						
1C	4.8(0.20)	6.8(0.58)	5.8(0.34)	7.6(0.65)	13(1.28)	6.25(0.44)
2C	1.0(0.10)	1.2(0.45)	0.8(0.15)	0.4(0.08)	2(0.50)	0.85(0.20)
3C	4.8(0.52)	5.2(0.45)	6.0(0.27)	7.4(0.29)	8(0.91)	5.85(0.38)
4C	3.2(0.07)	4.0,(0.33)	4.6(0.12)	5.0(0.23)	7(0.16)	4.20(0.19)
5C	0.6(0.19)	0.4(0.27)	0.6(0.30)	0.0(0.00)	1(0.22)	0.40(0.19)
6C	2.2(0.37)	2.4(0.53)	2.6(0.57)	3.4(0.53)	4(0.67)	2.65(0.50)
7C	3.4(0.06)	3.6(0.04)	2.8(0.05)	4.4(0.00)	5(0.00)	3.55(0.04)
8C	4.6(0.12)	5.0(0.13)	5.6(0.09)	8.6(0.13)	9(0.00)	5.95(0.12)
9C	1.6(0.34)	1.2(0.28)	1.4(0.30)	2.2(0.41)	5(0.66)	1.60(0.12)
10C	1.4(0.28)	1.6(0.33)	0.8(0.10)	2.2(0.19)	9(1.03)	1.50(0.22)
Group	2.8(0.23)	3.1(0.34)	3.1(0.23)	4.1(0.25)	6.3(0.54)	3.28(0.26)
Heavy users						
1H	5.0(0.21)	6.0(0.38)	6.6(0.38)	8.0(1.21)	13(0.94)	6.40(0.50)
2H	2.2(0.29)	3.0(0.47)	4.0(0.88)	5.4(2.17)	9(2.53)	3.65(0.95)
3H	5.2(2.18)	5.2(2.19)	4.2(1.30)	4.8(1.92)	10(1.99)	4.85(1.90)
4H	7.2(1.29)	7.6(1.62)	7.8(1.37)	9.6(1.94)	15(2.33)	8.05(1.56)
5H	7.6(1.53)	7.6(1.44)	9.2(1.49)	10.4(1.48)	20(3.12)	8.70(1.48)
6H	7.4(2.25)	6.0(1.28)	6.2(0.70)	7.6(0.64)	14(0.92)	6.80(1.22)
7H	4.4(1.29)	5.4(0.59)	7.8(1.47)	9.2(1.40)	15(1.74)	6.70(1.19)
8H	7.2(1.34)	6.4(1.21)	6.4(0.98)	9.0(1.39)	10(1.00)	7.25(1.23)
9H	6.2(1.60)	6.8(1.22)	9.0(1.03)	9.2(1.12)	10(1.02)	7.80(1.24)
10H	4.4(1.99)	4.2(1.55)	4.2(1.38)	5.2(1.68)	13(2.99)	4.50(1.65)
Group	5.7(1.40)	5.8(1.17)	6.5(1.10)	7.8(1.50)	13(1.86)	6.47(1.29)

the amount of marihuana consumed by many subjects on the last smoking day far exceeds any previously reported amount of observed marihuana smoking in a similar time span, there were no discernible differences in behavior from that occurring during the rest of the drug period. For example, of the 20 marihuana cigarettes smoked by subject 5H on the last day, ten were smoked within a span of five hours. Yet, even with this highly concentrated dose this subject followed his usual routines, participated in scheduled assessments, and, in general, appeared no different from when he was high from one or two marihuana cigarettes.

The use of marihuana increased over the 21-day drug period for both groups of subjects. In the casual user group there was a 46% increase in the use of marihuana during the fourth quarter as compared to the first quarter (Table 3.3). The increase was related to both the number of new initiations of smoking (cigarettes purchased) and the total amount of marihuana actually smoked (cigarettes purchased minus marihuana returned). An examination of consumption patterns for individual subjects showed that the trend toward increased use in the casual user group occurred primarily in those subjects who initially were the heaviest users of the drug. Subjects who initially were the least frequent users of the drug did not show an increase over the course of the study. These latter subjects (2C, 5C, 9C, and 10C) smoked an average of 1.2 marihuana cigarettes a day each during the first quarter of the drug period. Their daily smoking increased by a negligible 4% by the fourth quarter of the drug period. In contrast, subjects (1C, 3C, 7C, and 8C) who smoked an average of 4.4 marihuana cigarettes a day each during the first quarter increased their smoking by 59% by the fourth quarter. It is noteworthy that two of these latter subjects were among the three casual users who reported on the pre-study drug use questionnaire that marihuana had a relaxing effect—an effect reported by nine of the ten heavy users.

A similar trend toward increased marihuana consumption was observed in the heavy user groups. There was an average 37% increase in smoking in the fourth quarter of the drug period as compared to the first quarter. However, in direct contrast to the casual user group, subjects in the heavy user group who initially smoked the least during the first quarter (1H, 2H, 7H, and 10H) showed a larger increase in smoking in the fourth quarter (74%) than subjects who smoked the most during the first quarter (4H, 5H, 6H, and 8H) and showed less of an increase in smoking by the fourth quarter (25%).

In combining the data for both groups, it appears that the increase in marihuana smoking was least among subjects who initially had comparatively very low or very high marihuana consumption rates. The increase in smoking was highest among subjects who initially had comparatively moderate marihuana consumption rates.

Table 3.4

Casual Users' Responses to Question: How Typical Was Your Smoking Behavior during the Study?

Subject	Response
1C	I smoked much more than I normally do though I probably would have smoked as much if I had as much available outside.
2C	I smoked as often though not more often than I have in the recent past. I believe I will be smoking less in the near future.
3C	A little more than normal.
4C	Smoked more and, perhaps, for different reasons. Time passed much more quickly while stoned, and that was a desirable attribute of being constantly stoned.
5C	I feel that I smoked on the average as often as I had been on the outside— perhaps a bit less considering the availability factor. The environment was the primary reason I didn't smoke more. In the term environment I'd include my frame of mind—lack of freedom to move around.
6C	I smoked much more than normally because I felt that the reason I was here was to smoke. Also I thought maybe it would relieve the boredom. (I don't think it really did.)
7C	No (smoked more and usually don't smoke all day).
8C	My smoking increased because of the availability of dope. I would probably smoke as much outside if I could afford it and if it were as available.
9C	I smoked more during the study than I usually do. As to if it was typical, yes because of the situation.
10C	No, I would never smoke so much in so short a time because I have been in a similar type of atmosphere once before and, although important for the perspective such as experiment offered, I was left with a residual depression and feeling of futility for too long a time.

As expected from subject selection criteria, the heavy users consumed approximately twice as much marihuana as the casual users. There was some overlap, however, in individual subject consumption between the two groups. Three casual users (1C, 3C, 8C) had higher rates of marihuana consumption than three heavy users (2H, 3H, 10H). The ranges of average individual daily marihuana consumption were 0.8–6.2 for the casual users and 3.6–8.7 for the heavy users (Table 3.3).

In post-study interviews subjects were asked how typical their smoking behavior had been during the study compared to their usual smoking behavior. Their written responses to this question are presented in Tables 3.4 and 3.5. Seven of the casual users had smoked more marihuana during the study than usual; one smoked a little more than normal, and two smoked about their normal amounts. Only one of the heavy users had smoked more marihuana than normal during the study; one smoked slightly more; two

Table 3.5

Heavy Users' Responses to the Question: How Typical Was Your Smoking Behavior during the Study?

Subject	Response
1H	My smoking behavior was probably very typical in terms of times smoked, the effects, and for the most part the amounts. (If freely available, I would smoke more in a research project setting than typically.) I don't usually smoke until afternoon or early evening, but that is usually under a combination of drugs (grass + hash + tequila + beer). Considering the abnormal setting I think my smoking behavior was fairly typical.
2H	As far as quantity, my behavior was normal. But my usual wide variety of drug practices was curtailed by the restrictions. No passing of joints—highly atypical. No hash—atypical.
3H	The smoking was different in that (a) I smoked more grass at one time because of the hassles we had to go through to get a joint; (b) I was conscious of the money factor involved with each joint. Quite a few times I didn't smoke when I wanted to get high, suppressing the desire, or I smoked half a joint. (c) The environment was not conducive to getting high. I believe in a more natural setting a high is more powerful, sensory perception is heightened, enjoyed more because thought is less in fantasy, self-conscious. (d) I smoked more with other people because of added stimulus.
4H	My smoking behavior was just a bit above average considering the factor of pot being constantly present.
5H	Would have been more carefree, lively, active, would have smoked more, at least 15 grams a day.
6H	I was pretty much myself except that I really didn't open myself completely because these were all new people to me even though it shouldn't make any difference. I have felt much more open in the last 10 or 11 days. I guess it's because I feel I can relate with most of the people that have been around me. The last four days I guess I was like myself by always wanting to be active and rowdy. But that's my regular behavior more than my smoking behavior. When I smoke I usually like to relax and enjoy myself. I also sleep a lot when I smoke heavily.
7H	I don't usually smoke alone. Normally I do most of my weekday smoking at night and weekends anytime is cool.
8H	I tried to remain relatively high smoking as few joints as possible. This was the first time I had ever smoked grass without sharing it with my companions. I hadn't smoked any grass of this low quality for many years but it wasn't bad.
9H	Only the amount smoked was atypical. I smoked more in the study than I normally do. This is directly attributed to boredom. My smoking behavior and reactions to smoking may be different to a lesser degree. This is due to the environment we were confined to and the confinement itself.

Table 3.5 (Continued)

Subject	Response
10H	My smoking behavior was very much affected by the restrictive conditions of the ward, and also the expectation of having to fill out forms, have pulses taken, and knowing we might have tests or discussions after smoking. I feel I smoked less on the whole, and lesser than usual at one sitting. But I did enter the study hoping to make around $300; so I wanted to hold my smoking down a little. I also feel that I smoked with other people more than usual (smoking more times by myself on the outside), and thus my behavior after getting stoned might have been affected by group interaction.

smoked their normal amounts; and two smoked less than normal. Four of the heavy users were vague in regard to quantity used, but their responses suggest that their rate of marihuana consumption was normal during the study.

In comparing the responses of both groups of subjects, it appears that the quantity of marihuana used by the heavy users during the study was about normal for them, with two subjects smoking more and two less than normal. The quantity of marihuana used by casual users during the study was more than normal for all but two, or possibly, three subjects. Five of the casual users attributed their higher rate of marihuana consumption during the study to experimental conditions (including boredom and "expectation"). Two attributed increased consumption to availability (i.e., they would normally smoke more marihuana "outside" if it were as available as in the study). It is of interest that these latter two subjects (1C and 8C) had the highest rates of marihuana consumption among the casual users during the study.

The daily temporal distributions of subjects' marihuana smoking are presented in Figures 3.1 and 3.2. Marihuana smoking occurred during all times of the day including morning and early afternoon. Many of the subjects stated it was atypical for them to smoke marihuana other than in the evening (Tables 3.4 and 3.5), and there are no indications of why the morning and early afternoon smoking occurred during the study with such high frequency. If boredom of subjects was a factor contributing to their use of marihuana, the boredom should have been at its lowest ebb during those times of the day when subjects were busiest at scheduled assessments, i.e., during the morning and early afternoon.

It was mentioned earlier that there was a shift in temporal distributions of marihuana use toward later hours of the day for both groups of subjects (Figures 3.1 and 3.2). Thus, as each study progressed, there was an increase both in the amount of marihuana consumed (Table 3.3) and in the percent of daily consumption that occurred in later hours of the day. The concurrence of these two changes suggest that the *increase* in marihuana smoking that occurred during the study may have been related to subjects' boredom, since it would be expected that boredom would be greater during the later hours of the day and would increase as the study progressed. Alternate reasons for the increase in marihuana consumption are conceivable, however, and these are presented in the discussion section of this chapter.

2.3.   Other Reinforcements

Subjects were expected to participate in a number of daily and special assessments (see Chapter 1). A schedule of monetary reinforcements was established for accurate performance on some assessments (i.e., psychomotor, time estimation, memory, and risk taking tasks) and a standard $2.00 per day reinforcement was established for participation in all other assessments (e.g., taking of vital signs, interviews, psychological tests, etc.). The amounts that subjects earned for their participation are presented in Tables 3.6 and 3.7.

All of the casual users and five of the heavy users earned the maximum possible for participation in all assessments. Of the five heavy users who did not earn the maximum, three did not participate in some assessments on one day, and two did not participate in some assessments on two days. The failure of the heavy users to participate in assessments on one day occurred during the post-drug period when four subjects agreed among themselves not to participate in order to "tease" the research assistants. The data in Tables 3.6 and 3.7 indicate that the extent of the subjects' participation in scheduled activities over an extended period of 31 days was phenomenal for individuals of their age and background. In particular, there was no evidence that subjects' motivation to participate had been affected by their repeated use of marihuana.

Post-study interviews with all personnel connected with the research and an examination of the shift-logs in which staff recorded descriptions of ward activities suggested that no consistent changes had occurred in subjects' social and recreational behavior during the study. They regularly played group sports on a large lawn area adjacent to the ward, read newspapers and magazines, played cards and other games, wrote letters, and engaged in the constant horseplay that is normal for their age group. Subjects with personal interests, such as playing a musical instrument or creative writing, showed no change in these interests during the study. For example, one writer in each group had brought a typewriter onto the ward, and (oc-

Table 3.6

Subject Payments: Casual Users

	1C	2C	3C	4C	5C	6C	7C	8C	9C	10C	Total
Operant points	304.69	311.32	307.72	311.52	298.53	313.82	315.89	311.75	305.26	312.77	3093.27
Daily participation	62.00	62.00	62.00	62.00	62.00	62.00	62.00	62.00	62.00	62.00	620.00
Performance tasks	42.28	27.71	30.42	38.42	30.44	41.43	33.61	35.41	37.17	32.83	349.72
Total earned	408.97	401.03	400.14	411.94	390.97	417.25	411.50	409.16	404.43	407.60	$4062.99
Marihuana purchased	137.00	18.00	124.00	90.00	8.00	56.00	75.00	127.00	36.00	38.00	709.00
Tobacco purchased	—	—	20.00	—	—	—	—	12.00	14.00	10.00	56.00
Marihuana returned	−9.54	−4.46	−8.58	−3.89	−4.06	−10.64	−0.75	−2.35	−7.31	−5.56	−57.14
Total spent	127.46	13.54	135.42	86.11	3.94	45.36	74.25	136.65	42.69	42.44	$707.86
Subject payment	281.51	387.49	264.72	325.83	387.03	371.89	337.25	272.51	361.74	365.16	$3355.13

Table 3.7

Subject Payments: Heavy Users

	1H	2H	3H	4H	5H	6H	7H	8H	9H	10H	Total
Operant points	310.00	310.00	308.17	304.83	303.17	301.50	308.17	305.33	302.33	306.00	3059.50
Daily participation	58.00	62.00	62.00	62.00	60.00	58.00	60.00	62.00	60.00	62.00	606.00
Performance tasks	32.72	44.56	29.78	34.53	32.18	40.22	45.73	30.71	39.41	35.39	365.23
Total earned	400.72	416.56	399.95	401.36	395.35	399.72	413.90	398.04	401.74	403.39	$4030.73
Marihuana purchased	140.00	81.00	106.00	175.00	193.00	149.00	148.00	154.00	165.00	102.00	1413.00
Tobacco purchased	—	—	7.00	—	18.00	12.50	0.50	17.50	17.00	—	73.00
Marihuana returned	−10.88	−21.51	−39.90	−33.46	−32.74	−25.25	−25.48	−30.73	−25.88	−36.00	−281.83
Total spent	129.12	59.49	73.10	141.54	178.76	136.25	123.02	140.77	156.12	66.00	$1204.17
Subject payment	271.60	357.07	326.85	259.82	216.59	263.47	290.88	257.27	245.62	337.39	$2826.56

casionally to the consternation of other subjects), they showed no change in their initial habits of typing for long hours, often into the late hours of the night. Each group contained a few subjects who spent most of their time in passive, solitary activities such as spending long hours watching television or just lounging in their bedrooms listening to music. However, these latter subjects displayed these behavior patterns from the start of the studies, and the patterns did not appear to be either initiated or altered during the marihuana smoking period.

The ward was not staffed with housekeeping or kitchen personnel (meals were delivered to the ward on food carts), and the chores normally performed by these personnel were carried out by subjects on a rotating schedule. There was some dissatisfaction and begrudging compliance with these arrangements on the part of some subjects, but, overall, the cooperation of the subjects was consistently high during the study. They washed dishes, cleaned tables, swept floors, and performed other such tasks regularly, with no discernible alterations occurring either during or after the drug period.

3. DISCUSSION

The high rates of marihuana consumption by subjects in the present study are consistent with findings in other long-term studies of marihuana. Subjects in the Panama study (Siler *et al.* 1933) smoked between one and 20 marihuana cigarettes a day, with an average of five per day. Subjects in the LaGuardia study (Mayor's Committee on Marihuana 1944) smoked between two and 18 cigarettes a day with an average of 7.2 per day. Subjects in the Lexington study (Williams *et al.* 1946) averaged 17 marihuana cigarettes per day. These studies were carried out before the active ingredient in marihuana had been identified. The potencies of the marihuana used are therefore unknown and no direct comparison can be made of THC consumption between the three previous studies and the present investigation. The consistency of results regarding marihuana use in all four studies, however, supports the conclusion that despite the importance attributed to "setting" by many marihuana users, subjects in research environments will consume large amounts of marihuana on a free choice basis. This finding increases the prospects of developing a scientific body of knowledge concerning marihuana through laboratory research with human subjects.

The progressive increase in marihuana consumption that was observed during the present study is open to several interpretations. In post-study interviews some subjects attributed the increase to boredom (Tables 3.4 and

3.5), and a few others said that they increased their marihuana purchases after they had accumulated enough reinforcement points to assure them of a desired amount of money at the end of the study. However, while the study was in progress, many subjects complained that the marihuana was decreasing in potency. All the marihuana cigarettes came from a standard lot with uniform THC content, and deterioration in potency could not have occurred as rapidly as subjects asserted. In addition, although subjects in the first study complained of deteriorating potency of the marihuana, at the start of the second study subjects' estimates of the potency of the marihuana were as high as subjects' estimates at the start of the first study. The increase in marihuana use during both studies may thus have been at least partially the result of increasing tolerances for the drug. There are some reports in the literature that marihuana may be unique among psychoactive drugs in that habitual users develop a reverse tolerance for the drug. That is, the more the drug is used (up to a point) the less is needed to achieve a standard effect. There was no evidence of reverse tolerance occurring within the period of the present study insofar as quantity of marihuana consumption is concerned, and, as indicated above, there may have been some indications of regular tolerance.

Two main features of the design of this study were uniquely suited to investigate the effects of marihuana on motivation. First, subjects were given the opportunity to perform a task which produced two major reinforcements, marihuana and money. By making both reinforcements available to subjects on a free choice basis, the task was made sensitive to alterations in motivation for either reinforcer if they occurred over the duration of the study. Second, since subjects lived on a research ward for 31 days, there was an opportunity for intensive observation and acquaintance with their habitual behavior and interests. This made it possible to be sensitive to changes in behavior and interests if they occurred during the study.

All subjects performed close to the allowable maximum on the operant task before, during, and after the marihuana smoking period. Thus, there were no indications that the repeated use of marihuana adversely affected subjects' motivation to work for positive reinforcers. Rates of operant work output were much higher than needed to acquire the amount of marihuana consumed, and these high rates of work output continued during the post-drug period. Both facts indicate that the subjects' motivation for acquisition of money remained unchanged by the repeated use of marihuana. In addition, there was no indication of an acute effect of the drug on work output, since subjects often continued to work on the operant task while they were smoking marihuana or experiencing the maximum subjective effects of the drug (Figures 3.1 and 3.2). The absence of an observed relation between either acute or repeated use of marihuana and alterations in quantity of work output is made more meaningful by the fact that subjects maintained a high level of marihuana consumption. Further, in the case of the casual users, the level of marihuana consumption during the study was much higher than their normal consumption.

There was also no indication of an effect of repeated use of marihuana on other aspects of work and personal interest behavior of the subjects. With only a few, very minor exceptions among the heavy users, all subjects participated fully in all assessment procedures. They voluntarily adhered to a posted work schedule involving housekeeping and kitchen chores with no reinforcer other than social approbation. There were no discernible alterations in their customary recreational pursuits, ranging from passive listening to music to strenuous sports activities, even while they were high from the effects of the drug. For example, it was not unusual for some subjects to smoke marihuana before going out to play an hour or two of touch football.

In summary, there were no indications that the three-week period of daily marihuana use, often at very high rates, had any discernible effect on quantity of work-energy output. These results are in direct contrast to reports from two other long-term studies of marihuana which attributed a motivational decrement to marihuana smoking (Mayor's Committee on Marihuana 1944; Williams *et al.* 1946).

The contrast in results could stem from any number of reasons. Two possibilities relate to the nature of the subjects employed in the studies and subject–experimenter expectations. The two previous long-term studies which reported motivational decrements had employed prisoners as subjects. It may be that their usual work patterns were different and more susceptible to marihuana effects than subjects employed in the present study. The prisoners' activity levels may also have been artificially high during the initial phases of the studies, stimulated by the novelty of being removed from a prison cell to a hospital ward. The observed decrease in activity during those studies may thus have been related as much to waning novelty as to marihuana smoking. Finally, it is probable that the subject–experimenter expectations of the effects of marihuana on motivation were different when the previous studies were carried out from those of today. Recent work on the effects of these expectations has underlined their importance in behavioral science research (Orne 1962; Rosenthal 1966), although it has been known for some time that the psychological effects of drugs are partially determined by expectations (Mandler 1962).

Although quantity of work-energy output remained unaltered during the present study, there did appear to be a slight trend toward a shift of operant work toward the later hours of the day. The interpretation of this trend is not clearly evident. It may have been the beginning stages of a growing procrastination in performing work, a procrastination that might eventually lead to a decrease in quantity of daily work output over a longer period of time than that employed in this study. On the other hand, the observed shift may have been a secondary phenomenon related to some situational factors, such as an adjustment by subjects of their operant work patterns to more closely coincide with ward activities. It is also possible that the shift in work patterns was related to the fragmentation of sleep that occurred during the study (see Chapter 13). With the onset of marihuana smoking subjects slept more hours and there were more episodes of sleep (e.g., napping). This change in sleep behavior may partially account for the shift in work patterns, although the fragmentation of sleep remained relatively constant during the marihuana smoking period, while the shift in operant work patterns appeared to steadily increase over this same period.

The difficulty in arriving at a clear interpretation of the shift in work patterns points up one of the limitations of the present study in arriving at generalizations concerning the effects of marihuana on motivation. While the 21-day period of marihuana smoking and the measures employed in the present study represent important advances in the investigation of the effects of marihuana, it may require an even longer period of time and different measures to record marihuana-induced alterations in motivational behavior. Therefore, the results of the present investigation which indicate that marihuana had no discernible decremental effect on motivated behavior must be qualified (as in all research) by the phrase "under the conditions of this study."

4
Group Behavior: Patterns of Smoking

Thomas F. Babor, A. Michael Rossi,
Gerald Sagotsky, and Roger E. Meyer

Almost all aspects of the marihuana experience, from initial acquisition to possible psychological dependence, seem to be related to social psychological variables. Recent surveys (Haines and Green 1970; Goode 1969a) have shown that the initial act of "turning on" typically takes place in a small group setting in the company of close friends. In most cases the neophyte is guided through the important *rites de passage* by a more experienced smoker (Becker 1963), who helps to provide a set of meanings to attach to the physiological cues generated by the drug. It has also been found that initial experimentation is often motivated by curiosity and the desire to participate with friends in an "extraordinary" experience (Keeler 1968; Farnsworth 1967). In addition, the continuing use of marihuana seems to serve socializing and recreational functions (Haines and Green 1970).

Most of the reports dealing with marihuana use in a social context have been anecdotal or speculative. Despite this caveat, they have been useful in suggesting generalizations and hypotheses. Goode (1969a) has proposed that marihuana is highly "sociogenic," in contrast with opiates, amphetamines, and barbiturates. By this he means it is typically used in a group setting among close friends; it tends to maintain the group's cohesion; and it provides a basis of identity for individual group members.

Although Goode's analysis seems to accommodate many of the known sociocultural findings on marihuana, the sociogenic nature of the drug may derive more from the sociology of its use than from its pharmacological properties. In other words, since marihuana is illegal and symbolizes many of the values of the counterculture, its use has become a "group phenomenon." A question of equal heuristic interest relates to its pharmacological properties: Does marihuana, as a psychopharmacological agent, function to generate or enhance social behavior?

There is some retrospective evidence that the marihuana experience does not facilitate interactive behavior. Tart (1971) reports that at higher levels of intoxication, the user reportedly becomes less sociable and withdraws from his group in order to concentrate on the subjective aspects of the experience. Mirin *et al.* (1971) suggest that marihuana may produce paradoxically different social effects in heavy and casual users. Heavy users retrospectively reported more insightful and mystical experiences under the influence of marihuana, as well as a greater tendency to smoke alone. Casual users indicated that they felt more friendly and agreeable when high. Thus, casual users may be more responsive to the potential social effects of marihuana, while heavy users appear to be more responsive to the intrapsychic effects.

The present investigation provided an excellent opportunity to study social psychological factors associated with marihuana smoking. Casual and heavy user subjects were systematically observed before, during, and after periods of free access to marihuana. Special attention was devoted to observation of activity patterns, informal affiliation networks, variations in group size, and the overall quantity and type of communication.

1.   METHOD

The general context of the study, the nature of the subjects, and the experimental ward setting have been described in Chapters 1 and 2. The subjects were informed that they could smoke during the drug period whenever and wherever they chose, provided that each marihuana cigarette was consumed within the confines of the ward and in the presence of a staff member.

During the time each cigarette was being consumed, the following data were recorded: (1) name of smoker; (2) time smoking began and ended; (3) ward location; (4) names of other subjects present in the immediate proximity of the smoker; (5) frequency of verbal communication (e.g., constant, frequent, little, none); (6) type of activity which best characterized the individual or group; (7) self-ratings of subjective level of intoxication before and after smoking; (8) pulse rate before and after smoking. The latter two measures were obtained only from the heavy users and on alternate smoking days.

All staff members responsible for observing and recording marihuana smoking behavior were under 30 years of age. They dressed casually and were often mistaken for subjects by outside observers. These commonalities in age and appearance helped to minimize staff–subject differences. During the time that marihuana was being smoked, staff observers attempted to foster a cordial but neutral relationship with subjects, one in which the smokers would not feel that they were being judged or threatened. As a consequence, the general atmosphere during the smoking sessions was spontaneous, informal, and relaxed.

2. RESULTS

2.1. The Smoking Procedure

On a typical smoking occasion, one or two subjects would organize the session by asking a staff member to dispense marihuana in a specific location on the ward. Sometimes the initiator would recruit other subjects into the smoking group. At other times subjects merely chose a partner (usually the same person) and initiated the session without fanfare. Over 90% of the smoking took place in the T.V. and stereo lounge (fondly referred to as the "wreck room" by the heavy users). This location served as a central gathering place for the subjects who also had private bedroom accommodations.

On the average, subjects required between 10 and 15 minutes to finish a marihuana cigarette. On almost all smoking occasions subjects inhaled the smoke deeply and in large amounts. Most of each cigarette was smoked to the end. When the cigarette had been smoked to a point where it was difficult to hold between the fingers, various types of "roach" holders were often used to permit further smoking. Roach holders ranged from momentary improvisations, such as kitchen forks or folded matchbook covers, to homemade and commercial devices. Roach clips also permitted a procedure known as "snorting."[1] An analogous procedure, demonstrated by several of the heavy users, was called "shotgunning." One subject would place the lighted end of another's cigarette in his mouth. He would then exhale a stream of smoke which the other subject would inhale through his nose or mouth.

All of these procedures suggest that subjects were highly preoccupied with the technical aspects of smoking, especially those aspects which might help to obtain the maximum effect from the marihuana. For the more experienced smokers, these rituals served to demonstrate smoking skills, analogous to the connoisseur of fine wine who may ostentatiously proceed through various rituals during gustation.

The general consensus among both casual and heavy user subjects was that the standard one-gram cigarette was sufficient to produce a more than adequate level of intoxication. However, on some occasions a subject would purchase and consume a second or third cigarette immediately after finishing the initial "joint." The most commonly expressed motivations for repeated administration were: (1) failure to obtain a sufficient effect from the previous dose and (2) a desire to become as high as possible. The frequency of this "massing" was not randomly distributed among the subjects. Pearson product-moment correlations, computed between the number of instances of massing and the total number of cigarettes consumed during the study, showed a significant relation for both casual ($r = 0.74$, 8 df, p. < 0.01, two-tailed test) and heavy ($r = 0.73$, 8 df, p. < 0.01, two-tailed test) user subjects. In other words, the most frequent smokers in each group demonstrated the highest incidence of massing. These data are consistent with the development of tolerance.

2.2. Smoking in Groups

From the beginning of the first hour of the drug period, when nine of the ten casual users and all of the heavy users gathered for their first marihuana cigarette of the study, it became apparent that the smoking experience was an activity around which groups would form. Marihuana was smoked primarily in small groups, and it was unusual for one subject to smoke in isolation from others. Casual users consumed only 6.3% of their marihuana alone (i.e., with only the researcher present), and the figure was 4.3% for the heavy users.

In order to determine if the number of cigarettes smoked in isolation was related to the total quantity of marihuana consumed thorughout the study, Pearson product-moment correlations were computed between total marihuana consumed and the proportion of cigarettes smoked in isolation.

[1] Inhaling smoke through the nose.

For the casual users the correlation was -0.42 (8 df, n.s.), while the coefficient was 0.67 (8 df, p. $<$ 0.05, two-tailed test) for the heavy users. The significant coefficient for the heavy users indicates that the more marihuana a subject smoked, the more he tended to smoke in isolation from the group.

Over the course of the 21-day drug period, marihuana was distributed to casual users on a total of 271 occasions and to heavy users on 322 occasions. In view of the fact that the heavy users consumed almost twice as many cigarettes as the casual users (cf. Chapter 3), the difference in the number of smoking sessions (51) is not pronounced. Comparing frequency distributions of smoking sessions according to the number of smokers in each group, a chi square analysis revealed that the heavy user groups contained larger numbers of smokers than the casual user groups (χ^2 = 65.97, 9 df, p. $<$ 0.001). While 27.7% of the heavy user groups included more than five smokers, only 4% of the casual user groups contained as many. These data indicate that a primary difference in smoking patterns between the casual and heavy users is that the latter were smoking in larger groups during each session.

A related issue concerns the relationship between smokers and nonsmokers once the smoking session had begun. Do heavy users differ from casual users in their propensity to join other smokers? Frequently, nonsmoking subjects were present in the immediate vicinity at the time a smoking occasion was initiated. The data indicate that heavy users were more likely than casual users to join in smoking with their peers. For the heavy users the average number of subjects smoking per group was 3.98. The average size of the total group, which includes smokers and any nonsmoking subjects present in close proximity, was 4.15. The similarity of the averages suggests that rarely was a heavy user subject present in a group of smokers without also smoking. In contrast, the average group size for the casual users (3.58) was appreciably larger than the average number of smokers (2.56), indicating that nonsmoking casual users were frequently present while marihuana was being consumed by others.

The data suggest that marihuana smoking in isolation is more likely to occur in very heavy users, and that heavy users are less likely to resist the opportunity to smoke in a group in which smoking has already been initiated. These data are consistent with the presence of a degree of "psychological dependence" in the heavy user group.

2.3. Affiliation Structures and Role Differentiation

The following data are based on careful observations of the individuals who constituted each smoking group. From this record it was possible to derive a matrix of affiliation frequencies showing the number of times each group member smoked with every other group member. Since subjects were free to associate with whomever they chose, it was expected that the affiliation patterns would not be random.

One method of representing the affiliation structure of the casual and heavy user groups is by means of sociograms, shown in Figures 4.1 and 4.2. Each subject is represented by a numbered circle. The position of the circle on the vertical axis represents the frequency with which each subject smoked during the study. The arrows emanating from each circle indicate the two individuals with whom the subject smoked most frequently.

Looking first at the structure for the casual users (Figure 4.1), a number of interesting patterns may be noted. The five heaviest smokers differentiate into two "cliques" or subgroups of smokers, one a triad, the other a dyad. Subjects 1C, 3C, and 8C, the heaviest smokers in the group,

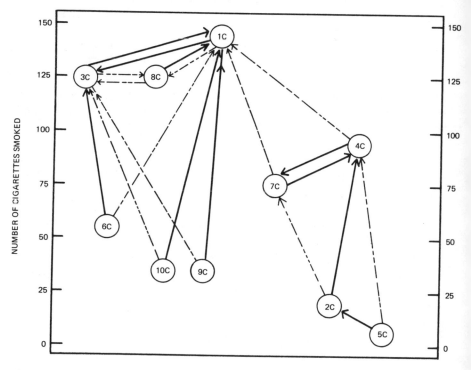

Figure 4.1. Affiliation structure of casual user group as defined by frequency of mutual marihuana smoking. Solid arrows indicate most frequent smoking companion; broken arrows indicate second most frequent smoking companion. Numbers in circles identify each subject; position of circle on vertical axis shows total number of marihuana cigarettes smoked during the 21-day drug period.

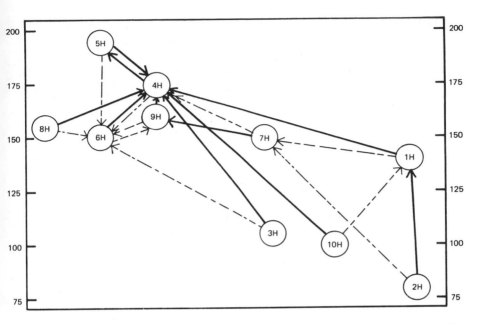

Figure 4.2. Affiliation structure of heavy user group as defined by frequency of mutual marihuana smoking. Solid arrows indicate most frequent smoking companion; broken arrows indicate second most frequent smoking companion. Numbers in circles identify each subject; position of circle on vertical axis shows total number of marihuana cigarettes smoked during the 21-day drug period.

form a triad of mutual affiliation. Each member of the subgroup has the two remaining subjects as his "most frequent" and "second most frequent" smoking companions. Subjects 1C, 3C, and 4C appear to be the most "popular" smokers, judging by the number of other subjects who affilitated with them frequently during smoking. The lightest smokers (2C, 5C, 6C, 9C, and 10C) smoked more frequently with the heavier smokers than they did with each other, and they tended to join one or the other subgroup of heavier smokers. This finding is not surprising in view of the probability that the former were more likely to be available for any smoking occasion. However, the distinctive patterning of the affiliation structure suggests that factors other than statistical probability were at play.

Although Figure 4.1 indicates who associated most frequently with whom during the smoking sessions, it does not provide information relevant to group role differentiation, i.e., the direction of the choices and the characteristic sequences of joining the smoking groups. Some of the subjects chose each other as mutual smoking partners before initiating a smoking session. Other subjects initiated distribution by themselves and were later joined by subjects who happened to be in the vicinity. In order to differentiate between the "initiators" and the "joiners," the smoking record was consulted to find the frequency with which each subject was the first to receive a marihuana cigarette at the beginning of a group smoking session.[2]

Applying these data to an interpretation of Figure 4.1, several interesting findings emerge. While subject 1C was frequently a smoking companion for most of the other subjects, he joined ongoing smoking groups for 71% of his cigarettes, while initiating only 29%. Subject 8C, another frequent smoker, initiated only 27% of his cigarettes, many of these late at night while he was alone. Subjects 3C and 4C, on the other hand, seemed to act as catalysts in their separate cliques, initiating 46% and 56% of their own marihuana cigarettes, respectively. Together, these two were first to smoke in over 44% of the total number of smoking occasions for the casual users. Thus, each subgroup or clique contained one member who served to initiate smoking for the others.

Other aspects of the casual user affiliation structure can be understood in terms of the personal histories and characteristics of the subjects. Two subjects, 4C and 7C, entered into a close friendship during the initial pre-drug period, and their continued friendship is reflected in the higher frequency of mutual smoking occasions. Subject 5C, who consumed the least amount of marihuana, smoked most of his cigarettes with subject 2C, his regular roommate prior to the study. Thus, it appears that smoking affiliation was influenced by personal relationships, and not merely by availability, convenience, or other impersonal factors.

The affiliation structure of the heavy user group is presented in Figure 4.2. The apparent absence of any subgroup structure among the heavy users is consistent with the finding that these subjects tended to smoke in larger numbers than the casual users. As with the casual user group, however, there is again a triad of the most frequent smokers in the center of the affiliation structure. The figure shows that the members of the triad (4H, 5H, and 6H) smoked most frequently with each other, while subjects 4H and 6H were the most "popular" smoking partners. Although subject 5H was the heaviest smoker in the group, he did not rank high as a smoking companion for any of the other smokers except 4H.

Taking into consideration the role differentiation among group members, the data indicate that the apparent centrality of subject 4H (the "star" in the affiliation structure) may be due more to his role as joiner than as initiator. Of the total number of smoking occasions, only 8.1% were

---

[2] While this is not an error-free measure of who actually asked the researcher to begin distribution, in most cases the subject who first asked to smoke was the first to receive a cigarette.

initiated by subject 4H. Only 15% of the 176 marihuana cigarettes he smoked were consumed in smoking sessions initiated by him. In contrast, subject 6H initiated 15.9% of the total smoking occasions, and was the initiator 35% of the time that he was involved in smoking.

2.4. Activities and Communication during Smoking

The type of activity in which the majority of subjects participated during each smoking occasion was used to categorize each smoking group. The numerical and percentage distributions of these smoking groups is presented in Table 4.1. The results indicate that watching television, listening to rock music, and engaging in conversation were the most frequent activities for both casual and heavy users. However, casual users showed a marked preference for watching television, while the heavy users tended to listen more to music. Excluding those instances where the activities noted were either miscellaneous (e.g., reading, taking tests, etc.) or undetermined, a comparison of the two groups by means of the chi square test showed these differences in activity preference to be highly significant (χ^2 = 122.63, 4 df, p. < 0.001).

Table 4.1 also shows that conversational groups occurred in approximately the same proportions for both types of user (casual users: 22.0%; heavy users: 24.8%). These statistics, however, do not reflect the frequency with which subjects conversed over all smoking sessions, including

Table 4.1

Activities Engaged in during Marihuana Smoking Sessions by Groups of Casual and Heavy User Subjects

Activity	Groups of casual users		Groups of heavy users	
	N	Percent	*N*	Percent
Watching television	111	40.1	50	15.5
Engaging in conversation	61	22.0	80	24.8
Listening to rock music	16	5.8	135	41.9
Playing games	19	6.9	5	1.5
Group discussion	11	4.0	8	2.5
Other (miscellaneous)	31	11.2	24	7.5
Undetermined	28	10.1	20	6.2
Total	277	100.01	322	100.00

Table 4.2

Frequency of Communication in Groups of Casual and Heavy Users
during Marihuana Smoking Sessions

Frequency of communication	Groups of casual users		Groups of heavy users	
	N	Percent	N	Percent
None	32	11.6	85	26.4
Little	70	25.3	114	35.4
Frequent	129	46.6	79	24.5
Constant	6	2.2	1	0.3
Undetermined	40	14.4	43	13.4
Total	277	100.1	322	100.00

those occasions when talking was not the dominant activity. Data presented in Table 4.2 show the numerical and percentage distributions of smoking groups according to the frequency with which individual marihuana smokers engaged in verbal communication, either among themselves or with the researcher. The data are based upon ratings of each smoker by the researcher during the smoking occasion. The ratings were combined to obtain a modal frequency for each smoking group. The results indicate that the casual users engaged in significantly more verbal interaction (χ^2 = 47.01, 3 df, p. < 0.01) while smoking than did the heavy users. The absence of communication was observed in 26.4% of the heavy user groups, as compared to only 11.6% of the casual user groups. Conversely, frequent communication was observed in 46.6% of the casual user groups, as compared to 24.5% of the heavy user groups.

2.5. Content and Quality of Communication

Systematic observations were not made of content and quality of the communication during marihuana smoking, in order not to inhibit spontaneous interaction and free choice smoking behavior. However, general observations were recorded by staff members in a log book twice daily. The record showed that few instances of anomalous behavior or conversation were noted. Subjects were rarely observed acting in a noisy or boisterous manner, and there were few instances of unusual or uncontrollable laughter. Many conversations were associated with the activities and conditions of the moment. Politics, drugs, personal experiences, and the experimental situation were frequent topics of conversation. It is our impression that casual observation would not be able to differentiate these marihuana smoking sessions from informal meetings among the same subjects during the pre- and post-smoking periods.

3. DISCUSSION

The present data suggest very strongly that marihuana smoking, in addition to being a subjective drug experience, is also a focus for social activity. The results offer support for Goode's (1969a) contention that, sociologically, marihuana is sociogenic. Subjects rarely chose to smoke alone. More than 94% of all marihuana consumed by either type of user was smoked in a place where other subjects were present. Although the data indicate that both types of user tended to smoke in groups, the results also suggest that heavy users were more inclined to join their comrades in smoking once a smoking occasion had been initiated. This readiness to indulge, but not necessarily to initiate, might indicate that the heavy users were more susceptible to group influences than the casual users. For the heavy users, marihuana smoking is a pivotal activity around which a good portion of their lives revolve. It is likely that the norm for heavy smoking would be stronger for the heavy users, not only because smoking was for them a primary means of reinforcing group solidarity, but also because each heavy user shared expectations of how other heavy users were supposed to act in that type of situation. Moreover, from a behavioral point of view, the heavy user's smoking patterns are strongly influenced by the visual and olfactory cues that are present when others are smoking. He is more psychologically dependent, and his behavior is more clearly under stimulus control than the casual user. The greater frequency of solo smoking among the heavy user group is also consistent with psychological dependence.

Considering these results in conjunction with the analysis of affiliation patterns, the data suggest that social influence and social reinforcement were also important factors in determining frequency of smoking. The smoking affiliation structures of both groups demonstrated a central structure dominated by a triad of the most frequent smokers. The heavier smokers in each group smoked most frequently with other heavier smokers. The lighter smokers also smoked most frequently with the heavier smoking subjects. Only one subject out of the twenty initiated as much as 50% of his own smoking occasions. By varying their roles as initiator and joiner, subjects were continually providing reciprocal role support for one another and thereby helping to perpetuate the smoking process.

The existence of friendship patterns is another factor related to the affiliation structure which may have influenced frequency of smoking. Subjects 4C and 7C, 2C and 5C, and 1H and 2H were found to be mutual smoking companions. They were also acknowledged by staff members as being "buddies" before marihuana became available. It is conceivable that friendship patterns partly account for the fact that members of these dyads consumed similar amounts of marihuana.

The results also indicated that even though marihuana smoking tended to be a group centered activity, subjects did not always engage in social interaction during and after the act of "turning on." It was not uncommon to observe some or all of the smokers withdrawing from interaction during the smoking occasion. This usually took the form of a passive activity such as watching television, listening to music, or simply looking at objects or other people. These findings suggest that while marihuana is "sociogenic" in the sociological sense indicated by Goode (1969a), it may not act to generate social behavior because of the psychopharmacological effect it has on the individual. On the contrary, subjects in the present study seemed to withdraw from interaction in order to enjoy the subjective experiences associated with being high.

Smokers shared common activities in a group setting when high, even when they were not engaging in verbal interaction. Two types of group behavior were observed during and after the smoking occasion. Prior to and during the smoking session, social behavior was characterized by verbal interaction in response to a common purpose and as a result of the presence of other participants. These groups might be termed *interacting* groups. As the marihuana began to take effect, however, the character of the group changed from interaction to co-action. In these *co-acting* groups, participants shared common subjective effects, common external stimuli, and common experiences, but they were not interacting with one another in response to these.

The results also revealed characteristic differences between the casual and heavy users in their social response to marihuana. The heavy users tended to be more withdrawn than the casual users during the smoking sessions, as indicated by their significantly lower frequency of communication and their distinctive preference for listening to music while smoking. The high noise level of the stereo phonograph may have imposed an artificial constraint on conversation among the heavy users, but further analysis of the data showed that even with type of activity held constant, they tended to interact less than the casual users. The heavy users were more inclined to seek the subjective, personal effects of the drug, while the casual users emphasized the social effects. This difference may account for the different patterns of communication and activity observed in the two groups. Thus, listening to rock music may have been the activity most conducive to the enjoyment of subjective states such as contemplation and introspection. Watching television, on the other hand, provided a greater opportunity for group entertainment and conversation. These findings are consistent with results obtained by Mirin *et al.* (1971) in interviews with casual and heavy marihuana users. Further research is necessary to clarify whether the observed differences represent a progressive development associated with a greater intensity of marihuana use, or whether the heavy users were initially less verbal and more interested in introspection and contemplation and used marihuana to enhance this tendency.

In conclusion, the findings presented in this chapter can be summarized in two main points. First, marihuana smoking was clearly a social activity around which groups formed. This finding is consistent with Goode's (1969a) hypothesis that marihuana is highly sociogenic. It also suggests that the sociogenic nature of cannabis derives more from sociological factors than from the pharmacological properties of the drug itself. In recent years the ritual aspects of marihuana smoking have become associated with a number of social meanings which, to a certain extent, determine how, why, and with whom the drug is used. They also anticipate the effects of the drug on the user. These social meanings appear to symbolize group solidarity, value consensus, defiance of the established authority structure, and identification with the so-called "hang loose" ethic (Suchman 1968). By sharing a pleasant marihuana experience with other group members, it is likely that these meanings receive validation each time the ritual is repeated, regardless of the specific social or psychological effect of the drug itself.

The second point, related to the above, concerns the psychopharmacological effect of marihuana on the group. Even though the marihuana smokers studied here remained participants in the group on a symbolic level, they often tended to withdraw from social interaction. These observations are corroborated by results presented in Chapter 5, which show a consistent decline in verbal interaction as a function of level of intoxication. It is not clear whether this quieting effect is the result of a general incapacity or a motivational unwillingness to engage in interaction. The results indicate, however, that the pharmacological effect of marihuana is not as "sociogenic" as anecdotal reports and survey data would suggest.

5
Group Behavior: Verbal Interaction

Thomas F. Babor, A. Michael Rossi,
Gerald Sagotsky, and Roger E. Meyer

Although marihuana smokers often report that verbal interaction is a typical part of the marihuana experience (Tart 1971; Haines and Green 1970), they sometimes encounter problems in expressing ideas clearly and in remembering trains of thought. These latter effects were investigated by Weil and Zinberg (1969), who suggest that marihuana intoxication may exert subtle influences on speech, possibly as a result of a marihuana-induced interference with short-term memory. Drawing their data from five-minute verbal samples gathered before and during marihuana smoking, the authors found that while marihuana did not impair the comprehension of a verbal monologue, there was a "strange" quality in the drug samples which was not easily quantified.

In another study, Haines and Green (1970) conducted personal interviews with 131 moderate and heavy marihuana smokers. Respondents were asked whether they usually become more quiet or more talkative when high. Thirty-six percent said they became more quiet, 19% said they became more talkative, 25% said both may happen, and 20% did not know.

The somewhat contradictory finding that some users become more quiescent while others become more talkative has also been reported in another survey. Tart (1971) asked 150 relatively young (mean age 22 years) users to report on various intoxicating effects of marihuana. In response to two separate questions concerning marihuana and social interaction, 45% of the respondents indicated becoming more talkative and 49% less talkative when high. These varying effects may be related to degree of intoxication, since Tart's subjects also indicated that the quieting effect tended to occur at higher levels of intoxication. Another possibility is that individual styles of interaction are influenced differentially by the drug. Conceivably, the garrulous are affected in one way, and the taciturn in another. These studies, although retrospective in nature, suggest that marihuana may have a quieting effect on social interaction, particularly at higher levels of intoxication.

In view of reports indicating a general elevation of mood during marihuana intoxication (McGlothlin and West 1968; Allentuck and Bowman 1942), changes in the quality of interaction might also be expected. Tart's respondents reported being more sensitive to humor; giggling was cited as a common reaction. It might be expected that laughter and other types of positive interaction would be more prevalent during marihuana intoxication than negativism, hostility, or task-related conversation.

In order to investigate these impressions, groups of casual and heavy marihuana users were observed in task-oriented discussions before, during, and after a 21-day period of marihuana availability. It was expected that the rate, quality, and quantity of interaction would vary according to the use or nonuse or marihuana. Furthermore, in view of recent findings suggesting that heavy users accommodate themselves better to the disruptive effects of marihuana (Meyer *et al.* 1971), it was hypothesized that these effects would be more pronounced for the casual users.

Another issue investigated in the present study concerns the relationship between marihuana intoxication, group discussion, and opinion change. When individuals make their views public in a group discussion, social influence is generally applied toward those members whose initial views are most deviant from the central tendency (Schachter, 1951). Often this pressure toward conformity takes the form of genuine attitude change, as measured by an individual's private views after group discussion. In view of findings that the marihuana high is typically associated with feelings of euphoria, sociability, and group solidarity (Bennett 1971; Tart 1971; McGlothlin and West 1968); it was expected that tendencies toward compromise and concession would be more pronounced during intoxication. In short, individual opinions would be more susceptible to pressure from others.

1. METHODS AND PROCEDURE

The overall context and rationale of the investigation, as well as the subjects studied, have been described in Chapters 1 and 2. In the present research, subjects were convened for task-oriented group discussions each weekday afternoon during the three phases of the study. They were separated into two five-person groups which met concurrently in separate rooms. Group composition was varied from session to session by systematically exchanging two randomly selected group members. This was done in order to prevent the formation of a permanent status hierarchy and to provide discussants with a greater variety of opinions and viewpoints. On some occasions, however, the same combinations of group members were repeated for special assessments of hostility and aggression (see Chapter 6).

At the beginning of each session subjects were presented with a questionnaire booklet containing a discussion topic and a set of questions. On alternate days the nature of the discussion topic varied. Approximately half the discussions were based on a series of moral conflict problems, modeled after those developed by Stouffer and Toby (1951) in their study of role conflict and personality. Each situation involved a conflict between obligations to a friend and obligations to the larger society. The remaining meetings were devoted to discussions of Charles Morris' "Ways to Live" (Morris and Jones 1955). Each "way" consists of a capsule summary of a different life style common to a particular cultural group or historical period.

All discussions were similar in terms of participant functions and interaction requirements. Following an initial reading of the topic, each subject was instructed to record his personal opinion. If he was considering a "Way to Live," he was asked to record on a seven point scale the degree to which he liked or disliked that particular life style. Similarly, if he was reviewing a moral conflict problem, he answered two questions about the position he would take in the conflict situation. Next, the subject was asked to discuss the topic with the other members of the group for approximately 30 minutes. The stated task of the group was to arrive at a consensus as to the response category or categories which best reflected the opinion of the group. After the discussion was completed and the group opinion recorded, subjects were asked to record their private beliefs (regardless of the way they differed from their initial answers or from the group choice). A final question, included only during the drug period, instructed the subject to record on an 11-point scale his subjective level of intoxication.

Each discussion was tape recorded by a staff member who also served as nondirective group moderator. The interaction tapes were analyzed by two trained coders according to a modified Bales (1950) category system. Coders were not aware of the state of marihuana intoxication of the subjects. Intercoder reliability was checked routinely and was found to be high [average Scott's (1955) reliability coefficient, 0.85 or greater].

For greater simplicity and reliability, only four categories of interaction were coded: (1) positive reactions, e.g., showing solidarity, showing tension-release, joking; (2) personal disagreement or antagonism toward other participants; (3) attempted answers, e.g., giving suggestions, opinions, or information; (4) questions. These correspond roughly to Bales four major content areas, with two exceptions. Laughter was coded separately instead of as an instance of positive reactions. In addition, person-oriented acts of disagreement or antagonism were differentiated from instances of general disagreement. The latter were coded as attempted answers.

Verbal output in each of the main categories of interaction was treated statistically in terms of the absolute number of units spoken (total units) and in terms of the proportions (percentages) of these units relative to the total amount of output. It was expected that total units would reflect the effect of marihuana on the quantity of interaction, while the percentage data would be sensitive to changes in the individual and group interaction profiles, i.e., in the relative proportions of interaction regardless of quantity of output in each category.

2.   RESULTS

2.1.   Overall Effect of Marihuana on Verbal Interaction

The initial data analysis examined the relationship between various aspects of verbal interaction and the mere presence of intoxicated individuals in the group. The interaction data for each subject was averaged for each successive five-day segment of the study. The resulting segments were composed of the pre- and post-drug periods, as well as each quarter of the drug period. Analysis of variance was used to determine whether there were trends in verbal interaction which could be related to marihuana use.

The averages for the first series of analyses are shown in Table 5.1. The table first shows the number of group meetings observed during each five day segment of the study. A total of 36 five-person group meetings were observed among the casual users, and 40 groups were observed among the heavy users. On the average, both casual and heavy users rated themselves in the "mildly high" to "moderately high" ranges on the 11-point subjective intoxication scale after the group discussions. Comparing the individual mean intoxication levels over the four quarters of the drug

Table 5.1

Averages of Intoxication Level, Rate of Interaction, and Total Interaction Output: Casual and Heavy Users

			Marihuana smoking period: quarter				
		Pre-drug	1st	2nd	3rd	4th	Post-drug
Number of groups	Casual	6	6	6	6	6	6
observed	Heavy	8	6	6	6	6	8
Individual level	Casual	—	3.56	3.63	2.87	3.93	—
of intoxication	Heavy	—	3.73	4.23	3.63	3.85	—
Rate of interaction	Casual	13.03	13.07	13.27	15.98	12.74	15.73
	Heavy	13.15	11.71	11.21	12.31	12.98	13.24
Total output	Casual	325.5	206.0	199.5	194.5	153.5	180.2
	Heavy	137.0	88.3	161.5	128.3	151.8	185.4

period, a repeated measures analysis of variance indicated no significant differences for either the casual users ($F = 0.219$, df = 3, 36, n.s.) or the heavy users ($F = 0.238$, df = 3, 36, n.s.). The average group levels of intoxication during the discussions were remarkably consistent, even though some of the subjects characteristically were more intoxicated than others.

Casual user group discussions varied in length from 7 to 32 minutes, with an average duration of 16 minutes. Heavy user discussions ranged from 2.5 to 30 minutes, with an average length of 11.5 minutes. Using the number of verbal units per minute as a measure of rate of interaction, the results shown in Table 5.1 indicate that the pace of the discussions remained relatively constant for both types of user over all phases of the study. One-way analysis of variance revealed no significant differences between the means (F, casual users = 0.747, df = 5, 27, n.s.; F, heavy users = 0.367, df = 5, 34, n.s.).

Total verbal output decreased sharply during the initial part of the drug period for both casual and heavy users (Table 5.1). Whereas the total output of the casual users averaged 325.5 units of interaction during the pre-drug period, it dropped to less than two-thirds of this level (206.0) when marihuana became available to group members. The amount of interaction continued to decline throughout the drug period, but showed a slight increase during the post-drug phase. Repeated measures analysis of variance indicated significant differences between the means of six periods (F = 5.73, df = 5, 45, p. < 0.01).

It would be expected that such factors as progressive familiarity with the discussion task or developing friendships among the subjects produced certain systematic changes in verbal interaction independent of the use or nonuse of marihuana. A supplementary trend analysis was therefore performed to determine whether variations in verbal interaction occurred as a function of variables other than repetition of the task. The results of the trend analysis of the casual users' data indicated the existence of both linear (F = 7.64, df = 1, 9, p. < 0.05) and quadratic (F = 15.27, df = 1, 9, p. < 0.01) trends. The linear trend gives evidence of a repetition effect, whereas the quadratic or curvilinear trend is related directly to the use of marihuana. The findings indicate that marihuana contributed to the steady reduction of total verbal interaction over the course of the study for the casual user group.

Within the heavy user group total verbal interaction declined from the pre-drug period average of 137 units per discussion to a low of 88.3 units during the first quarter of the drug period. Total output tended to decrease during the remaining portion of the drug period, but showed an increment in the post-drug phase. Analysis of variance showed the difference between means to be significant (F = 3.81, df = 5, 45, p. < 0.01). The trend analysis indicated a significant (F = 9.73, df = 1, 9, p. < 0.05) linear tendency for verbal interaction to increase progressively over the course of the study. The quadratic trend was not significant (F = 2.56, df = 1, 9, n.s.), indicating that marihuana was not an influence in the variations in verbal interaction.

2.2. Specific Effects of Marihuana on Verbal Interaction and Laughter

The foregoing results give an indication of the general effect exerted on verbal interaction when some of the group members are mildly or moderately intoxicated. Further analyses are necessary in order to separate direct marihuana-related effects from indirect effects. For example, it is possible that the decrements in group interaction are not a function of marihuana but reflect a general withdrawal by nonintoxicated group members from interaction with their intoxicated peers. This would be an "indirect effect."

For this reason partial correlation coefficients were computed between numerical and percentage data, on the one hand, and subjective level of intoxication, on the other. In each case, the study day was partialed out to control for a possible repetition effect. To arrive at an overall evaluation of the significance of the relationship, each subject's partial correlation coefficient was transformed using Fisher's "z" transformation. The transformed coefficients were averaged across subjects and the student's "t" test was applied to the mean z score to determine the significance of the mean sample correlation from zero. To summarize the magnitude of the relationship, the average Fisher's z transformation was reconverted into a correlation coefficient, here referred to as the *average Pearson r.*

Table 5.2 summarizes the relationship between the amount of verbal interaction and the level of intoxication. A positive correlation in any category indicates an increase in amount of that interaction when the subject was high; a negative correlation reflects a decline in interaction.

The results for casual users indicate that total verbal interaction tended to decline as marihuana intoxication increased (r, total interaction $= -0.305$). These results corroborate the findings presented in the previous section, showing a significant decrement in total amount of verbal interaction during the drug period. Examining the data by individual categories of interaction, the casual user results show significant correlations in the categories of attempted answers ($r = -0.399$, p. < 0.05) and personal disagreement ($r = -0.187$, p. < 0.01), with the coefficient for laughter approaching significance ($r = 0.10$, p. < 0.10).

The results for the heavy users indicate a significant marihuana-related decrement in total interaction ($r = -0.178$, p. < 0.05), but the magnitude

Table 5.2

Average Pearson Correlation Coefficients: Amount of Interaction Correlated with Subjective Level of Intoxication, with Study Day Partialed Out

Interaction category	Casual users ($N = 7$)[a]			Heavy users ($N = 10$)		
	Average Pearson r	t	Level[b]	Average Pearson r	t	Level[b]
Positive reactions	0.073	0.87	n.s.	−0.056	−1.24	n.s.
Personal disagreement	−0.187	−2.42	0.05	0.029	0.41	n.s.
Attempted answers	−0.399	−3.98	0.01	−0.179	−2.48	0.05
Questions	−0.130	−0.79	n.s.	−0.171	−2.22	0.10
Laughter	0.100	1.82	0.01	0.188	1.9	0.05
Total interaction	−0.305	−4.04	0.01	−0.178	−2.57	0.05

[a] Three of the casual users (2C, 5C, and 10C) smoked marihuana so infrequently before group discussion that correlation coefficients could not be computed. The average Pearson r is therefore based on a sample of seven subjects.
[b] All significance levels were determined by the one-tailed test, except for questions, where no directional hypothesis was proposed.

of the r is smaller than that of the casual users ($r = -0.305$). Despite the decline in total interaction and attempted answers ($r = -0.179$, p. < 0.05), the incidence of laughter tended to increase ($r = 0.188$, p. < 0.05) with subjective intoxication.

The correlations of degree of marihuana intoxication with proportional (percentage) variations in verbal interaction are presented in Table 5.3. For the casual users level of intoxication correlated significantly with the relative proportion of positive reactions ($r = 0.33$, p. < 0.05). There was also a trend toward a decrease in proportion of attempted answers ($r = -0.31$, p. < 0.10). Although the incidence of laughter was not analyzed as a proportion of the total amount of verbal interaction, a standardized measure was obtained by computing the number of laughter units (i.e., discrete episodes of laughter) per minute of discussion. The results show that the higher a subject rated his level of intoxication, the more his rate of laughter tended to increase ($r = 0.29$, p. < 0.05).

In the heavy user sample, only the proportion of attempted answers decreased significantly with subjective intoxication ($r = -0.158$, p. < 0.05), while positive reactions showed a tendency to increase ($r = 0.09$, p. < 0.10).

2.3.   Effect of Marihuana on Opinion Change after Group Discussion

Responses to the "Ways to Live" questionnaire were analyzed in order to evaluate the effect of marihuana on opinion change and conformity to the

Table 5.3

Average Pearson Correlation Coefficients: Percent of Interaction Correlated with Subjective Level of Intoxication, with Study Day Partialed Out

Interaction category	Casual users ($N = 7$)[a]			Heavy users ($N = 10$)		
	Average Pearson r	t	Level[b]	Average Pearson r	t	Level[b]
Positive reactions	0.332	2.67	0.05	0.090	1.80	0.10
Personal disagreement	−0.093	−1.04	n.s.	0.010	0.17	n.s.
Attempted answers	−0.313	−1.77	0.10	−0.158	−2.56	0.05
Questions	0.120	0.66	n.s.	−0.067	−0.74	n.s.
Rate of laughter	0.294	2.02	0.05	0.066	0.52	n.s.

[a] Three of the casual users (2C, 5C, and 10C) smoked marihuana so infrequently before group discussion that correlation coefficients could not be computed. The average Pearson r is therefore based on a sample of seven subjects ($N = 7$).
[b] All significance levels were determined by the one-tailed test, except for questions, where no direction hypothesis was proposed.

group norm. Difference scores were computed between the pre-discussion and post-discussion responses. Post-discussion changes in the direction of the group norm (i.e., the response category reflecting the group consensus after discussion) were coded as positive, while changes away from the group norm were coded as negative. These difference scores were then correlated with ratings of subjective level of intoxication. As in previous analyses, study day was partialed out to control for repetition effects.

For the casual users, only four coefficients could be computed, each one based on 11 observations. The data from three of the casual users (2C, 5C, and 10C) were unusable because they smoked marihuana too infrequently before discussions. Three other subjects (1C, 3C, and 9C) failed to vary any of their opinions from the pre-discussion ratings. The resulting average Pearson r, summarizing the correlations of the four remaining subjects, was found to be 0.278 ($t = 0.87$, 3 df, n.s.). Although the correlation is in the predicted direction, it does not approach statistical significance because its magnitude is strongly determined by the high positive coefficient of subject 8C ($r = 0.80$).

Ten coefficients were computed for the heavy users, each one based on 12 observations. The resulting average Pearson r was close to zero ($r = 0.056$, $t = 0.58$, n.s.) and not statistically significant. Thus, the results for both groups indicate that there was no significant tendency for marihuana intoxication to be related to opinion change during group discussion.

3. DISCUSSION

The findings relating marihuana intoxication to variations in verbal interaction tend to offer general support for the hypotheses initially proposed in this study. Before discussing the findings, however, it should be emphasized that the results pertain to mixed groups of intoxicated and non-intoxicated individuals. Some subjects were characteristically more intoxicated than others, before and during the discussions. Since the basic design of the study required that subjects have free access to marihuana, it was neither possible nor desirable to control for levels of intoxication.

With respect to the overall effect of marihuana on verbal behavior, the most consistent finding from both the casual and heavy user studies was the marked decrement in total interaction during the initial quarter of the marihuana smoking period. These results are not surprising in view of the fact that the subjects had not smoked marihuana for at least five days prior to the morning of the first discussion session. They were also unfamiliar with the quality and potency of the "grass," which undoubtedly was stronger than that which they were accustomed to smoking (see Chapter 1).

These factors may have intensified the marihuana effect during the initial part of the drug period.

While the heavy users tended to exceed pre-drug levels of verbal interaction after the first quarter of the drug period, total interaction among the casual users continued to diminish. These results suggest that the heavy users accommodated themselves better to the long-term effects of marihuana. The findings are consistent with anecdotal reports describing the differential manner in which users with different levels of experience typically function under marihuana.

The findings describing the overall effect of marihuana on group discussion received strong confirmation from the results of individual correlational analyses. These results showed that changes in the quantity and quality of interaction were directly related to variations in marihuana intoxication. For both types of user, the total amount of verbal interaction tended to decrease at higher levels of intoxication, and this relationship was found most consistently in the category of attempted answers. These findings are consistent with the self-report data presented by Tart (1971), and they suggest that marihuana has a general quieting effect on social interaction. At the same time, however, the results showed that the incidence of laughter tended to increase during intoxication.

When changes in percentage profiles were analyzed, the evidence pointed to a general decline in the proportions of attempted answers, and a concomitant increase in percent of positive reactions. Again, these results were more pronounced for the casual users than for the heavy users.

These changes in interaction quality and talkativeness may be interpreted either of two ways. On the one hand, the observed changes may indicate that verbal facility is impaired when under marihuana. This general impairment in verbal facility could have resulted in a diminished capacity to engage in goal-related discussion. While this hypothesis is intriguing, other evidence does not support it.

Casual user groups averaged 66.2% attempted answers during the period of marihuana availability, as compared to 75.0% during the pre- and post-drug periods. The figures were 60.4% and 67.6%, respectively, for the heavy user groups. These data suggest that while the quality of the discussions may have shifted away from task-oriented responses, there was by no means a general disruption of verbal interaction, nor were the groups diverted or prevented from reaching their stated goal of consensus. Furthermore, differences in verbal behavior at various levels of intoxication were not clearly apparent. Few anomalies in speech or sentence structure were observed which could be attributed to marihuana intoxication. There was no evidence to suggest that subjects were incapable of engaging in intelligent discourse when high.

An alternative hypothesis is that a marihuana-related reduction in motivation caused subjects to withdraw from verbal interaction. Casual users interviewed at the end of the study stated that they found the task more boring and uninteresting when high. They felt more aware of the artificiality of the experimental situation. Marihuana may alter the way an individual perceives a social situation or a task; and he may make subtle modifications in the quantity and quality of his interaction as a result. A related possibility is that intoxicated subjects merely withdraw from interaction in order to concentrate on the subjective experience.

The findings also showed that there was no tendency for subjects to modify their private opinions after discussion when under the influence of marihuana. This tends to contradict an observation by Smith and Mehl (1970) that the marihuana user is particularly susceptible to the influence of other individuals in the immediate social environment. While this generalization may apply more to naive users under more threatening conditions, there was no evidence that subjects became more susceptible to the opinions of the majority. The findings presented here indicated that the compliance necessary to reach group consensus was public rather than private, and that subjects maintained rather than modified their differences of opinion.

A question can be raised about the applicability of the findings of this study to nonexperimental situations. While it can be argued that the setting and the task were artificial, the situation was not as atypical as one might suppose. Almost all of the subjects who volunteered for the study stated that they had interacted at one time or another with "straight" people when intoxicated. Many of them typically "turn on" with friends before a recreational activity, a college lecture, or even a day at work. Thus, it is not unlikely that during their daily activities many of these subjects come into contact with mixed groups of intoxicated and nonintoxicated individuals, and find it necessary to engage in some form of goal-oriented discussion. The present findings indicate that while subjects are capable of accommodating their speech and behavior according to the demand characteristics of the situation, they did show evidence of subtle but significant modifications in their verbal interaction when intoxicated.

4. SUMMARY

During the long and controversial history of its use, marihuana has been condemned as a social evil and extolled as a social facilitator. The present investigation studied several issues related to a small part of this controversy, the effect of marihuana on verbal interaction, laughter, and opinion change. While the results tended to show that individuals will reduce the amount and alter the quality of their conversation when high, the subjects were nevertheless found to be capable of engaging in intelligible, goal-directed discussion. The general tendency to withdraw from verbal interaction may be related to changes in motivation during marihuana intoxication. When intoxicated subjects did interact, their responses were more positive and less task-oriented than when they were not intoxicated. Furthermore, intoxication did not affect the modification of an individual's private opinion by group pressure.

6

Group Behavior: Hostility and Aggression

Carl Salzman, Gerald E. Kochansky,
and Linda J. Porrino

The possible relationship between marihuana and hostile human behavior has been debated for nearly half a century. Early reports that marihuana increased hostility were based on anecdotal evidence and came primarily from law enforcement agencies. Kaplan (1969), Grinspoon (1971), and Goode (1970) trace the development of opinion among law enforcement agencies that marihuana use is associated with increases in hostile human behavior such as aggressive and assaultive crime. Indeed, based on such opinion, the 1937 Marihuana Tax Act established marihuana as a harmful substance. According to these three reviewers, current police opinion concerning the role of marihuana in human hostility has not changed perceptibly.

Although objective research was scarce, early observation by physicians tended to dispute the reputed association between marihuana and aggression or hostility. Bromberg, writing in 1934, for example, commented on the difficulty of logically associating marihuana use and crime. He further speculated that alcohol was probably more responsible as an agent for crime than marihuana. Supporting evidence for Bromberg's speculations came a decade later. In the oft-quoted LaGuardia report (Mayor's Committee on Marihuana 1944), several observations were made which led to the conclusion that marihuana did not increase hostile or aggressive human behavior; on the contrary, it likely decreased it. In this report, Allentuck noted that "no aggressive or violent behavior (was) observed" in response to anxiety. Halpern, also writing in the LaGuardia report noted less aggression following the smoking of marihuana cigarettes. Recent writings tend to support the LaGuardia report observations that marihuana has no association with an increase in aggression or hostility. For example, Chopra and Chopra (1957) reported habitual users to be less offensive and obnoxious than nonusers; acts of violence were rarely committed by users. Murphy (1966) commented that "most serious observers agree that cannabis does not, *per se*, induce aggressive or criminal activities." Hollister *et al.* (1968) noted that responses to the aggressive factor of the Clyde Mood Scale went down after ingestion of tetrahydrocannabinol, the active ingredient of marihuana.

It would seem, therefore, that the basis of association between marihuana and aggressive or hostile human behavior is limited to non-research reports, while refutation of this position is given by research and clinical observation. Yet within some of these research reports are comments which suggest that marihuana may have indeed produced an increase in aggressive, hostile, antagonistic, or obnoxious behavior in certain subjects. Within the LaGuardia report, Allentuck (1944) reported an increase in "antagonism" at high doses of marihuana and a "spirit of antagonism or belligerence" in two subjects. Halpern noted that 88% of the marihuana users studied considered themselves aggressive after they had the drug as compared with only 42% in the undrugged state. In a summary of the LaGuardia report, Wallace commented:

> "In a limited number of the subjects there were alterations in behavior giving rise to antisocial expression. This was shown by unconventional acts not permitted in public, anxiety reactions, opposition and antagonism, and eroticism. Effects such as these would be considered conducive to acts of violence. However, any tendency toward violence was expressed verbally and not by physical actions."

Our laboratory has had a general interest in the effects of psychotropic agents upon hostility. During the past two years, we have been developing a series of research methods through which verbal hostility can be measured as an inner affective state as well as an interpersonal communication.

A review of the literature (Feshbach 1964; Kaufman 1965; Berkowitz 1962) suggests that "hostility" is a multidimensional construct which is related in a complex fashion to other constructs such as aggression, violence, and anger. We conceptualize hostility as an intervening variable in which the goal response is injury to some object; it is subsumed under the term "aggression," but must be distinguished from it. For this study of marihuana effect, we have focused upon verbal, interpersonal hostility, in which the goal response is nonphysical injury to another person through speech. The deprecation, ridicule, criticism, or denouncement of a colleague or of the experimenter is a readily apparent example of hostile verbal interpersonal behavior.

1. METHODS

The experimental focus for this study was two groups of five volunteer subjects who convened to discuss topical issues. The particulars of these groups have been described in Chapter 5. We shall present data for one group of heavy users of marihuana.

Two interactive sessions for each group were analyzed. The first occurred during the pre-drug period of the study; no subjects were marihuana intoxicated. The second group interaction occurred during the drug period of the study; all subjects were intoxicated some of the time. Although data for a post-drug interactive session were also collected, these have not been included in the present report since some of the heavy user subjects allegedly were marihuana intoxicated during this period (see footnote 3, Chapter 1). Subjects were asked to rate themselves and each other for various affects, including hostility, at the end of each of the two group sessions. Group interaction was tape recorded, and subsequently scored for verbal interaction hostility.

Three assessment procedures were used to conceptualize different dimensions of the hostility construct.

1.1. Assessment of Hostile Inner States

At the termination of each group discussion, the Buss–Durkee Hostility Inventory (BDHI), a paper-and-pencil test, was administered to each subject. This is a self-report scale (Buss and Durkee 1957) which has been widely used to assess absolute levels and changes in levels of hostility as an inner affective and motivational state. The BDHI yields two first-order factor scores, motoric and attitudinal, plus eight subfactor scores in addition to a total score.

1.2. Interpersonal Perception of Hostility

In order to assess the degree to which each group member perceived each of his fellow group members as hostile during any given group session, our laboratory developed the Hostility Interpersonal Perception Scale (HIPS) and administered it to each subject in the present study at the end of each group discussion. The scale is similar to many self-rated mood adjective checklists. On the HIPS, however, the subject is asked to rate each group member on each of the ten adjectives which comprise the scale. Most of the ten adjectives describe affective aspects of hostile mood states (e.g., "irritable," "openly antagonistic," "feeling angry," etc.), while others describe affects which may be opposite to hostile mood states (e.g., "cooperative," "friendly," etc.), and "filler" adjectives (e.g., "anxious," etc.). By means of the HIPS it becomes possible to assess the degree to which each group member *is perceived* as either "positive" or hostile by fellow group members.

1.3.   Assessment of Verbal Interpersonal Hostility

The verbal interpersonal dimension of hostility was assessed by an observer rating system developed by Kochansky, Salzman, and Porrino in 1971 and still undergoing revision and refinement. The rating system was devised to enable asessment of the quantity and quality of verbal hostility which is emitted during interpersonal interactions. Most, though not all, of the categories of hostility included in the scale are based upon the content, as opposed to the formal or affective qualities of the verbal communication. Often, however, the affective tone of the communication may determine the scoring of the relative intensity of a particular kind of hostility expressed, since the rating system was designed to assess three levels of intensity (mild, moderate, and severe) for each category of verbal hostility included in the system. The rating system is composed of eight categories of verbal interpersonal hostility:

1.   Criticisms of another's performance.
2.   Verbal assaults upon another's worth.
3.   Interruptions.
4.   Nonsequential behavior.
5.   Threatening behavior.
6.   Hostile attempts to alter or control interpersonal fields.
7.   Sarcasm.
8.   Threats of physical assault.

In the present study the three authors independently rated audio tapes of the group discussions. Final scores of verbal interpersonal hostility consisted only of those ratings which all three raters agreed were hostile, according to the system.

2.   RESULTS

2.1.   Hostility as an Inner Affective State

Mean Buss–Durkee scores are presented in Table 6.1. Total hostility as an inner motivational and affective state was significantly decreased following

Table 6.1

Mean Buss–Durkee Scores: Pre-Drug vs. Drug Periods

	Pre-drug period	Drug period	Significance[a]
Motoric factor	14.10	12.50	n.s.
Attitudinal factor	1.60	1.30	n.s.
Assaultiveness	3.30	3.10	n.s.
Verbal hostility	6.80	6.10	n.s.
Indirect hostility	0.80	0.60	n.s.
Irritability	1.30	0.90	<0.05
Negativism	1.80	1.50	n.s.
Resentment	0.60	0.50	n.s.
Suspicion	1.00	0.90	n.s.
Total	15.70	13.70	<0.05

[a] Paired t test, two-tailed, df = 9.

group sessions in which subjects had been marihuana intoxicated. Most of this decrease can be accounted for by a lessening in the irritability subfactor, although all subfactor scores show a slight decrement. By inspection, the items which showed the largest decrease in scores following marihuana intoxication are shown in Table 6.2. There was no difference between casual and heavy users.

2.2. Perception and Expression of Hostility in Others

Subjects when intoxicated with marihuana are consistently seen by their colleagues as more friendly, receptive, understanding, and cooperative (correlated t = 2.5349, p. < 0.05, two-tailed). There is also a nonsignificant trend for intoxicated subjects to be seen by their colleagues as less irritable,

Table 6.2

Buss–Durkee Items Reflecting Greatest Decrease in Hostility during Drug Period

Item number	
25.	I would say nasty things if I got mad (Verbal Hostility).
33.	I feel I would raise my voice if I got into an argument (Verbal Hostility).
41.	If someone made a rule I didn't like, I would be tempted to break it (Negativism).
57.	I feel I am unlikely to have a fit of temper over something (Indirect Hostility). (This item is scored in a reversed direction.)

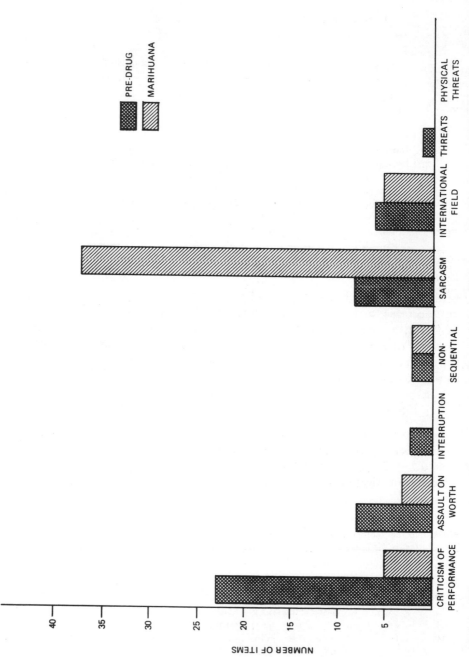

Figure 6.1. Frequency of verbal hostility units during pre-drug and marihuana smoking periods.

disagreeable, openly antagonistic, annoyed, or angry (t = 1.8698, p. < 0.10, two-tailed).

2.3.   Verbal Interactional Hostility

Since the Verbal Interactional Hostility Scale is still being refined, data will be presented as qualitative changes rather than statistical differences. The overall effect of marihuana upon verbal hostility can be seen in Figure 6.1. It is clear that in these group settings marihuana qualitatively affected the style of hostile communication. When subjects were not intoxicated, the primary form of hostile communication consisted of hostile criticisms of colleagues' performances during the group discussion. When intoxicated, however, criticisms markedly declined, and the use of sarcasm markedly increased. This observation is consonant with findings presented in Chapter 5, that marihuana increased laughter. Sarcastic comments directed at fellow subjects, at the experiment, or at the researchers, were invariably followed by laughter. Sarcasm, as a communicative style, is indirect or oblique, as opposed to a more direct criticism. However, it is often an extreme and potent means of expressing hostility, despite its humorous components.

In summary, subjects who have smoked marihuana and then interact in a group setting seem to perceive themselves and their group colleagues as less hostile and more friendly. These subjects, however, when rated by nonintoxicated experimenter observers, evince a *shift in style* of hostile communication, rather than any readily apparent quantitative change.

3.   DISCUSSION

We wish to emphasize caution in interpreting data presented here. Only ten subjects in four group interactions were studied; the group interactions occurred within the larger context of this collaborative experiment. We have no way of assessing the effect on hostility that may have occurred from sources outside these groups. In addition, since we could not use data from post-drug group interactions for comparative purposes, there is no statistical way of isolating marihuana effects from repetition, or group process effects. We may state, however, that our observation of the post-drug group interactions suggested that most of the subjects returned to their earlier (pre-drug) style of communication, i.e., more overt criticism, and less sarcasm.

For these reasons we must consider our data as preliminary, and suggestive of further research endeavors. It would seem that our observations on the effect of marihuana on hostility are consonant with commonly reported antihostility effects of this drug. Our observations also confirm earlier unpublished research which had incidently commented upon marihuana and hostility; the drug in general produced a decrease in hostility as experienced internally and externally. The tendency toward sarcasm would indicate that if hostility is not markedly decreased, then it is converted into an indirect and humorous *verbal* communication. Sarcastic hostility may also provide tension relief, thereby leading to less antagonistic interpersonal relationships among group members.

Our data on hostility as an inner affective state, derived from Buss–Durkee Hostility Inventory scores, are also consonant with Q-sort data from this study, presented in Chapter 10. On the basis of these findings, we feel it likely that marihuana, per se, has little tendency to increase hostility, as has been suggested by earlier reports. It may be, however, that *under conditions of frustration* the marihuana-intoxicated person may in fact report an *increase* in hostility. Earlier data from the LaGuardia report (Mayor's Committee on Marihuana 1944) and recent data on tetrahydrocannabinol lend credence to this supposition (Chopra and Chopra 1957; Murphy 1966; Hollister *et al.* 1968). The conditions of the present study, and the group interactive phase in particular, do not allow for prediction of marihuana effect under such adverse social conditions as frustration or fear. Although the present data are consonant with the growing literature which considers marihuana as a hostility decreasing substance, we feel that further investigation is warranted to study the effect of marihuana on hostility individually and in social settings under conditions of frustration.

7

Group Behavior: Problem Solving Efficiency

Thomas F. Babor, A. Michael Rossi,
Gerald Sagotsky, and Roger E. Meyer

Numerous researchers have explored the effects of marihuana on various aspects of cognitive performance. In general, the more complex the cognitive manipulation involved, the greater the marihuana-related impairment (Melges *et al.* 1970a; Clark *et al.* 1970). Melges *et al.* (1970a) have summarized these observations under the term "temporal disintegration," which is defined as difficulty in retaining, coordinating, and indexing goal-related information.

In contrast with data obtained in the experimental laboratory, experienced users are not consistent in their retrospective reports on the effects of marihuana upon cognitive function. Tart (1971) obtained survey data suggesting that marihuana resulted in dulling of attention, fragmentation of thought, and impaired immediate memory. In general, logical reasoning ability was reduced, but intuitive and creative thinking were more original during intoxication. These reports are consistent with the experiences of some artists, writers and musicians who maintain that marihuana actually enhances creative thinking [e.g., Alan Ginsberg (1966) and William Burroughs (1966)]. The data obtained in the experimental laboratory on "temporal disintegration" and the retrospective reports of users in surveys and personal reminiscences are all consistent with the notion that marihuana facilitates intuitive, nonlogical kinds of thought processes at the same time that it interferes with logical, "rational" forms of thinking.

The present study was undertaken to investigate problem solving behavior in a social setting utilizing the familiar parlor game, "Twenty Questions." Participants were presented with pictures of a finite set of objects. They were instructed to determine which object the experimenter had in mind by asking questions which he could answer "yes" or "no." The task was chosen because one can differentiate two distinctive problem solving strategies (Mosher and Hornsby 1956) whose relative frequencies might be altered by marihuana intoxication. The most efficient strategy is called "*constraint seeking*"; the participants attempt to eliminate exactly half the alternatives with each question. The least efficient strategy is "*hypothesis scanning*." Here participants ask questions applying to one object at a time; testing only specific, self-sufficient hypotheses. In an investigation of cognitive behavior, these strategies can be studied as representing either a logical (the former) or an intuitive (the latter) approach.

It was anticipated that groups containing marihuana-intoxicated subjects would: (1) require more questions to arrive at a correct solution; (2) tend to use a hypothesis scanning strategy rather than a constraint seeking approach; and (3) manifest a reduced motivation to participate.

1. METHOD AND PROCEDURE

The general experimental design and research procedures, as well as the characteristics of the subjects studied, have been described in Chapters 1 and 2. Assessments of problem solving ability were conducted on six occasions during both the casual user and the heavy user studies. During these six sessions, subjects were organized into two five-person teams.

During each session, the teams each played four or five games of Twenty Questions concurrently while in different rooms. At the first meeting, the rules of the task were explained. Several practice games were played in order to familiarize subjects with the task and to minimize the effect of practice on later sessions. Subjects were seated in full view of a large poster board which contained 42 pictures, each depicting a familiar object (such as a boat, an automobile, a flower, etc.). Participants were informed that before each game one of the objects had been selected at random by the research staff. It was the task of each team to determine which object the researcher had in mind. In order to enhance motivation and involvement, as well as to generate a spirit of competition, participants were told that the team achieving the correct answer in the least number of questions would win $1.00 (i.e., 20 cents for each team member).

Subjects were instructed to work as a team in formulating the questions they considered to be the most efficient. Before each question, the team was given a three-minute time interval to exchange suggestions and to discuss the merits of each. Immediate notification was provided to the winning and losing teams after each game.

Excluding a practice session on study day 2, all subjects met to play Twenty Questions on five occasions. The sessions were equally spaced over the three phases of the study. Casual users played four games per meeting, while heavy users played five. Except for one instance of apparatus failure during the casual user study, tape recordings were made of all sessions. These tapes, as well as a written record of the questions kept by the staff member, provide the basis for the present analyses.

The tape recordings of each session were analyzed by a trained coder according to the number and type of suggestions proposed by each subject in the course of the group discussions. Four types of problem solving behavior were coded: (1) A count was made of the total number of suggestions proposed by each subject during each session.[1] This variable was used as a *measure of motivation* since it appears to be a good index of willingness to participate in task-oriented discussions. (2) The number of original suggestions actually adopted by the group and formally proposed to the researcher was coded for each participant. This measure was considered an index of the "quality" of the suggestion, as judged by the group. (3) A count was made of the number of questions which each subject formally proposed to the staff member on behalf of the team (regardless of whether it was originally his suggestion or not). This measure was used as an index of willingness to assume the leadership role, since such an initiative required that the subject become the spokesman for the group. (4) Each original suggestion proposed by a group member was analyzed according to whether it applied to only one object on the board (i.e., "hypothesis scanning") or whether it was general enough to include two or more objects (i.e., "constraint seeking"). As indicated above, this measure was used to evaluate individual problem solving efficiency (and logical vs. intuitive thinking).

The main part of the data analysis consisted of relating these measures to variations in the level of intoxication, as measured by an 11-point self-report rating scale. The scale, as well as the procedures and rationale for computing the partial correlation coefficient, are discussed in Chapter 5.

---

[1] Suggestions which were repetitions of those of other subjects, or which had been proposed previously, were not counted in this total.

2.   RESULTS

In order to evaluate the overall motivation and performance of competing groups, team averages were computed summarizing the number of original suggestions proposed per game, and the number of questions per game required to arrive at the correct solution. The results for the casual users are shown in Table 7.1, which also lists the average level of intoxication for all participants. Since group membership in the casual user teams varied from session to session, the team results were combined rather than presented separately.

The results for the casual users show that both suggestions and questions declined slightly up until study day 20. At this point, one of the teams indicated a change in both indices, with suggestions dropping to an average of 7.7 and questions increasing to 12.6. This trend became pronounced in the post-drug session (study day 28), when subjects on both teams ceased making suggestions within the group. As the post-drug mean suggests ($\bar{x}$ questions – 22.1), performance was least efficient during the last session.

The data indicate no consistent relationship between number of questions and level of intoxication. Although the worst team performance during the marihuana smoking period took place on study day 20 ($\bar{x}$ questions = 8.8), when the highest average level of intoxication was reported ($\bar{x}$ intoxication = 4.6), a further analysis of the data revealed that, in fact, the team with the highest reported average intoxication ($\bar{x}$ intoxication = 5.6) actually arrived at problem solutions with the least number of questions ($\bar{x}$ questions = 5.0).

The overall team results for the heavy users are presented in Table 7.2. A moderate reduction in the incidence of both suggestions and questions

Table 7.1

Averages of Original Suggestions, Questions, and Level of Intoxication: Casual Users (N = 10)

Study period	Study day	Original suggestions	Questions	Level of intoxication
Pre-drug	5	11.8	6.7	—
Drug	8	11.0	6.2	3.9
	13	—[a]	5.7	2.9
	20	9.2	8.8	4.6
Post-drug	28	0	22.1	—

[a] Data incomplete due to apparatus failure.

Table 7.2

Team Averages of Original Suggestions, Questions, and Level of Intoxication: Heavy Users (N = 10)

Study period	Study day	Original suggestions		Questions		Level of intoxication	
		Team A	Team B	Team A	Team B	Team A	Team B
Pre-drug	5	12.6	13.2	8.0	10.8	—	—
Drug	7	6.0	7.6	4.6	5.6	3.2	4.6
	14	8.6	6.2	5.8	5.8	5.6	4.4
	21	5.8	8.6	5.0	7.0	5.6	3.0
Post-drug	28	10.8	7.0	6.0	7.6	—	—

can be noted on study day 7, the first session of the marihuana smoking period. Performance remained stable during the remaining sessions of the drug period. In the post-drug session, efficiency decreased slightly for both teams, while the number of suggestions increased for team A only. The results summarizing average team intoxication show no consistent relationship to differences in performance. For example, team A performed more efficiently (i.e., required fewer questions to arrive at the solution) than team B on study days 7 and 21; yet the average intoxication level for team A was lower than that of team B on study day 7 and higher on study day 21. The only apparent relation between overall performance and marihuana use occurs when the results of the drug period are compared with those of the nondrug periods (study days 5 and 28). These data indicate that efficiency for both teams was the highest when marihuana was available.

In order to evaluate more specifically the relationship between marihuana intoxication and problem solving behavior, the results were analyzed for individual subjects. Unfortunately, the data for the casual users were incomplete for study day 13. This, coupled with the infrequent marihuana smoking on the part of some subjects, made it impossible to analyze the data properly. Thus, only the results for the heavy users are reported (Table 7.3).

The average Pearson correlations indicate that there were no apparent changes in the two indices of problem solving efficiency related to marihuana intoxication. There was no tendency for the proportion of constraint questions to decrease during intoxication ($r = 0.062$), nor was there a decline in the proportion of suggestions accepted by the team ($r = -0.096$). The proportion of original suggestions was moderately correlated

Table 7.3

Average Pearson Correlation Coefficients Summarizing Relationship
between Four Measures of Problem Solving Behavior and Subjective
Level of Intoxication with Study Day Partialed Out: Heavy Users
(N = 10)

	Average Pearson r	t	Significance level[a]
Constraint[b]	0.062	0.25	n.s.
Suggestions adopted[c]	−0.096	−0.29	n.s.
Original suggestions[c]	−0.382	−0.90	n.s.
Questions asked[c]	−0.355	−2.73	0.05

[a] All tests of significance were by the two-tailed method, using nine
degrees of freedom.
[b] Based on the proportion of an individual's total suggestions for that
session that reflected a constraint-seeking strategy.
[c] Based on the proportion of the group total for each session.

with level of intoxication, but the average Pearson correlation ($r = -0.382$)
did not attain statistical significance. This was because the coefficients for
four subjects were in the positive direction. With respect to questions ver-
balized to the staff member while the subject was intoxicated, the significant average Pearson correlation ($r = -0.355$) indicates that the higher a
subject's level of intoxication, the less he acted as team spokesman.

3.   DISCUSSION

In general, teams of both types of users performed the Twenty Questions
task more efficiently during sessions when marihuana was used by group
members. In view of the individual analysis of the heavy users' data, it does
not appear that this change was directly related to the effect of marihuana
on motivation or cognitive functioning. It is still conceivable, however, that
the quality of the constraint questions improved under marihuana intoxication, and that this resulted in better performance. It was not possible to
evaluate this possibility adequately with the present data, but further research is planned to explore this question more thoroughly.

     In spite of the fact that overall team efficiency increased during the pe-
riod of marihuana smoking, there was also a tendency for suggestions to
diminish. Although the improved performance may have reduced the
necessity for considering many suggestions, this change may also reflect an

overall reduction in motivation to perform the task. This is best illustrated by the performance of one of the casual user teams. In the last game of study day 20, subject 1C suggested that his team switch from the more usual constraint seeking strategy to a hypothesis scanning or guessing approach. Thus, instead of generating numerous suggestions, considering the merits of each, and then proposing the best one to the staff member, the team members decided to take turns guessing at the objects one by one. In switching to the least efficient strategy, these subjects indicated a reduction in motivation both to perform the task efficiently and to compete with the other team.

This trend was carried over into the final post-drug session, however, suggesting that it was boredom rather than the drug which precipitated the change. Before the final series of games, members of both casual user teams agreed to compete according to the least efficient guessing strategy, and this is reflected in the sharp increase in questions and the total absence of suggestions.

No such radical change took place during the games between the heavy user teams. The findings presented in Table 7.2 show that the increase in efficiency of overall performance was unrelated to the average intoxication level of team members. This conclusion is corroborated by the results of the individual correlational analysis, which revealed no tendency for the proportion of constraint questions to vary under marihuana intoxication. These results indicate that marihuana did not interfere with subjects' ability to formulate a conceptual strategy and to efficiently employ new information to arrive at a correct solution. The results also indicate that marihuana intoxication did not increase hypothesis scanning or guessing tendencies. If, as some reports have suggested (e.g., Tart 1971), marihuana smoking does stimulate intuitive thinking, then it is apparent that this generalization does not apply to the particular kind of problem solving situation employed in the present investigation.

The individual correlational results also showed that heavy user subjects were less prone to assume a leadership role in the group when intoxicated. This finding is consistent with data presented in Chapter 5, demonstrating a general tendency for subjects to withdraw from verbal interaction when intoxicated. Thus, whereas marihuana may not have affected an individual's ability to perform the task, the effect of intoxication may have been sufficient to inhibit verbalizations directed at the researcher. This hypothesis also receives some support from the nonsignificant tendency for original suggestions to decline with degree of intoxication (average Pearson $r = -0.382$).

Unfortunately, it was not possible to determine whether these findings apply also to the casual users. It is conceivable that casual and naive users may not be capable of maintaining their normal level of performance while intoxicated with marihuana, and that our findings relative to heavy users may reflect their ability to compensate for or to suppress the effects of marihuana. Alternatively, it may suggest behavioral tolerance.

In summary, heavy users who were intoxicated with marihuana were quite capable of retaining information gained from previous questions, and demonstrated a normal ability to organize and coordinate feedback while pursuing a goal-directed task. It is possible that the disruptive effects of marihuana upon problem solving were not observed in the present study because of the group testing situation, the nature of the task, or the nature of the dependent measures that were selected. Alternatively, marihuana-related decrements in performance observed in other settings (Melges *et al.* 1970*a*) may be related to the specific monitoring task, the testing procedure, or exposure to doses of marihuana or tetrahydrocannabinol which are selected by the experimenter rather than by the subject.

8
Memory and Time Estimation

A. Michael Rossi and John O'Brien

The ability of marihuana to alter the sense of time has been noted by many authors (Bloomquist 1968; Cohen 1968; Goode 1969c; Jaffe 1965; Kaplan 1969; Hollister 1971; Grinspoon 1969; Gershon 1970; Walton 1938). The alteration has been described in various terms, but there is near total agreement that the basic change produced by marihuana is a subjective impression that real time is passing slowly. The occurrence of this effect has been documented in a number of research studies which have employed a wide range of techniques to assess time perception (Allentuck and Bowman 1942; Bromberg 1934; Clark *et al*. 1970; Hollister and Gillespie 1970; Isbell *et al*. 1967a; Melges *et al*. 1970a, 1970b; Meyer *et al*. 1971; Tinklenberg *et al*. 1970; Weil *et al*. 1968). In the only research study which failed to find some evidence of altered time perception, very short time intervals (one, two, and five seconds) had been used in the assessment procedures (Dornbush *et al*. 1971).

Although the occurrence of a marihuana-induced altered time sense has been well documented, there is still much to be learned about this effect and its behavioral consequences. For example, the basic mechanism by which marihuana alters time perception is still to be elucidated. It is not known whether the alteration in time sense is brought about by some direct pharmacological action on neuronal systems serving as a "biological clock," or whether the alteration is a secondary phenomenon occurring as a consequence of changes in either ideational or memory processes. The latter possibility has been suggested by Clark et al. (1970), who have stated that "It is likely that distortion of time sense is incidental to . . . effects on perception, memory, and organization of thought" (p. 198). The general suppositions underlying this view are: (1) The disinhibiting properties of marihuana lead to both a loosening of ideational associations and a rapid flowing of ideas which speeds up the subjective sense of time; (2) a marihuana-induced short-term memory impairment interferes with a sense of continuity in passing events which is an essential element in time perception.

Despite the fact that impaired memory function also has been widely described to be an effect of marihuana (Bloomquist 1968; Cohen 1968; Goode 1969a, 1969b; Jaffe 1965; Kaplan 1969; Hollister 1971; Grinspoon 1969; Gershon 1970; Walton 1938), attempts to obtain research evidence of a marihuana-induced memory dysfunction have not been universally successful. Some studies have documented this effect (Abel 1970; Abel 1971a; Melges et al. 1970a, 1970b; Clark et al. 1970; Mayor's Committee on Marihuana 1944; Waskow et al. 1970), but other studies have produced negative or mixed results (Clark and Nakashima 1968; Dornbush et al. 1971; Hollister and Gillespie 1970; Jones and Stone 1970; Meyer et al. 1971; Williams et al. 1946).

The fact that results have been mixed in documenting a marihuana-induced memory impairment would seem to weaken the hypothesis that the well-documented altered time sense is a function of impaired memory processes. However, the fact that memory processes are exceedingly complex may partially explain the inconsistent research results. There are many inherent difficulties in devising appropriate assessments of memory functions which are not seriously affected by variables such as subjects' motivation, attention, concentration, and intelligence. In addition, it has been stated that "impairments in immediate memory from marihuana intoxication do not follow a smooth time function, but rather are episodic, brief in duration, and not always under volitional control . . . " (Grinspoon 1971, p. 142). If true, this waxing and waning of the marihuana effect would be a further obstacle in obtaining consistent research results.

It has been reported that the acute effects of marihuana on a variety of subjective experiences and psychomotor skills have been either enhanced or diminished by repeated exposure to the drug (Weil, et al. 1968; Williams et al. 1946; Carlini 1968; McMillan et al. 1970). Although there has been some research evidence that the acute effects of marihuana on memory become less pronounced with habitual use (Weil et al. 1968), there is no data regarding possible changes in effects on time perception with habitual use. One of the purposes in including assessments of both time perception and memory function in the present study was to determine whether the acute effects of the drug on these functions are changed with prolonged use.

The research design includes repeated measurements and the use of each subject as his own control. These features provide certain advantages over previous research designs used in this area. For example, the use of subjects as their own controls partially avoids the possibility of the results being confounded by the large individual differences that have been reported in marihuana research (e.g., Clark and Nakashima 1968; Pivak *et al.* 1972; Melges *et al.* 1970*a* and 1970*b*). Also, if the effects of marihuana wax and wane as reported (Grinspoon 1971), these effects are more likely to be found with repeated measurements than with one or two assessments. The use of repeated measurements also makes it possible to record changes in these effects if they occur with repeated marihuana use.

1. METHOD

The general design of this study and subject selection have been described in Chapters 1 and 2. Two groups of experienced marihuana users were employed as subjects in two separate but identical studies. One group of ten subjects, defined as casual users, had at least a one-year history of marihuana use and were currently averaging approximately eight smoking sessions per month. The other group of ten subjects, defined as heavy users, had a two-to-nine-year history of marihuana use and were currently averaging 33 smoking sessions per month. Each group of subjects lived on a closed hospital research ward for 31 days, under living conditions made as comfortable as possible, consistent with security and experimental requirements.

From the sixth through the twenty-sixth day of the study subjects were permitted to purchase and smoke *ad lib* one-gram marihuana cigarettes with approximately 2.0% delta 9 THC content. The method by which subjects could purchase marihuana and the amount and temporal distribution of their marihuana consumption are described in Chapter 3.

Subjects were tested for time estimation and short-term memory beginning at approximately 10:00 a.m. on each of the 31 days of the study. These assessments are termed *daily assessments* in this report, and they were carried out each day regardless of whether or not subjects smoked marihuana. However, accurate records were kept of exactly when subjects chose to smoke marihuana, and these records made it possible to know how much time had elapsed between the smoking of marihuana and the

assessments. Assessments that were made less than 90 minutes after a subject chose to smoke marihuana are referred to as *daily marihuana-related
assessments* in this report. Subjects were under the impression (correctly
so) that the daily assessments were being carried out to evaluate changes
related to long-term use of marihuana. There was no indication that they
were aware that these assessements also could be related to the time of
their most recent marihuana intake and used to evaluate the acute effects
of the drug. Thus, the daily marihuana-related assessments are relatively
free from the bias introduced by subjects who would be motivated to distort
their performances to coincide with how they believe they should behave
after smoking marihuana.

In addition to the daily assessments, each day during the 21-day drug
period, two subjects were scheduled for time estimation and short-term
memory assessments one-half hour after smoking a marihuana cigarette.
The schedule was arranged so that any one particular subject would be
scheduled for these marihuana-related assessments four times during the
21-day drug period. These assessments are referred to as *special
marihuana-related assessments* in this report. Subjects were aware that
these assessments were to be used to evaluate the acute effects of
marihuana. Thus, one of the major differences between the *daily*
marihuana-related assessments and *special* marihuana-related assessments
was the degree of subject awareness that the results would be examined for
evidence of the acute effects as well as the repeat dose effects of marihuana.

The short-term memory and time estimation assessments were always
carried out in conjunction with each other and in the named order. The
assessments were conducted in a large room on the research ward, and a
testing session lasted between 35 and 45 minutes. Daily assessments were
group administered, with the subjects sitting in two columns of five seats
lined up against two side walls, facing the front wall of the room. The seats
were spaced so that subjects could not easily communicate with each other or
observe each other's responses without being observed by the experimenter
who always remained in the rear of the room.

1.1   Memory

Short-term memory was assessed by the Digit Span Forward and Backward Test. This test consists of presenting subjects with a progressively
increasing number of digits which are to be reproduced in either the given
order or reverse order according to directions. The test was administered to
subjects by projecting the digits with a Carousel slide projector. Each slide
contained one digit, and the slides were placed in the slide tray with three

blank spaces separating the digit series, which progressed in length from three to nine digits. Pressing the "forward" button on the slide projector advance controls automatically projected each digit for one second until the button was released. The appearance of a blank projection was the signal for the experimenter to release the button and for subjects to record their responses with pen and paper. After all subjects had signaled (by placing their pens behind an ear) that they were finished recording their responses, the next series of digits was projected. Subjects were constantly monitored to ensure that none wrote digits while they were being projected; reproduced a digit series backward by writing the digits right to left, or reproduced a series backward after first writing the series in a forward order.

A different set of digits was used for each testing session. Sixty sets were compiled by selecting digits from a table of random numbers and rearranging sequences to insure that each digit appeared in each position (e.g., first, last) with equal frequency; no digit appeared more than once in any series; no two series in a set began or ended with the same digit; no strongly associated digit sequences occurred (e.g., 2-4-6-8); and no two naturally successive digits occurred (e.g., 7-8; 2-1).

In order to maintain subjects' motivation for accurate performance, they were paid five cents for each series of digits reproduced correctly.

1.2.   Time Estimation

Time estimation was assessed with two six-channel event recorders. Five channels on each recorder were connected to hand button-switches which were activated by subjects during a testing session. The remaining channel on each recorder was activated by the experimenter. Depression of the button on a hand switch produced a deflection of a pen on the recorder, and the pen would remain deflected until the button was released. The paper drive on each recorder moved at a constant speed (2 mm/sec), and measurement of the length of a line produced by a deflected pen provided a direct and exact measure of how long any button had been depressed. Subjects were instructed to make their time estimates by pressing the button on their hand switches for the length of the specified intervals to be judged. The experimenter depressed his button on a random basis to assure that subjects received no auditory cues from activation of the recording pens.

During each testing session subjects were required to make eight time estimations which bracketed four time intervals of 10, 60, 90, and 180 seconds. For example, during one session subjects estimated time intervals of 75-50-180-9-70-105-11-180 seconds in that order; the next session they estimated time intervals of 60-7-170-85-190-13-95-60 seconds, and so on. A total of 28 different time intervals in different combinations were estimated during the course of each study to partially offset practice effects. The test was group administered, and subjects were paid five cents for each correct time estimation within plus or minus 10% error.

The procedure used during special marihuana-related assessments was identical to those used during the daily assessments, with the exception that the tests were administered individually rather than in groups.

2. RESULTS

2.1. Short-Term Memory

Data from the assessments of short-term memory were analyzed by a Stepwise Multiple Regression Analysis of Variance computer program.[1] This analysis is designed to examine interrelations between several predictor variables and a dependent variable within the framework of an additive model. In the present study, the analysis indicated how a number of independent variables (e.g., cumulative number of marihuana cigarettes smoked, time elapsed since marihuana smoked, etc.) related both singly and jointly to the dependent variable (e.g., digit span score). For a variety of technical reasons only data collected in the daily assessments during the drug period were included in the analysis. The exclusion of data from pre- and post-drug periods and from the special assessments increased the probability of a type II error (real differences not reaching statistical significance), rather than a type I error (chance differences reaching statistical significance). The results of the analyses of variance are presented in Table 8.1.

2.2. Improvement with Practice

None of the variances in the digit span scores attributable to "groups" (casual vs. heavy) reached statistical significance. Therefore, the digit span scores for the two groups were combined for purpose of discussion. Mean performances for the subjects during the pre-drug, drug, and post-drug periods were 7.91, 8.03, and 8.32, respectively, on the Digit Span Forward Test, and 6.91, 7.67, and 8.14, respectively, on the Digit Span Backward Test. The mean scores reflect the expected differences in difficulty between the Digit Span Foward and Digit Span Backward tests. In addition, the mean scores show a progressive improvement in performance with

---

[1] This technique was suggested by Dr. Robert H. Harrison, of Boston University, who served as statistical consultant for this research.

Table 8.1

Summary of Analyses of Variance of Scores for Digit Span Forward, Digit Span Backward, and Time Estimates of 180 Seconds

Variable	df	Digit span forward		Digit span backward		Time estimation	
		F	P	F	P	F	P
Group[a]	1	0.05	n.s.	0.49	n.s.	0.04	n.s.
Day linear[b]	1	187.32	<0.001	233.93	<0.001	134.15	<0.001
Day linear × group	1	0.16	n.s.	0.25	n.s.	5.31	<0.05
Day quadratic	1	7.51	<0.05	9.53	<0.01	16.05	<0.001
Day quadratic × group	1	1.74	n.s.	0.27	n.s.	22.66	<0.001
Time[c]	1	7.19	<0.05	6.72	<0.05	9.97	<0.01
Time × group	1	0.01	n.s.	1.09	n.s.	0.23	n.s.
Cumulative cigarettes	1	1.31	n.s.	0.08	n.s.	2.74	n.s.
Cumulative cigarettes × group	1	0.14	n.s.	0.35	n.s.	1.91	n.s.
All error terms for above	18						
Cumulative cigarettes × time	1	5.17	<0.05	0.00+	n.s.	6.32	<0.03
Cumulative cigarettes × time × group	1	1.73	n.s.	2.92	n.s.	0.01	n.s.
Error term	17						

[a] Casual vs. heavy users.
[b] Study day.
[c] Time elapsed since marihuana was smoked.

repetition of the task, indicating that repeated use of marihuana did not interfere with the ability of subjects to improve with practice.

Correlations of study days with Digit Span Forward and Backward scores average 0.41 and 0.40, respectively, for the casual users and 0.37 and 0.40, respectively, for the heavy users. These correlations were significant beyond the 0.001 level (cf. "Day linear," Table 8.1), and there were no differences between the casual and heavy users in this relationship (cf. "Day linear × group," Table 8.1). These statistically significant correlations support the interpretation that repeated use of marihuana did not block the ability of subjects to improve performance with practice.

Table 8.2

Digit Span Forward and Backward, Means, and Standard Errors of the Means

| | | Pre-drug period | Marihuana smoking period | | | Post-drug period |
			Non-marihuana related	Daily marihuana related	Special marihuana related	
Casual users						
Forward { Mean		7.68	8.23	7.39	7.88	8.18
σ̄x		0.18	0.07	0.21	0.17	0.14
Backward { Mean		7.16	7.54	7.08	7.42	8.04
σ̄x		0.20	0.10	0.21	0.27	0.15
Heavy users						
Forward { Mean		7.15	8.22	7.57	7.77	8.47
σ̄x		0.20	0.09	0.16	0.21	0.12
Backward { Mean		6.66	7.99	7.08	7.36	8.25
σ̄x		0.22	0.10	0.19	0.20	0.14

2.3.   Acute Effects of Marihuana

A breakdown of scores obtained during the drug period into those that followed marihuana use (within one and one-half hours), and those that did not, suggests that marihuana did have an acute decremental effect on digit span scores. Both groups of subjects obtained higher scores during non-marihuana-related assessments than during marihuana-related assessments (Table 8.2). Correlations of elapsed time since the last marihuana cigarette was smoked (up to two hours), and performance scores during the drug period were 0.22 and 0.17 for Digit Span Forward and Backward, respectively, for the casual users, and 0.24 and 0.24, respectively, for the heavy users. These correlations were significant beyond the 0.05 level (cf. "Time," Table 8.1), and there were no differences between the heavy and casual users in this regard (cf. "Time × groups," Table 8.1). These correlations remained essentially unaffected by the amount of marihuana previously smoked (cf. "Cumulative cigarettes × time," Table 8.1).

2.4.   No Changes during Drug Period

These results suggest that marihuana had a slight, but statistically significant, decremental effect on performance on the digit span tests. The independence of the correlations from amount of previous marihuana smoked suggests that the acute effect did not change significantly during the 21-day period of marihuana smoking. The latter finding provides indirect evidence that no tolerance for this acute effect developed within the time span of this research.

2.5. Volitional Control of Effects

Subjects obtained higher mean scores during the special marihuana-related assessments than during the daily marihuana-related assessments (Table 8.2). One interpretation of this finding (other interpretations are presented in the discussion section of this chapter) is that subjects performed better when they were aware that the performance was to be directly related to marihuana use, i.e., the acute effect of marihuana on digit span performance was at least partially susceptible to subjects' control. This interpretation would help us to understand how the three heaviest smokers in the casual user group (1C, 3C, 8C) achieved their highest digit span scores during special marihuana-related assessments, and lowest mean scores during daily marihuana-related assessments, compared to the non-marihuana-related assessments.

2.6. Time Estimation

The same computer program used in the analysis of digit span scores was used for the analysis of the 180-second time estimation scores. Financial and time costs for repeating this analysis for the 10-, 60-, and 90-second time estimation scores were not warranted, considering the little additional information that could be provided by additional separate analyses. The 180-second time estimates were chosen for the computer analysis because it was believed that these larger estimates would be most likely to reflect effects that might have occurred during the study. The results of this analysis of variance are presented in Table 8.1.

2.7. Pre-Drug Estimates

Estimates of 10, 60, 90, and 180 seconds by the casual users during the pre-drug period resulted in mean estimates of 9.88, 61.00, 91.22, and 180.70, respectively (Table 8.3). These mean scores are each based on approximately 100 estimates, and they are approximately 1% in error. Thus, time estimates made by casual users during the pre-drug period were similar to those that would be expected from a sample of normal subjects. That is, a series of repeated subjective measurements from a sample of normal subjects will usually result in a range of scores with a mean close to the true mean.

Table 8.3

Mean Time Estimates and Standard Error of the Means

		Pre-drug period	Marihuana smoking period			Post-drug period
			Non-marihuana related	Daily marihuana related	Special marihuana related	
Casual users						
10 sec	Mean	9.88	9.76	10.23	9.47	10.26
	$\sigma\,\bar{x}$	0.30	0.15	0.31	0.25	0.15
60 sec	Mean	61.00	63.78	58.52	58.02	67.41
	$\sigma\,\bar{x}$	1.40	0.60	0.95	1.47	0.95
90 sec	Mean	91.22	94.32	88.00	85.34	98.21
	$\sigma\,\bar{x}$	1.92	0.85	1.22	2.70	1.30
180 sec	Mean	180.70	185.94	171.17	164.00	195.99
	$\sigma\,\bar{x}$	4.84	1.73	2.57	5.81	3.57
Heavy users						
10 sec	Mean	11.13	11.31	10.35	10.78	10.93
	$\sigma\,\bar{x}$	0.25	0.15	0.25	0.23	0.13
60 sec	Mean	71.98	69.16	68.65	63.20	69.95
	$\sigma\,\bar{x}$	1.99	0.98	2.33	1.78	1.47
90 sec	Mean	95.98	100.64	93.65	95.97	102.93
	$\sigma\,\bar{x}$	2.64	1.23	3.09	2.94	2.00
180 sec	Mean	188.95	192.83	167.46	176.17	194.45
	$\sigma\,\bar{x}$	5.34	2.98	4.94	5.44	5.60

During the same pre-drug period, however, the mean time estimates of the heavy users were consistently high: 11.13, 71.98, 95.98, and 188.95, respectively. These mean time estimates are in error from 5% to 20%. The size of the errors and the fact that they are all in the same direction (i.e., overestimates), suggests that during the pre-drug period the heavy users' subjective sense of time was faster than both normals and casual users.

2.8.   Overestimate vs. Underestimate

It may be helpful to digress here to discuss the terms underestimate and overestimate, since these terms are often confusing when used in connection with time perception. The terms are descriptive of a relation between two measurements, one subjective and one objective (usually). The correctness in use of either term depends on which measure is being referred to in comparison with the other. While the objective measurement is almost always used as the standard in such comparisons, there are some exceptions in common use, and one of these exceptions relates to time perception. For example, it is not uncommon to hear the expression "time passed quickly," or "time passed slowly," stated with implication that the subjective sense of time was being used as the standard with which to compare the passage of real time. This common usage interferes with unambiguous meaning being attached to the phrases overestimation and underestimation of time. In research studies the tendency is to use the term that best fits the operational procedure. Thus, when a subject is presented with a tone that is activated for 60 seconds and he estimates that the tone was activated for 70 seconds, the recorded response is an overestimate. When a subject is requested to activate a tone for 60 seconds and activates the tone for 50 seconds the recorded response is an underestimate, i.e., he has underestimated the length of a true 60-second time interval. Of course, the interpretation of results in both procedures would be the same and could be stated in either of two complementary ways, i.e., "real time is slower than subjective time," or "subjective time is faster than real time." The procedures and data display used in the present research make it appropriate to use the term underestimate when subjects' time estimation scores are less than the time interval being estimated (implying that subjective time is faster than real time). However, the reader should be aware that other investigators, using different measurement procedures, sometimes use the term overestimation when describing results with the same implication.

2.9. Acute Effects of Marihuana

Mean time estimates obtained during marihuana-related assessments were consistently lower than mean times obtained during other assessments (Table 8.3). This suggests that an acute effect of the drug is to speed up the hypothetical internal clock so that real time appears to pass slowly. The presence of this acute effect was further suggested by the correlation of the 180-second time estimate scores with time elapsed since marihuana was smoked (up to two hours). This correlation was 0.17 ($p. < .01$) for both groups combined, and indicates that subjects tended to make shorter time estimates when they were under the influence of marihuana (cf. "Time," Table 8.1).

2.10. Tolerance

The results of the analysis of variance indicated that this acute effect was influenced by the amount of marihuana previously smoked during the study ($p. < 0.03$; cf. "Cumulative cigarettes × time," Table 8.1). The size and direction of the partial correlation reflecting this influence (0.13) suggest that there was a mild but statistically significant trend toward an attenuation of the acute effect with repeated use of marihuana. There were no significant differences between the heavy and casual users in this trend (cf. "Cumulative cigarettes × time × group," Table 8.1). These results indicate that tolerance for the acute effect of marihuana on time perception was beginning to develop during the 21-day smoking period.

2.11. No Volitional Control of Effects

In contrast to results obtained in assessments of short-term memory function, there appeared to be no consistent differences in time estimations made during special and daily marihuana-related assessments (Table 8.3). Mean time estimates made during special assessments (when subjects were aware that their performances would be directly related to marihuana smoking) were unchanged from mean time estimates made during daily marihuana-related assessments. This finding suggests that subjects either could not or would not modify their time estimation performance while intoxicated.

2.12. Changes in Time Estimates during Drug Period

Subjects in both groups showed a tendency to increase their time estimation during the 21-day drug period ($p. < 0.001$; cf. "Day linear," Table 8.1). Mean time estimates for the casual user group increased by approximately 7% from the pre-drug to post-drug periods (Table 8.3). Subjects in the heavy user group showed a similar trend only for the 90- and 180-second time intervals. The rate in increase in time estimates that occurred during the drug period differed for the casual and heavy users ($p. < 0.05$; cf. "Day linear × groups," Table 8.1). However, the difference was slight according to the partial correlation reflecting the differences (0.07) and can probably be attributed to the fact that the time estimates of the heavy users were already elevated during the pre-drug period. There was a limit to the amount of increase that occurred during the drug period ($p. < 0.001$, cf. "Day quadratic," Table 8.1). The heavy users reached this limit sooner than the casual users ($p. < 0.001$, cf. "Day quadratic × group," Table 8.1), but again this can probably be attributed to the heavy users' elevated pre-drug time estimates.

The relationship between initial and other time estimates made during the study are seen clearly in Figures 8.1 and 8.2. Daily and special marihuana-related assessments are combined in these figures because there appears to be no consistent differences in the results of these assessments. Both groups of subjects demonstrated a similar trend during the drug period. Marihuana-related time estimates became lower and nonmarihuana-

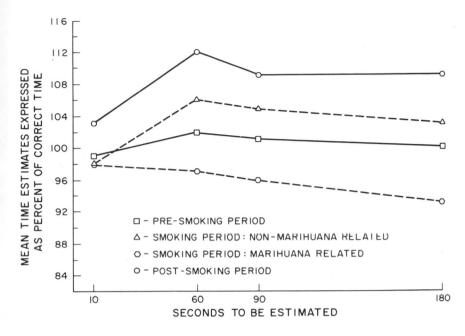

Figure 8.1. Casual users (N = 10).

related time estimates became higher than they were during the pre-drug period (Figures 8.1 and 8.2). During the post-drug period, time estimates by the casual users continued to increase over pre-drug and drug period levels, while the time estimates of the heavy users remained approximately at the elevated drug period, nonmarihuana-related levels. It should be noted that the increase in time estimates by the casual users resulted in their post-drug estimates closely resembling the pre-drug estimates of the heavy users. The possible significance of this resemblance after an extended period of heavy smoking by the casual users will be discussed later.

2.13.   Net Effects on Accuracy of Time Estimates: Heavy vs. Casual Users

The relations between time estimates made during different periods of the studies were essentially the same for both casual and heavy users (Figures 8.1 and 8.2), but the time estimate levels of the heavy users were all higher than those of the casual users. Thus, although both groups of subjects made their lowest time estimates during the marihuana-related assessments, these latter assessments for the heavy users were among their most accurate approximations of true time intervals. That is, because the time estimates by

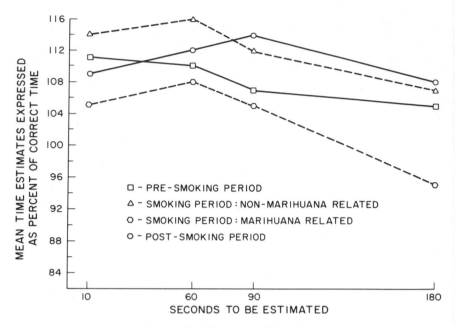

Figure 8.2.   Heavy users (N = 10).

heavy users during the pre-drug period were elevated, the acute effect of the drug was to make their time estimates more accurate by bringing them down closer to true time intervals. The mean estimates of the casual users during the pre-drug period were very accurate, so the acute effect of the drug was to make their time estimates more inaccurate. Thus, although marihuana had the same acute effect on the relative time estimates of both groups, this effect led to an increase in accuracy for the heavy users and a decrease in accuracy for the casual users. Hollister and Gillespie (1970) also found that THC led to closer approximation of accurate time estimations in experienced users.

3.   DISCUSSION

Marihuana is often described as having the effect of interfering with short-term memory. However, research studies have not provided consistent evidence of this effect. It was mentioned that some studies have produced results clearly indicating an impairment in short-term memory performance associated with marihuana use (Abel 1970, 1971*a*, 1971*b*; Melges *et al.* 1970*a*, 1970*b*; Tinklenberg *et al.* 1970; Clark *et al.* 1970). Other studies have yielded negative or mixed results in regard to impairment of short-term memory (Clark and Nakashima 1968; Jones and Stone 1970; Hollister and Gillespie 1970; Dornbush *et al.* 1971; Meyer *et al.* 1971; Mayor's Committee on Marihuana 1944; Weil *et al.* 1968). Failures of research studies to document a marihuana-induced memory impairment have been attributed to such variables as dose, experience of subjects, setting, and memory task, among others. The results of the present research suggest another possible explanation for the variability in previous research findings, as well as contributing to an understanding of the nature of the effect of marihuana on short-term memory.

In practically all previous studies of marihuana, subjects were fully aware that their performances would be directly related to marihuana use. Ethical and legal considerations also required that the great majority of these studies employ as subjects persons who had previous experience with marihuana, i.e., persons who would be biased toward demonstrating that marihuana has only beneficial effects. It may be significant that most of the studies that have produced unambiguous indications of a marihuana-induced memory impairment have employed either nonusers or very occasional (e.g., once a month) marihuana users. This latter fact is usually interpreted to mean that inexperienced users are more susceptible to deleterious effects of the drug and/or experienced users have developed tolerance for these effects. An alternate interpretation is that the impairment in short-term memory performance is not mediated through some direct effect of delta 9 THC on neuronal memory storage systems, but rather the impairment in performance is a secondary by-product of subjects' wandering attention. This interpretation would lead to the prediction that when subjects had adequate motivation to maintain attention to a memory task (e.g., experienced users motivation to demonstrate that marihuana is harmless), no decrements in performance would occur.

The results of the present study lend support to the latter interpretation. A unique aspect of the design of this study made it possible to obtain marihuana-related assessments of short-term memory both when experienced subjects were and were not aware that their performance would be directly related to acute marihuana use. A comparison of "aware" (special) and "unaware" (daily) marihuana-related assessments indicated that subjects displayed less impairment in performance when they were aware that their performance would be related to marihuana. In fact, a few subjects (1C, 3C, 8C) obtained higher memory performance scores during the "aware" assessments than during nonmarihuana-related assessments, although these same subjects obtained their lowest memory performance scores during "unaware" marihuana-related assessments. Subjects did show some impairment in performance during the special marihuana-related assessments. This impairment may be attributable to the fact that the drug period extended over three weeks, and subjects' motivation to maintain concentration while intoxicated may have been less intense or less effective than it might be in a short-term acute study.

The results of a series of studies by Abel (1970, 1971a, 1971b) led him to conclude that marihuana has no significant effect on the retrieval of stored information in memory, but it may affect the storage of information by interfering with concentration. Abel's conclusion is consistent with the interpretation of the results in the present study. The implication of his interpretation is that the reported acute deleterious effect of marihuana on short-term memory may not be a reflection of direct impairment of neuronal memory systems, but rather a reflection of what a person chooses to attend to while under the influence of the drug. Evidence that attention can be maintained under the influence of marihuana is provided by the results of studies which showed that marihuana did not affect tests of sustained attention, the Continuous Performance Test (Weil and Zinberg 1970; Meyer et al. 1971), and the Rod and Frame Test (Jones and Stone 1969).

There are alternate interpretations of the difference in results obtained between "aware" and "unaware" marihuana-related assessments. The "unaware" assessments always occurred at approximately 10:00 a.m. each day. The "aware" assessments occurred at various times of the day or evening, whenever subjects chose to smoke a marihuana cigarette on days they were scheduled for the assessments. Thus, it is possible that diurnal variations, either in the effects of marihuana or in short-term memory ability, produced the obtained differences. The "unaware" assessments were always group administered, while the "aware" assessments were administered to one or two subjects at a time. It is possible that performances during the group administrations suffered from distractions not present during individual administrations. Finally, the "aware" assessments always occurred approximately 30 minutes after marihuana was smoked, while the "unaware" assessments occurred anywhere from immediately after to 90 minutes after marihuana was smoked. It is possible that the acute effects of the drug on short-term memory were less potent during the "aware" assessments. These alternate interpretations are all possible, but it is believed that the original interpretation discussed above best fits not only the results of the present study, but the results of other studies as well.

There were no indications in the present study that the repeated use of marihuana significantly interfered with the ability of subjects to improve with practice. Their performance on the digit span tests showed consistent improvement during the study, and it is conceivable that if the subjects had not obtained such high scores initially, perhaps even more improvement may have been achieved. The high scores that subjects obtained on the digit span tests can be attributed to both their above average intellectual levels (see Chapter 2) and the fact that the test items were presented visually rather than orally. Whatever the acute effect of marihuana on short-term memory, the results of this study indicate no effect of the drug on short-term memory as a consequence of smoking over a three-week period.

In comparison to the variable results of research on the acute effects of marihuana on short-term memory, results of similar research on time perception are remarkably consistent. Almost every investigation in this area has yielded results which indicate that marihuana has the acute effect of making time appear to pass slowly. The results of the present research provide further confirmation of this acute effect. Both casual and heavy users made significantly shorter estimates of time while under the influence of marihuana than at other times (Figures 8.1 and 8.2).

A finding in the present study that has not previously been reported is that time estimations progressively increase over an extended period of marihuana smoking. This finding is contrary to what would be expected under normal conditions. Repeated testing on time estimations over a period of many days usually leads to either a stabilization of initial estimates or a trend of estimates toward true time intervals. The increase in time estimates was in the opposite direction from the acute effect of the drug, suggesting that the increase represented a compensating or rebound reaction to the acute effect. This, in turn, suggests that the acute effect of marihuana on time perception is produced by direct action of delta 9 THC within the central nervous system. Assumption of this direct action would make the results consistent with the law of denervation (Sharpless 1964) which states that compensatory processes occur as a result of induced changes in the level of activity of neuronal pathways. Further, the assumption of direct pharmacological action in both the acute and compensatory effects of the drug on time perception would be consistent with other findings in this study.

In contrast to results obtained in assessments of short-term memory, there were no consistent differences in time estimations made during "aware" and "unaware" marihuana-related assessments. This similarity in performance under both conditions would be predicted if the acute effect of the drug on time perception was brought about by direct action on neuronal systems, thereby being less susceptible to either volitional control of subjects or other influences. Further, the indication that tolerance for this acute effect was beginning to develop during the 21-day drug period would also be consistent with a direct pharmacological action. Finally, the mean time estimates by casual users during the pre-drug period were very accurate, while those of the heavy users were overestimates, with approximately 8% error. Since the heavy users, by definition, most likely had been smoking marihuana almost daily just before the start of the study, it would be predicted, from the assumption of a compensatory reaction, that their time estimates would be elevated during the pre-drug period. During the post-drug period, mean time estimates by the casual users had risen from normality to overestimations, approximately equal to those of the heavy users. These factors provide further indication of the presence of a rebound reaction to the acute effect of marihuana.

Clark *et al.* (1970) have suggested that the acute effect of marihuana on time perception may be a secondary effect mediated through impairments in attention, short-term memory, and systematic thought. The results of the present study suggest that the effect is mediated directly through the action of delta 9 THC on the central nervous system. This interpretation is supported by the findings of McIsaac *et al.* (1971) that THC is concentrated within neocortical and hypocampal areas of the brain in squirrel monkeys. While a similar concentration has yet to be demonstrated in humans, the location of the concentrations would be consistent with the assumption of a direct effect of THC on neuronal systems involved in time perception.

The relation between the short-term acute effect of marihuana on time perception and its longer-lasting compensatory effect (as found in this study) parallels the temporal relation between the stimulatory and depressant effects of the drug found in many studies (Gershon 1970). Braude *et al.* (1971) have stated: "The overall actions of marihuana on the brain are a mixture of apparent stimulatory sensory effects with superimposed depressant elements. Temporally, the activation is followed by sedation, but there is considerable overlap" (p. 9). It may be that the acute effect of speeding up the biological internal clock is associated with the stimulant effects, and the subsequent slowing of the internal clock is associated with the depressant elements.

9

Cognitive Effects of Marihuana

Homer B.C. Reed, Jr.

The amount of objective data relating marihuana ingestion to psychological test performances is very small. In the now famous LaGuardia report (Mayor's Committee on Marihuana 1944), marihuana was found to produce dose-related impairment of complex reaction time, static equilibrium, and hand steadiness. On tests of higher mental abilities (e.g., Army Alpha, Koh's Blocks, Form Boards, etc.), the drug produced decrements in overall functioning. Degree of impairment was found to be related both to drug dosage and to task complexity. Marihuana produced no apparent impairment in simple tasks such as speed of tapping, perception of length of lines, and auditory acuity. Subjects for these studies included both users of marihuana and nonusers, and the effects of the experimentally administered drug were generally more apparent among nonusers.

Clark and Nakashima (1968) reported a series of pilot studies investigating the effects of marihuana on a wide variety of tasks. These tasks included: (1) hand and foot reaction time to both simple and complex visual stimuli; (2) digit code learning; (3) depth perception; (4) visual flicker fusion; (5) auditory frequency discrimination; (6) Archimedes spiral after-images; (7) mirror tracing; and (8) visual motor coordination measured by a pursuit rotor apparatus. Subjects for this study were limited to medical students, medical residents, and graduate students in psychology, none of whom had previous experience with marihuana. Each subject performed each task under differing dosage levels, thus utilizing an experimental design which permitted each subject to serve as his own control. The results of the pilot studies were characterized by generally high inter- and intrasubject variability. The most consistent impairment was found on complex reaction times and on digit code learning, but even on these tasks there were marked individual differences. No consistent effects of marihuana were found on tasks involving mirror tracing, pursuit rotor learning, depth perception, perception of auditory frequencies, and duration of Archimedes spiral effects.

From the findings of the studies cited above, it is clear that our knowledge of the effects of marihuana on cognitive and motor abilities is very limited. Transitory impairment on certain kinds of tasks is demonstrable for certain individuals. However, the impairment is not consistent, and it is imperfectly related to dosage level. It is probably related to the subject's prior experience with marihuana, since it apparently is more pronounced in subjects with little or no prior experience with the drug. Knowledge concerning the effects of chronic marihuana usage on cognitive and motor abilities is even more limited than knowledge of acute effects. Meyer *et al.* (1971) administered marihuana to both casual and heavy users. Their findings support the impressions from the studies cited above which indicate that the effects of marihuana on task performance tend to be more pronounced for casual users than for heavy users.

In the present investigation, ten heavy and ten casual marihuana users were studied in two separate but identical studies. The procedures employed in defining and selecting these groups are described in Chapters 1 and 2. The present chapter focuses specifically on how these groups performed on a variety of cognitive and motor tasks under conditions of both recent and remote marihuana usage.

1. METHODS

1.1. Introduction

The acute and repeat dose effects of marihuana on cognitive function were studied through serial evaluation of all subjects with a battery of psychological tests known to be sensitive to organic brain dysfunction. All subjects were evaluated on three occasions. The initial evaluations were carried out during the pre-drug period, on study days 1 and 2. The second evaluations were made during the drug period, on study days 22 and 23, and the third evaluations took place on the last drug period day, study day 26. Thus, the initial evaluation occurred at a time when subjects were judged to have been drug-free. The second evaluation occurred 20 days later, during the period of marihuana availability. The third evaluation was designed to investigate the possible acute effects of marihuana ingestion on psychological test performance. For this reason, each subject was required to smoke at least one marihuana cigarette on the last day of the drug period and the test battery was administered approximately 30 minutes after marihuana ingestion.

1.2.   Evaluation Instruments

The psychological assessments used in this study were derived from a battery of tests that has been extensively employed during the past two decades to evaluate the influence of brain dysfunction on adaptive behavior. The specific tests used in evaluating the subjects participating in this study included the Wechsler Adult Intelligence Scale, and the following instruments.

1.2.1.   *The Halstead Category Test.*   The test measures complex nonverbal concept formation ability. The test requires the subject to form and apply concepts on the basis of recurring similarities and differences of visual stimuli. The stimulus materials include 208 35-mm slides which are divided into seven groups. In the first six groups a concept is presented, and if the subject infers the concept correctly, he can then apply it to stimuli delivered in each of the subsequent slides. The subject was instructed to press an answer button for each slide and was "rewarded" or "punished" with a bell–buzzer system. The bell informed the subject that his answer was correct, and the buzzer if the answer was incorrect. The task of the subject was to modify his answers on the basis of the feedback information so as to attain the correct answers as quickly as possible. The seventh group of the Category Test was a memory subtest. The subject's score for the Category Test was the number of incorrect answers.

1.2.2.   *Tactual Performance Test.*   This procedure measures complex psychomotor problem solving ability. The test consists of a eight-block form board which is placed on an upright stand in front of the subject. Before the test begins, the subject is blindfolded and instructions for the test are given. The subject is told to put each block in its correct place as rapidly as possible, using only his dominant or preferred hand. Upon completion of the first trial, the subject is then told to perform the same procedure again, using only his nondominant hand. Finally, a third trial is administered with the subject using both hands. Upon completion of the third trial, the board and blocks are put away and the blindfold is removed from the subject. The subject is then told to draw the outline of the board from memory and to draw as many of the blocks as he can remember, putting each block drawing in its correct location.

The Tactual Performance Test yields three scores. One score is the total time the subject uses over all three trials. A second score is based on the number of blocks that the subject correctly remembers. The third score is the number of blocks that the subject can correctly localize.

1.2.3. *Seashore Rhythm Test.* This test consists of 30 pairs of rhythms which are presented with a tape recorder. For each rhythm pair the subject must decide whether the members of the pair are similar or different. He indicates his answer by writing S for same and D for different on an answer sheet provided for him. The test is scored in terms of the total number of correct answers.

1.2.4. *Finger Tapping Test.* The instrument used for this test is a manually operated counter attached to a short tapping arm. The subject is instructed to tap, using the index finger of the dominant hand, as rapidly as possible for a ten-second interval. The subject is given a few practice trials and then is required to tap for a series of ten-second intervals. When the subject achieves five consecutive trials in which there is a range of no more than five taps, the test is discontinued. The score for this test is the average of the five trials. This test is also administered to each subject using the index finger of the nondominant hand.

1.2.5. *Trail-Making Test.* The Trail-Making Test is a two part measure of perceptual speed and accuracy. Part A requires the subject to connect, in sequence, numbers 1 to 25 which are circled and scattered over an 8 by 11 in. sheet of paper. In part B the subject has to alternate between ascending numerical (1 to 13) and alphabetical (A to L) series in connecting circled numbers and letters (1-A-2-B-3-C-4-D, etc.). Each part of the test is scored in terms of the seconds required for completion.

2. RESULTS

The means obtained during each testing session by the casual and heavy marihuana users are presented in Table 9.1 and 9.2 respectively. The two groups did not differ significantly on any of the test procedures on any of

Table 9.1

Group Means on Cognitive and Motor Tests: Casual Users

| Sessions | Age | I.Q. | Trail-making | | Halstead category | Tactual performance | | | Seashore rhythm | Finger tapping | |
			Part B	Total		TPT total	TPT memory	TPT localize		Dominance	Non-dominance
1	23.8	122	51.0	72.2	35.4	5.4	6.3	5.0	27.1	52.8	41.9
2	—	—	40.7	57.9	13.2	4.5	6.9	5.8	27.4	52.1	45.9
3	—	—	42.9	58.2	4.7	3.2	7.3	6.7	28.7	49.6	45.4

Table 9.2

Group Means on Cognitive and Motor Tests: Heavy Users

| Sessions | Age | I.Q. | Trail-making | | | Halstead category | Tactual performance | | | Seashore rhythm | Finger tapping | |
			Part B	Total			TPT total	TPT memory	TPT localize		Dominance	Non-dominance
1	21.8	117	58.3	83.7	27.1	6.5	6.1	3.6	27.8	53.8	46.8
2	—	—	51.2	73.3	13.3	5.5	6.8	4.6	28.1	55.4	49.1
3	—	—	52.8	68.2	6.7	3.9	6.9	5.6	28.0	54.4	49.5

the three evaluations. The practice effects occur where expected, with one exception: Neither group improved its performance from evaluation 2 to evaluation 3 on part B of the Trail-Making Test. This finding is contrary to normal expectations and suggests that impairments in both perceptual speed and accuracy for certain kinds of complex tasks may be an acute effect of marihuana ingestion. This finding corresponds with earlier investigations reporting impairment in complex reaction times associated with marihuana ingestion (Clark and Nakashima 1968). In the present study the magnitude of the impairment is small and without obvious clinical significance. One can, of course, think of situations in which even very slight impairment of abilities may have drastic consequences (e.g., competitive race car driving). Such situations are rare, however, and slight impairments in perceptual speed and accuracy ordinarily have few practical consequences.

The data in Table 9.1 and 9.2 indicate clearly that both groups of subjects are of superior intellectual ability. On the neuropsychological tests the groups perform at about the level that would be predicted for them on the basis of their I.Q. scores (see Chapter 2). Thus, with the one exception discussed above, the group data fail to suggest any alterations in cognitive or motor abilities associated with marihuana smoking. The heavy users do not perform less well than the casual users, and both heavy and casual users show the same acute effects.

The analysis of the group data was augmented by a detailed individual analysis of all 20 test protocols. This was done because impairment of cognitive and motor abilities may be reflected in changes in the interrelationships among abilities rather than in a depressed level of functioning. The analysis of the individual protocols was done by a psychologist specially trained in the interpretation of this battery of tests. The analysis revealed several interesting but difficult-to-interpret findings. For two individuals in each group, the analysis revealed impairment in some aspect of cognitive or motor functioning. For example, two of the heavy users performed quite poorly on the Trail-Making Test. In addition, these same two individuals did not show consistent patterns of improvement on one or more of the tests. Two of the casual users also demonstrated unexpected impairment either in initial level of performance or in their patterns of improvement. For all four of these individuals, there was unequivocal evidence of impairment, but it is not possible to assign any specific interpretation to this finding. The impairment may be related to any of the number of factors, such as previous drug histories, residual effects of some traumatic injury to the brain, etc. For the two heavy users who demonstrated impairment, inquiry revealed excessive use of LSD prior to this study (cf. Chapter 2). No such drug histories, however, characterized the casual users. One would certainly not expect 20% of any randomly selected group of healthy, bright, young adults to manifest impairment in cognitive or motor functions, and thus the groups included in the present study show a greater incidence of impairment than one would expect to find. This finding clearly warrants further investigation, but the present data offer no basis for presuming that the impairment is a consequence of marihuana use.

3. SUMMARY

Ten casual and ten heavy users of marihuana were individually administered a battery of psychological tests designed to measure general intelligence and specific cognitive and motor abilities. Each subject was completely evaluated on three occasions. The first evaluation was at the beginning of the study when all subjects were drug-free. The second evaluation was three weeks later, during which time all subjects had access to marihuana. The data revealed no significant differences between the heavy and casual users on any of the test procedures. Practice effects occurred where they were expected, with one exception. Neither group demonstrated a positive practice effect between the second and third administrations of one test measuring perceptual speed and accuracy. Effects similar to this have been demonstrated in other studies focusing on the acute effects of marihuana ingestion. Individual analysis of the 20 test protocols revealed two subjects in each group who performed significantly less adequately on the tests than would be predicted on the basis of their I.Q. scores. This kind of impairment rarely occurs in normal subjects, but in this particular case there is nothing in the data to suggest that the impairment is attributable to marihuana smoking.

10
Mood States

A. Michael Rossi, Thomas F. Babor, Roger E. Meyer, and Jack H. Mendelson

Marihuana is used primarily to achieve pleasant subjective mood states, according to the results of numerous surveys of marihuana users (Freedman and Rockmore 1946; Haines and Green 1970; McGlothlin and West 1968; Mizner et al. 1970). The results of these surveys are summarized in a statement by Cohen (1968): "What most users seek is a feeling of relaxation with the dissolution of the tensions and frustrations of the day." The typical sequence of feelings occurring with marihuana use are reported to be a sense of calmness, followed by a mild to strong sense of euphoria which alternatively rises and falls in wavelike fashion, with the fall sometimes associated with unpleasant sensations (Walton 1938; Jaffee 1965; Allentuck and Bowman 1942; Grinspoon 1971). Occasionally, some initial anxiety or apprehension occurs immediately after ingestion and before the feeling of calmness emerges (Bromberg 1934; Walton 1938; Jaffee 1965; Mayor's Committee on Marihuana 1944; Hollister, Richards, and Gillespie 1968). The duration of the subjective effects is reported to be one and one-half to four hours after smoking (Grinspoon 1971; Haines and Green 1970; Isbell et al. 1967a, 1967b; Hollister 1971), with peak effects occurring within an hour.

In the vernacular of the marihuana smoker, a number of generic terms are typically applied to the feeling states associated with the marihuana experience. Most familiar are abstract nouns like "stoned," "high," "spaced," "ripped." Like their counterparts in the parlance of alcohol use, these words convey the user's impression of the totality of subjective effects accompanying intoxication.

The typical pattern of subjective effects has been reported to be liable to many variations as a function of the dose, user's personality, expectations, and previous experience with the drug (Grinspoon 1971; Hollister 1971). The setting in which smoking occurs also has been reported to have an influence on the effects of marihuana, but this has not been confirmed by preliminary research results (Waskow et al. 1970). The most frequently documented sources of variation are dose and the amount of previous experience with the drug. Inexperienced users are reported to experience a wider range of subjective effects ranging from practically no effects to predominantly unpleasant effects (Becker 1967; Pillard 1970; Bromberg 1934; Hollister 1971; Waskow et al. 1970). However, two out of three of the 131 respondents in a survey by Haines and Green (1970) reported that they had experienced a euphoric high the first time they had smoked marihuana. Extended use of the drug over several years apparently produces a gradual diminishing of the euphoric feelings. This may be one of the reasons that "heavy users described a search for insight and/or a wish for a sense of harmony or union as part of the motivation for continued use" (Meyer et al. 1971, p. 90).

The almost universal agreement on the nature of subjective effects of marihuana is based largely on anecdotal accounts (e.g., Baudelaire (1858), retrospective reports from nonintoxicated marihuana users (Haines and Green 1970; Hekimian and Gershon 1968; Tart 1971), and a relatively few studies of the acute effects of the drug in which subjects were either interviewed (Mayor's Committee on Marihuana 1944; Bromberg 1934; Meyer et al. 1971) or tested (Waskow et al. 1970; Hollister et al. 1968) while intoxicated. Only three studies have been published in which subjective effects have been assessed while subjects were using the drug over an extended period of time (Mayor's Committee on Marihuana 1944; Siler et al. 1933; Williams et al. 1946). It is noteworthy that the subjective effects found in these three studies were not clearly as euphoric as would be expected from the other literature. The discrepancy usually has been ascribed to the fact that deviant individuals had been employed as subjects in the long-term studies. However, there are alternative possible explanations for the discrepancy between the results obtained in the few long-term studies and the results as usually reported in the bulk of the literature.

Experience in alcohol research has indicated that there may be important differences between reports of subjective effects of a drug when subjects are and are not intoxicated. For example, there is voluminous literature based almost entirely on retrospective reports which indicated that alcoholics experience anxiety reduction while intoxicated. However, assessments made while alcoholics were undergoing an extended period of intoxication indicate that many experienced an increase in anxiety rather than a reduction (Mendelson and Mello 1966a; Nathan *et al.* 1970). It is possible that a similar situation may be found in regard to marihuana, with a discrepancy between what experienced users report retrospectively and what they report while intoxicated. Second, many authors have described the ability of subjects to control the effects of marihuana in order to meet the demands of specific tasks (Mayor's Committee on Marihuana 1944; Hollister 1971; Grinspoon 1971). In short-term studies experienced users may be motivated enough to control the effects and report what they believe they should feel rather than what they actually feel. The motivation to control the effects may be difficult to maintain in long-term studies.

In the present study an investigation was made into both acute and repeat dose effects of marihuana upon subjective mood states. In addition to investigating these specific aspects of the marihuana experience, general ratings of subjective levels of intoxication were also routinely elicited. Since it is often at this more general level of verbalization that the drug effect is described by the user, it was hoped that by monitoring introspective reports, valuable information could be obtained about the magnitude and duration of the marihuana effect, as well as its variability in different settings. Furthermore, it was anticipated that the subjective reports would be useful in determining whether marihuana smokers develop tolerance to the subjective effects of the drug. Tolerance is said to develop when a response to a standard dose of a drug decreases with repeated use. There are numerous biological, behavioral, and psychological responses that a drug may influence, and tolerance to these different responses may develop at different rates. Thus, while there is some evidence that human subjects develop tolerance to the behavioral and physical effects of cannabis (Meyer *et al.* 1971), this may or may not be true for the subjective effects as well.

1. METHOD

The general design of this study and the subject selection procedure have been described in Chapter 1 and 2. Two groups of experienced marihuana users were employed as subjects in two separate but identical studies. One group of ten subjects, defined as casual users, had at least a one-year history of marihuana use, and were currently averaging approximately eight smoking sessions per month. The other group of ten subjects, defined as heavy users, had a two-to-nine-year history of marihuana use and were currently averaging approximately 33 smoking sessions per month. Each group of subjects lived on a closed hospital research ward for 31 days, under living conditions that were made as comfortable as possible, consistent with security and experimental requirements. From the sixth through the twenty-sixth day of each study, subjects were permitted to purchase and smoke *ad lib* one-gram marihuana cigarettes with approximately 2.0% delta 9 THC content. The method by which subjects could purchase marihuana and the amount and temporal distribution of their marihuana consumption are described in Chapter 3.

1.1. Mood Assessments

At approximately 10:45 a.m. on each of the 31 days, subjects were required to rate their mood states with a *Q*-sort modification of a self-report instrument developed by Raskin and associates (1967). These assessments are termed daily assessments in this report. The daily assessments were carried out each day regardless of whether or not the subjects smoked marihuana. However, accurate records were kept of exactly when subjects chose to smoke marihuana, and these records made it possible to know how much time had elapsed between the smoking of marihuana and the mood assessments. The mood assessments that were made less than 90 minutes after a subject chose to smoke marihuana are referred to as *daily marihuana-related assessments* in this report. Subjects were under the impression (correctly so) that the daily assessments were being carried out to evaluate mood changes related to long-term use of marihuana. There was no indication that they were aware that these assessments also could be related to their most recent marihuana intake and used to evaluate the acute effects of the drug. Thus, the daily marihuana-related assessments are relatively free from the bias introduced by subjects who would be motivated to distort their mood ratings to coincide with how they believe they should feel after smoking marihuana.

In addition to the daily assessments, each day during the 21-day smoking period two subjects were scheduled to rate their moods before and one-half after smoking a marihuana cigarette. The schedule for these assessments was arranged so that any one subject would be scheduled for the assessments four times during the 21-day smoking period. These assessments are referred to as *special marihuana-related assessments* in this report.

The *Q*-sort instrument used to assess mood states consists of 64 5 × 5 in. cards. The cards contain different adjectives or phrases which describe mood states (e.g., "depressed," "full of pep," etc.). Subjects were instructed to describe their moods by sorting the cards into four bins according to how accurately the adjectives or phrases matched their current mood. The bins were labeled: (1) "Not at all"; (2) "A little"; (3) "Quite a bit"; (4) "Extremely." Tamerin *et al.* (1970) have reported that a factor analysis of results with this instrument had yielded eight factors: anxiety, hostility, guilt-shame, friendliness, carefulness, cognitive-loss, fatigue, and depression.

1.2.   Intoxication Ratings

In addition to mood assessments, self-ratings of subjective level of intoxication were also solicited during the 21-day smoking period. These ratings were obtained systematically only from the heavy user subjects, after preliminary results with the casual user group indicated the feasibility and utility of the procedure. In order to minimize inconvenience to the subjects, these ratings were obtained only on alternate smoking days. The procedure consisted of simply presenting the subject with an 11-point subjective intoxication scale both immediately before and after each marihuana cigarette was consumed. The scale was based on the following question: "In comparison to the highest you've ever been on grass, rate on the scale below how stoned you feel now." The response categories ranged from (0) "No effect, not high at all," through (2) "Mildly high," (5) "Moderately high," (8) "Very high," and (10) "Highest ever." In addition, on each occasion when the subject smoked marihuana, the following information was noted by a staff member: (1) the time of day; (2) the ward location; and (3) the type of activity which best characterized the smoker's behavior.

2.   RESULTS

2.1.   Mood Assessments

In the design of this research, subjects' mood states at given times can be compared to their own mood states at other times and not to hypothetical or statistically normal mood states. Therefore, statements regarding either an increase or decrease in specific mood states during specific assessment times are made solely in relation to assessments made at other times of the study. For example, even when subjects rated themselves highest on the depression mood scale, the only interpretation permissible is that they rated themselves as being more depressed at those times than at other times, and not that they were clinically or seriously depressed (which they may or may not have been).

Subjects used the *Q*-sort instrument to rate their moods every day, so that approximately 31 daily scores were obtained for each subject on each of the eight mood scales. The maximum possible scores for each of the

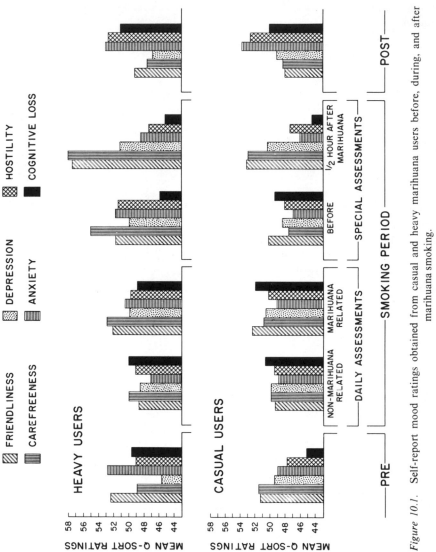

Figure 10.1. Self-report mood ratings obtained from casual and heavy marihuana users before, during, and after marihuana smoking.

eight mood scales varied, so that the obtained mean scores also varied for each scale. The means and standard deviations of the daily scores for each subject on each scale were used to convert the scale scores to T-scores, with a mean of 50 and a standard deviation of 10. This conversion, which does not change the basic relations between daily scores, was carried out to facilitate a comparison of changes occurring on different mood scales.

In the tabulation of results, mood scale scores were deleted when they were more than three standard deviations from a subject's mean score for any particular mood scale. These extreme scores occurred infrequently and appeared to be unrelated to specific assessment times. They appeared to be errors in ratings or scoring and were deleted to minimize distortions of results. Scores on the guilt-shame and fatigue mood scales were so unstable that results for these scales were discarded. The instability may have been related to the fact that scores for each of the two scales were based on only three Q-sort cards.

The results of the mood ratings are presented in Figure 10.1. There was a great deal of similarity in the mood ratings between the casual and heavy users, but there were also some notable exceptions. The mood ratings for both groups of subjects during the pre-drug period adequately reflected clinical impressions during this time. Both groups of subjects appeared to be friendly and sociable, but the casual users seemed more relaxed and carefree than the heavy users, who appeared to be more anxious.

The daily nonmarihuana-related assessments during the smoking period revealed no predominance of any specific moods for either group of subjects. The stability may be a reflection of the fact that subjects had settled down and adjusted to ward routine after the initial pre-drug period.

2.2. Moods after Smoking

Some interesting and potentially significant differences occurred between marihuana-related mood assessments that were obtained when subjects were and were not aware that the assessments would be directly related to marihuana smoking. When subjects were not aware that the assessments would be directly related to marihuana smoking (cf. daily marihuana-related assessments, Figure 10.1), there was a trend toward an increase in all mood state ratings. Ratings of friendliness and carefreeness appear to have the largest increase, but the presence of even modest increases in other mood states would tend to suggest that the effect of marihuana was to intensify prevailing moods rather than change them.

However, when subjects were aware that assessments would be directly related to marihuana smoking (cf. special marihuana-related assessments, Figure 10.1), a different pattern of results was obtained. Ratings of positive mood states (carefreeness, friendliness) increased, but ratings of negative mood states (anxiety, hostility) decreased. The apparently anomalous rise in ratings of depression within this pattern will be discussed separately. Thus, the daily marihuana-related assessments indicated that marihuana intensified all prevailing moods, while the results of the special marihuana-related assessments seem to suggest that the effect of marihuana is to change mood states toward a more euphoric pattern. It is interesting to note that increases in ratings of friendliness and carefreeness which characterized both sets of marihuana-related assessments were much more pronounced during special assessments.

2.3.   Moods before Smoking

Mood ratings obtained just before marihuana was smoked during special assessments were compared to daily nonmarihuana-related mood ratings, to determine whether unique mood patterns existed just prior to marihuana use. However, no consistent pattern of differences emerged in this comparison. The mood ratings of the heavy users were all increased just prior to smoking marihuana while the mood ratings of the casual users showed a trend toward a decrease. Ratings of friendliness were increased for both groups just before marihuana smoking (slightly so for the casual users), and the increase in this rating is consistent with the finding that marihuana smoking was a gregarious activity (see Chapter 4).

2.4.   Depression

Ratings of depression were elevated for the heavy users during the smoking period (compared to pre- and post-drug periods). The ratings of depression for both groups increased during both daily and special marihuana-related assessments. An examination of the adjectives used in the depression scale (sad, down-hearted, worthless, unhappy, useless, depressed, blue, troubled, lonely) clarifies that the rise in depression ratings reflected psychological rather than psychomotor depression. The consistency in the results indicates that the rise in depression ratings was a reliable effect of marihuana. The strength of this effect is suggested by the fact that the increase in depression ratings was present during the special marihuana-related assessments, when the pattern of mood ratings was generally more positive than during the daily marihuana-related assessments.

During the post-drug period both groups of subjects displayed a similar pattern of mood ratings (Figure 10.1). This pattern was decidedly negative in relation to patterns that had been obtained in earlier phases of the study. The mood ratings that were predominant were of anxiety and hostility, and ratings of friendliness and carefreeness were as low or lower than at any other previous assessment time. It is unfortunate that the design of this study does not make it possible to determine how much of this dysphoric mood pattern occurred as a sequelae to the three weeks of relatively heavy marihuana smoking, and how much of the pattern reflected the subjects' uncertainties regarding their future plans at the imminent end of the study. However, the patterns of mood ratings did coincide with clinical impressions that during the post-drug period subjects were less happy and more hostile than during previous periods. The agreements between clinical impressions and mood ratings does not demonstrate the validity of the latter, but it does increase our confidence that the mood ratings were adequate reflections of subjects' moods.

2.5. Subjective Level of Intoxication

Before presenting the findings based on ratings of subjective level of intoxication, data pertaining to the validity of the measure will be discussed. Since there is widespread agreement that the physiological and chemical effects of THC decrease as a function of time, it was suspected that the subjective effects would also vary in the same fashion. In order to test this hypothesis, ratings obtained from each subject just before smoking were correlated with elapsed times from the previous smoking episodes. For example, if a subject smoked three marihuana cigarettes at varying time intervals during the day, his rating before each successive smoke was used to provide an estimate of the deterioration of effect from the time of his last "after" rating. The level of the rating after the preceding cigarette was partialed out of the correlation in order to control statistically for variations in previous levels of intoxication. The average Pearson r was found to be -0.67, a correlation significant at the 0.001 level ($t = 13.4$, 9 df). The procedures used in the statistical analysis have been described in Chapter 5.

The ratings obtained immediately after marihuana was smoked varied from 0 to 9 on the 11-point scale. This variation was reflected in the average ratings for individual subjects, which ranged from a low mean response of 3.05 for subject 2H, to a high mean rating of 6.85 for subject 5H. The mean for the heavy user group was 5.82 and the average of the standard deviation was 1.28.

2.6. Duration of Subjective Effect

The duration of the subjective effect is suggested by the data in Figure 10.2, in which the average "before" subjective ratings are plotted as a function of the elapsed time since the previous smoking session. Approximately 15 minutes was required to smoke each marihuana cigarette. As the results show, the subjective effect was at its maximum (5.82) immediately after the

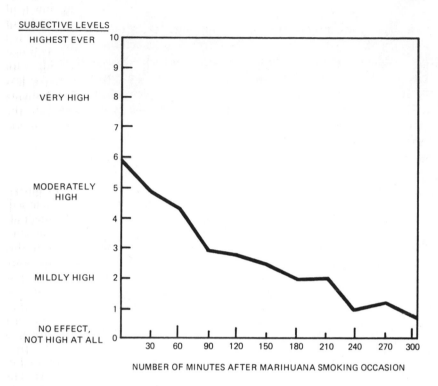

Figure 10.2. Average ratings of subjective level of intoxication made within 30-minute time intervals after a marihuana smoking occasion. Points represent averages of individual means for ten heavy users. Dosage and accumulated delta 9 THC not controlled.

subject finished smoking. Thirty minutes later, subjects still rated themselves in the "moderately high" range (4.93), as they did one hour after the cessation of smoking (4.25). The subjective effect declined sharply to 2.97 after 90 minutes, and it remained relatively stable in the "mildly high" range until four hours after smoking. In some cases, lingering effects were reported for as long as eight or nine hours.

Although these results provide a clear picture of the duration of the "typical" marihuana experience, they do not indicate how the subjects regulated their degree of intoxication over the course of a "typical" day of free access to marihuana. How high did subjects usually report themselves before they returned for their second, third, and subsequent "joints" of the day? Did they allow the effect to dissipate completely before initiating another smoking episode, or did they attempt to maintain some constant level of intoxication throughout the entire day? An analysis of the data excluding the first cigarette of the day showed that the smoking occasion was more likely to be a discrete episode of "getting stoned" rather than part of a continuous process of "staying stoned." On more than 61.5% of the smoking occasions, ratings before smoking were at the level of 3 ("mildly high") or below.

2.7. Tolerance

In order to determine whether tolerance develops to the subjective effects of marihuana, correlation coefficients were computed for each subject between the level of intoxication after each cigarette and the cumulative rank of that cigarette in the subject's total over the entire smoking period. If the subjects were becoming tolerant to the subjective effects, a negative correlation should be found between the two variables, i.e., as the subject smoked more marihuana, the magnitude of his high would not be as great as it was on previous occasions. In order to assure that the analysis of the relationship was not confounded with differences in the time intervals between smoking occasions, the effect of this variable was partialed out. The results indicated that that correlation was negative (consistent with tolerance) but it did not achieve statistical significance.

Changes in ratings of subjective effects were also examined on a daily basis. For each heavy user subject, comparisons were made between the average ratings of the first and last cigarettes of the day. On the average, the first cigarette was rated 5.04, while the last was rated 6.39. The differences between the individual means were highly significant ($p. > 0.001$), as determined by the Wilcoxon matched-pairs signed-ranks test. The direction of the differences indicated that subjects were experiencing a greater high at the end of a day of smoking than at the start of the day. This is directly contrary to what would be expected if tolerance to the subjective effects had occurred.

2.8. Effect of Setting

Each time a rating of subjective level of intoxication was recorded, the setting of the smoking occasion was also noted. For three types of settings there were sufficient observations (at least five per subject in each setting) to provide an adequate sample for statistical analysis. The three settings were: (1) watching television; (2) listening to rock music; and (3) engaging in conversation. The ratings obtained from each subject in each of the settings were averaged, and these means were used in a one-way analysis of variance to test for significance of difference. The results indicated that the average ratings varied little from one setting to another (5.57 watching television; 5.63 listening to music; 5.51 engaging in conversation), and that the differences were not statistically significant ($F = 1.05$, df $= 2, 29$, n.s.).

3. DISCUSSION

There were a number of findings in the present research which indicate that the effects of marihuana on mood are complex and not invariably euphoric. Differences in results were obtained between times when subjects were and were not aware that their ratings would be related directly to the acute effects of marihuana smoking. The "aware" mood ratings obtained following marihuana use reflected a pattern of euphoria consistent with anecdotal accounts of the effect of the drug. The "unaware" mood ratings reflected a simple rise in all prevailing moods (with perhaps a slightly greater increase in pleasant moods). The difference in results from the two sets of marihuana-related mood assessments is subject to various interpretations.

One obvious interpretation is to regard the "unaware" mood ratings as the more valid indicator of the pharmacologic effect of the drug, and to regard the "aware" mood ratings as manifestations of experienced users' motivation to demonstrate that marihuana has beneficial effects on mood. This interpretation has a number of appeals. It is consistent with the conclusions of a number of authors who have stated that the effects of marihuana on mood are mixed and variable (Jaffe 1965; Walton 1938; Allentuck and Bowman 1942; Bromberg 1934; Bloomquist 1968; Ames 1958; Schwartz 1969; Weil *et al*. 1968). Weil *et al*. (1968) state: "It is not clear that marihuana has any specific pharmacologic effect on mood; in fact, the traditional euphoria of a high may well come from set and setting rather than drug" (p. 998). If the conclusions of these authors are correct, it would be expected that averaging mood ratings from a number of subjects after a number of different marihuana smoking occasions should result in a rise or fall of all mood states, with no specific moods predominant in the average marihuana-related change. This is what was found in averaging the results of the "unaware" marihuana-related mood assessments in the present study. This interpretation is also consistent with the pharmacological effect of most disinhibiting drugs on mood which commonly facilitate the expression of all moods, rather than selectively enhancing positive moods while attenuating negative moods. Finally, the interpretation is also consistent with common sense that would predict that experienced marihuana users would be biased (consciously or unconsciously) to rate their moods in a positive direction when they were aware that their ratings would be examined for an acute effect of marihuana. The acceptance of results in the present study as confirmation of this prediction would have obvious implications for the design of research on the mood effects of marihuana.

There are alternate interpretations of the difference in results obtained between "aware" and "unaware" marihuana-related mood ratings. The "unaware" ratings were always obtained during the late morning hours, while the "aware" ratings were obtained at all hours of the day (but predominantly during early afternoon). It is possible that differences in patterns of mood ratings reflected diurnal differences in the effect of THC on moods. Furthermore, the "aware" mood ratings were all obtained approximately one-half hour after marihuana was smoked, while the "unaware" ratings were obtained anywhere between immediately after to 90 minutes after marihuana was smoked. It is possible that the effect of marihuana on mood is consistently euphoric a half-hour or so after smoking, but that this effect changes with additional elapsed time. This interpretation is consistent with both some preliminary alcohol research which suggests that different mood effects are found during rising and falling blood alcohol levels (Eggleton 1941; Meerlo 1947; Young 1970), and with results reported in the present chapter in regard to subjective ratings of "highness" which indicate that subjects are still "moderately high" at 30 minutes, and only "mildly high" at 90 minutes after smoking marihuana.

Whatever the interpretation of the differences found between "aware" and "unaware" marihuana-related mood ratings, the differences do indicate that the effect of marihuana on mood is not always euphoric. The consistent findings of increases in ratings of depression during both "aware" and "unaware" marihuana-related assessments raises still another question about the nature of the reported marihuana-induced euphoria. Other authors have indicated that increased depression is not an uncommon reaction to marihuana in some persons at some times. Jaffe (1965) states that ". . . occasionally depressed mood may be the initial and predominant reaction (to marihuana)." In a survey of drug use among college students, Robbins *et al.* (1970) found that marihuana smokers rated themselves as more moody and unhappy than nonsmokers. The authors pose the question ". . . whether the marihuana smokers were more tense than the others before they began to smoke; or whether smoking made them more moody and depressed" (p. 1749). Kant (1930) administered hashish to manic-depressives and found that the drug produced depression in these patients. Hollister *et al.* (1968) found that one hour after oral ingestion of THC subjects' self-ratings indicated an increase in friendliness and a decrease in unhappiness, but five hours later the self-ratings indicated a significant decrease in friendliness and an increase in unhappiness. (The effects of oral ingestion are more slowly manifested than the effects of smoking THC.) In a study of the psychological effects of synhexyl (a THC homologue), Pond (1948) concluded that the drug had no utility in the treatment of patients with predominantly depressive characteristics, and that to use the word euphoria to describe the effect of the drug is to change the meaning of the word "from its original sense of normal bodily well-being to a sense of abnormal well-being such as characteristically occurs in alcoholic intoxication." (p. 278).

The increased ratings of depression during marihuana-related assessments in the present study also suggest that the euphoria produced by the drug is not an entirely benign state. The apparent insignificance of the presence of this element for the marihuana user is reminiscent of the insignificance of the presence of anxiety in the alcohol high for the alcoholic (Mendelson and Mello 1966a; Nathan et al. 1970). Accumulated results to date, while far from definitive, do indicate that suggestions that marihuana may be useful in alleviating clinical depression must be received with caution.

There were no major differences in the mood ratings of casual and heavy users that would imply differences in mood reactions to marihuana between the two groups. The heavy users were relatively more anxious during the five-day pre-drug period than during the smoking period, and they had more elevated mood ratings both before and after special marihuana-related assessments than the casual users. Outside of these, not clearly interpretable, differences, the mood ratings of both groups of subjects were similar during similar assessment times. The failure to find differences related to previous marihuana use histories, as reported by others (Hollister 1971; Grinspoon 1971; Meyer et al. 1971; Mirin et al. 1971), may be a function of either the subject selection procedures employed in the present study or the fact that both groups of subjects engaged in relatively heavy marihuana smoking during this study. The marihuana use histories of the casual users (see Chapter 2) indicated that they used marihuana less than the heavy users in the present study but more than casual user groups employed in other studies. Perhaps differences in mood reactions between the groups would have been found if the casual users had less previous experience with the drug. Marihuana consumption during the study for both groups of subjects was higher than their self-reported habitual consumption (see Chapter 3). This relatively heavy smoking may have obliterated mood reaction differences that initially may have existed.

It is interesting to note that the mood ratings that were obtained during the post-drug period were almost the obverse of those obtained during special marihuana-related assessments (Figure 10.1). If the latter ratings can be accepted as a valid indication of the pharmacological action of the drug on mood states (factors which limit this acceptance have been discussed earlier), the reciprocal relation would suggest that a rebound reaction possibly occurred during the post-drug period. It was mentioned earlier that the predominantly negative mood state patterns that emerged during the post-drug period may have been related to subjects' concerns about their future plans. However, it is also possible that the negative mood state patterns were a compensatory reaction to the extended period of repeated marihuana-induced positive mood state patterns. This interpretation is consistent with hypotheses regarding pharmacological interference with normal activity within the central nervous system (Cannon and Rosenblueth 1949). The possibility of a rebound reaction occurring with extended marihuana use may help explain the findings of Robbins *et al.* (1970) that marihuana smokers tend to describe themselves as being more moody and depressed than nonsmokers.

The mood ratings obtained from subjects just prior to smoking marihuana (cf. special assessments, Figure 10.1) failed to disclose any unique mood patterns related to the initiation of marihuana smoking. Mood ratings obtained from heavy users at those times were all elevated compared to ratings obtained during daily nonmarihuana-related assessments, but similar ratings from the casual users tended to be lowered rather than elevated just prior to smoking. However, the exception of this trend for the casual users was a slight rise in ratings of friendliness (compared to daily nonmarihuana-related assessments). This exception, and the fact that their ratings of friendliness were relatively higher than ratings of other moods just prior to smoking, suggest that the feeling of friendliness may be the most characteristic mood existing at the initiation of marihuana smoking. This would be consistent with other results in the present study which indicate that most occasions of marihuana smoking occurred with two or more participants and subjects often solicited or waited for other participants rather than smoke alone (see Chapter 4). Numerous surveys have yielded results indicating that marihuana smoking is primarily a social activity in this country (Haines and Green 1970; National Commission on Marihuana and Drug Abuse 1972; Goode 1970; Tart 1971). The findings of the present study suggest that feelings of friendliness may be the best mood predictor of the initiation of marihuana smoking.

The results of the global ratings of subjective level of intoxication indicated that the magnitude of the subjective marihuana effect deteriorates progressively with time. Although it was not possible to control adequately for dosage level and accumulated THC, the results presented here are consistent with those reported by Weil *et al.* (1968) and others.

In the absence of any consistent objective behavioral, physiological, or metabolic measures of the reaction to the presence of THC in the body, the subjective report still remains the most common criterion by which to judge the duration of the marihuana effect. The self-report can be considered an empirically useful index to the extent that it demonstrates some degree of association with behavioral and physiological responses. One such association which merits further study is the relationship between the self-report and the initiation and cessation of marihuana smoking.

Although social factors have been strongly implicated in marihuana consumption (see Chapter 4), the present data suggest that subjective cues may also be determining factors. Heavy user subjects rarely attempted to achieve maximum levels of intoxication, even though most of them demonstrated at one time or another that they were capable of reaching such extremes by means of repeated self-administration. Rather, on approximately 92% of the smoking occasions, heavy users attained a satisfactory level of intoxication after a single one-gram delta 9 THC cigarette. Their intoxication level at this cutoff point rarely exceeded the "moderately high" range on the 11-point rating scale. Furthermore, heavy users gave evidence of employing their internal cues as a criterion for initiating a new smoking episode. The results showed that the majority (61.5%) of the smoking episodes (after the first cigarette of the day) were initiated when the smoker's level of intoxication was 3 or below. This finding indicates that subjects tended to wait until the marihuana effect had dissipated to a low level before initiating another cigarette. However, on a sizeable proportion of the smoking occasions (39.5%), subjects reported themselves at a level of 4 or above, suggesting that they were attempting to maintain or augment an already moderate effect, or were influenced by other factors such as social pressure.

The present results indicate that the heavy users did not become tolerant to the subjective effects of marihuana. The implications of this finding are suggested by the National Commission's report (1972), which states that ". . . if tolerance develops slowly or not at all to the desired mental effects but more rapidly to the behaviorally or physically disruptive effects, no dosage increase or only a slight one would be necessary . . ." (p. 63). Furthermore, the report notes that under these conditions the behavioral and physical disruptions would progressively diminish, with the result that experienced marihuana smokers would become capable of exhibiting normal behavior even when they perceive themselves to be quite intoxicated.

The heavy user subjects reported themselves higher after the last cigarette of the day than after the first. Further research is necessary to ascertain whether this difference is attributable to a general increase in physiological sensitivity toward the end of the day, to the accumulation of THC, or to other, undetermined factors. Since dosage was not controlled, it is also conceivable that subjects were ingesting more marihuana from their last cigarette. However, our records indicate that there was little variability in the amount of marihuana returned unsmoked over the course of the study. The present data suggest that continuous marihuana smoking over a relatively short time (less than 24 hours) may result in a form of reverse tolerance whereby less marihuana is required to attain a desired level of intoxication.

It has been suggested (Grinspoon 1971; Weil *et al*. 1968) that effects of marihuana intoxication are partially influenced by set and setting. While the term *set* refers to the expectations, motivations, and attitudes of the user regarding the drug, the *setting* applies to the social context and physical environment in which the drug is taken. In the present study, ratings of subjective intoxication were obtained in three different social settings. The results indicate that the smoker's perception of his degree of intoxication did not vary with the setting. These findings are consistent with the results of the only other study where the effects of a setting variable (i.e., the presence or absence of music) were systematically investigated (Waskow *et al*. 1970). In that study the setting had no significant influence on a variety of behavioral and psychological measures, as well as on reports of subjective drug experiences.

A direct comparison between mood states and subjective level of intoxication was not possible in the present study because the two assessments were not systematically carried out at similar time intervals after marihuana ingestion. However, data relating to both assessments do provide the basis for speculation on the complexity of the phenomenology of marihuana intoxication. Conceptual models developed by Tart (1971) and Schacter and Singer (1962) to account for variations in the effects of psychoactive drugs seem applicable to the results of the present study.

Schacter and Singer's model proposes that emotional states are functions of interactions between physiological arousal and situationally determined cognitions. Given a state of arousal, an individual will label this state and describe his feelings in terms of the cognitions available at the time. One implication of this theory is that identical states of physiological arousal may give rise to different emotions as functions of environmental factors. This implication has been supported by research investigations (Schacter and Singer 1962). In a related theory, Tart (1971) proposes that a basic distinction be made between "pure" and "potential" drug effects. The pure effects are those that are manifested whenever the drug is taken, regardless of time, place, or person. The potential effects are those that vary with the influence of such factors as set, setting, mood, and the personality of the user.

Applying these conceptual models to the present findings, an outline of hypothesized relationships between physiological, psychological, and intervening variables is presented in schematic form in Figure 10.3. It is proposed that the "pure" effect of marihuana is to generate a physiological state of arousal, perhaps as a direct function of the influence of THC on the sympathetic nervous system. This effect is reflected in an increase in heart rate, swelling of the conjunctival blood vessels, and, possibly, mild cerebellar dysfunctioning (see Chapter 12). Higher brain centers may also be affected, with consequent cognitive distortions including dulling of at-

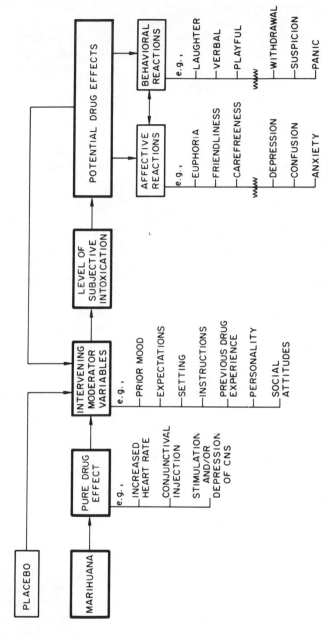

Figure 10.3.   Schematic diagram of pure and potential effects of marihuana.

tention, altered sense of time, and unusual ideational associations. These distortions, as well as their physiological concomitants, are the internal cues employed by the individual to define how high or stoned he thinks he is. Given this subjective perception of arousal, intervening or moderator variables next determine how the subjective experience will be labeled and reacted to. If the subject's mood, expectations, and previous experiences with marihuana are positive, if the setting, social events, or experimental instructions are nonthreatening, and if his personality is relatively stable, then it is likely that the affective label will be one of euphoria, friendliness, carefreeness, etc. Behaviorally, any number of positive responses are possible, including laughter, relaxation, conversation, and recreation.

On the other hand, if the subject's prior mood, expectations, and previous experience are negative, if the setting, social events, or experimental instructions are threatening, misleading, or ambiguous, or if his personality is relatively unstable, then the drug effect may be interpreted as one of anxiety, fear, confusion, or paranoia. Under these conditions, the person may withdraw from social contact, act suspiciously, and, in some cases, develop an acute psychotic reaction.

In the schematic diagram of these processes (Figure 10.3), feedback loops have been inserted between the major variables to indicate the presence of continuous dynamic interactions between subjective feelings of intoxication, intervening variables, and affective and behavioral reactions. It is these interactions which allow for the possibility of placebo-induced highs, and for intra- and intersubject variations to identical drug doses. The absence of invariant relationships between "pure" and "potential" effects contraindicates any attempts at simple predictions of the affective and behavioral effects of marihuana.

11
Physiological Assessments: General Medical Survey

Jerrold G. Bernstein, Roger E. Meyer,
and Jack H. Mendelson

Despite long-standing use of marihuana throughout the world and an extensive number of research studies on this drug, many questions remain to be answered regarding its physiological effects. Some of these questions remain, not because the answers have not been sought, but because certain controls have been lacking, i.e., as in outpatient studies where patients have had the opportunity to take other drugs prior to coming to the laboratory. Recalling the old pharmacological adage, "enough of anything will do anything," dosage is another major problem with many clinical studies. Some of the previous studies have utilized marihuana of unknown or variable potency. Other studies have utilized higher doses of marihuana or marihuana constituents (e.g., pyrahexyl compound and delta 9 tetrahydrocannabinol) than those ordinarily encountered when marihuana is smoked for pleasure. Although it is true that such investigations have provided interesting and valuable data about potential pharmacological effects of marihuana, much of this data is difficult to confidently extrapolate to what may be observed clinically with the social use of marihuana.

In the present investigation we performed a wide range of medical and physiological tests on normal human volunteers who were experienced marihuana smokers during a 31-day period of hospitalization on a closed research ward. The various tests and examinations were done at frequent intervals on all subjects during 21 days of free choice smoking of standardized one-gram marihuana cigarettes (2% THC) and during a five-day drug-free period prior to and following marihuana smoking.

1.   METHODS

The general research paradigm employed in these studies is discussed in Chapter 1. Two groups of ten experienced marihuana users, all males age 21–31, were investigated in two separate but identical studies, according to their prior history of either casual or heavy marihuana use. The recruitment, selection, and characterization of the research subjects is discussed in detail in Chapter 2.

Comprehensive medical, physiological, and biochemical tests were done during the course of pre-drug, drug, and post-drug periods of this study in order to acquire four types of information:

1.   To learn whether marihuana, as it is normally consumed, produces any clinically significant cumulative effects in healthy human subjects. For this reason comprehensive clinical observations were made frequently throughout the 31-day period of the study.

2.   Acute pharmacological effects of marihuana were investigated by correlating our findings with detailed records of marihuana consumption during the observation period.

3.   To learn whether these were long-range health consequences of marihuana use, we did comprehensive medical evaluations of the subjects at the beginning of the study, since all of them had used marihuana previously for 2 to 17 years.

4.   Subjects were thoroughly examined with respect to the development of signs and symptoms of tolerance and physical dependence during and following marihuana consumption to assess any addiction liability of the drug.

All medical examinations were performed by the same physician who also supervised all other physiological and biochemical testing of the subjects and examined subjects whenever medical complaints arose. Subjects were not permitted to consume any medication except that provided by the physician. We endeavored to avoid giving medication to the subjects except when absolutely necessary and then only certain medications were permitted. The allowable medications and their indications were as follows: analgesic: acetaminophen; antacid: magnesium and aluminum hydroxide gel; laxative: milk of magnesia; sore throat gargle: cetylpyridinium (Cepacol).

A complete medical history, mental status examination, and physical examination were done on each subject on the first day of hospitalization in the research ward. A 12-lead standard electrocardiogram and chest X-ray were also done on the first study day. The physical examination was repeated on the third, seventh, twelfth, eighteenth, and twenty-first days of marihuana smoking (study days 8, 12, 17, 24, and 27), and on the first, second, and fourth day after the smoking period (study days 28, 29, and 31). An electrocardiogram was done on arising and at bedtime on all subjects every second day throughout the study.

Urinalysis was done on the first morning urine on study days 2, 10, 17, 24, and 31. A complete blood count was done on study days 2, 17, and 31, and a hematocrit and white blood cell count were done on study days 10 and 24. Automated blood chemistry profiles were done on study days 2, 17, and 31. The chemistry determinations done on fasting blood included the following: glucose, blood urea nitrogen, uric acid, cholesterol, total protein, albumin, total bilirubin, alkaline phosphatase, lactic dehydrogenase, glutamic-oxaloacetic transaminase, calcium, and phosphorus.

All subjects were weighed each morning on arising. Lung vital capacity and one-second timed forced expiratory volume ($FEV_{1.0}$) were measured on arising and at bedtime each day in all subjects. The following measurements were done three times daily (on arising, 5:00 p.m., and at bedtime) in all subjects: oral temperature, blood pressure, and radial pulse; the latter two parameters were recorded each time first with the subject sitting and then repeated with the subject standing. The results of the blood pressure, pulse, electrocardiograms, exercise endurance, and pulmonary function tests are discussed in detail in Chapter 12. All other medical and physiological data are discussed in the present chapter.

2. RESULTS

2.1. Initial Medical History and Physical Examination

All subjects in both the casual (C) and heavy (H) marihuana smoking groups were in good general health based on the initial medical assessment. There was no history of major physical illnesses. Two relevant historical findings were that subject 4C had bronchial asthma in childhood but was not recently symptomatic, and subject 9C had a history of intermittent wheezing associated with tobacco smoking.

The initial physical examination findings were generally negative, with the exception of the following. Subject 2C had nonpainful, moderately enlarged tonsils. Subjects 5H, 8H, and 10H had conjunctival injection on the initial examination. Subjects 2C, 9C, 10C, 6H, and 8H and a fine tremor of the outstretched fingers on this examination. Subject 8H had a fine tremor of the head which had been present for many years. Lateral gaze nystagmus was present on the initial physical examination in subjects 10C, 3H, 4H, 5H, 6H, 8H, 9H, and 10H.

Chest X-rays done in all subjects at the beginning of the study were normal. No clinically significant abnormalities were noted in the initial electrocardiograms, which were read by two physicians independently.

2.2. Laboratory Studies

Urinalyses were done on five occasions throughout the study in all subjects, utilizing a dip-stick for pH, protein, sugar, ketones, and blood, and a hygrometer for specific gravity. All urinalyses were normal. First voided morning urines were tested in all cases and no defect was noted in urinary concentrating ability.

The mean urine specific gravity in the ten casual users was 1.023, both in the pre-drug period and the post-drug period. However, in the ten heavy users the mean urine specific gravity was 1.018 in the pre-drug period and 1.028 in the post-drug period.

Complete blood counts including hemoglobin, hematocrit, white blood cell count, differential WBC, and examinations of the peripheral smear were all within normal limits, with the exception of two interesting observations. In both the casual and heavy user groups all subjects generally had slightly elevated monocyte counts (in the range of 7–11% of total leucocytes). Five subjects in the casual user group and three in the heavy user group had mildly increased eosinophile counts occasionally observed (4–6% of total leucocyte count).

Comprehensive blood chemistry profiles done on study days 2, 17, and 31 were all within normal limits, except for the following minor abnormalities: Subject 10C had a mild elevation of serum glutamic oxaloacetic transaminase (SGOT = 85 units) on study day 2, and subject 7H had a mild SGOT elevation (65 units) on study day 31. Subject 2C had elevated alkaline phosphatase determinations of 100, 105, and 125 units, respectively, on the three occasions that these tests were done (upper limits of normal = 85 units). It is not felt that any of these minor biochemical abnormalities are of clinical significance.

Although blood urea nitrogen (B.U.N.) was within the normal range in all subjects throughout the study, there was a slight fall in the mean B.U.N. at the end of the second week of marihuana smoking in both casual and heavy user groups. On the fifth post-drug day the mean B.U.N. was slightly higher in both groups than it had been in the initial control determination.

All fasting blood sugar determinations were within normal limits. However, the mean initial pre-drug glucose in the heavy user group was slightly higher (93 mg percent) than in the mean pre-drug glucose in the casual user group (79 mg percent). There was relatively little variation among the three fasting glucose determinations in an individual subject, and the mean of the ten heavy users' glucose determinations were essentially the same on three separate occasions throughout the study. The second and third glucose determinations in the casual user group yielded identical means which were slightly higher than the pre-drug mean glucose in this group.

2.3. Body Weight

None of our subjects showed evidence of poor nutrition upon entrance into the study. All 20 subjects, except for 7C, gained weight during the course of the study. The maximal weight was almost always reached at the end of the marihuana smoking period. During the five-day post-drug period, all subjects except 2H lost weight. However, only three subjects of the total group of 20 weighed less at the end than at the outset of the study. In both the casual and heavy marihuana smoking groups, the period of marihuana

Table 11.1

Body Weight: Casual Users

Subject number	Initial weight	Minimal weight	Maximal weight	Study day of maximal weight	Final weight	Maximal weight gain	Net weight gain
1C	154	149	158	D-27	149	+4	−5
2C	147	145	150	D-22	145	+3	−2
3C	204	204	219	D-27	214	+15	+10
4C	144	144	154	D-27	145	+10	+1
5C	142	140	148	D-21	144	+6	+2
6C	125	124	132	D-27	126	+7	+1
7C	153	146	153	D-14	146	0	−7
8C	136	134	142	D-27	136	+6	0
9C	185	183	194	D-26	190	+9	+5
10C	141	141	154	D-26	149	+13	+8

Table 11.2

Body Weight: Heavy Users

Subject number	Initial weight	Minimal weight	Maximal weight	Study day of maximal weight	Final weight	Maximal weight gain	Net weight gain
1H	154	151	160	D-27	158	+6	+4
2H	134	130	140	D-31	140	+6	+6
3H	176	176	193	D-20	186	+17	+10
4H	140	139	147	D-28	144	+8	+5
5H	139	137	145	D-26	141	+6	+2
6H	160	155	163	D-25	155	+3	−5
7H	155	153	170	D-25	160	+15	+5
8H	116	116	134	D-27	129	+18	+13
9H	140	140	149	D-21	142	+9	+2
10H	164	163	180	D-27	170	+16	+6

smoking was associated with weight gain, although there was no apparent quantitative correlations between the amount of marihuana smoked and the amount of weight gain by a given individual. Mean maximal weight gain for the casual users was 7.8 pounds, and for the heavy users, 10.4 pounds. Comparing the mean weights on the first and last days of the study, there was a mean net increase of 1.3 pounds for the casual users, and 4.8 pounds for the heavy users. These data are shown in Tables 11.1 and 11.2.

Although we kept records of the subjects' estimated food consumption at each meal, variability in individual food preferences and eating habits makes these data difficult to evaluate. It was noted, however, that all subjects tended to consume particularly large quantities of fruit juices, desserts, and other sweets during the marihuana smoking phase of the study.

2.4. Temperature

Oral temperature was measured three times daily in all subjects with a mercury thermometer. It was generally somewhat below the usually cited "normal" of 98.6°F throughout the pre- and post-drug periods. During the marihuana smoking phase of the study, all subjects tended to maintain temperatures in the range of 97–98°F, generally about one degree lower than in the control periods, although there was no apparent correlation between marihuana dose and body temperature.

2.5. Respiratory Tract

All subjects experienced some throat discomfort occasionally throughout the course of the marihuana smoking period. The pharyngeal irritation was most marked in subjects consuming larger quantities of marihuana cigarettes, and, when more severe and persistent, was correlated with objective evidence of pharyngeal inflammation.

Three subjects experienced brief, mild upper respiratory tract infections associated with pharyngitis, rhinorrea, mild muscle aching, and low grade fevers (99–100°F). They were treated symptomatically and symptoms generally abated within three days.

Subject 4C, who had a history of bronchial asthma in childhood, was noted to have some high-pitched wheezes in both lungs on study days 24 and 27 only. Subject 9C, who had a prior history of wheezing associated with tobacco smoking, was noted to have high-pitched wheezes bilaterally on auscultation of the lungs on study day 12. Two subjects, who had no prior history of wheezing or asthma, developed a mild degree of high-pitched wheezing, noted on pulmonary auscultation. Subject 8H had wheezing on study days 8, 12, 17, 27, 28, 29, and 31, and subject 9H had wheezing on study days 12, 24, 27, and 28. Neither of these subjects had any abnormality of breath sounds on the initial physical examination at the beginning of the study. In no case was wheezing associated with any discomfort or respiratory distress. Results of the pulmonary function tests will be discussed in Chapter 12.

2.6. Eyes

No visual changes were noted by any of the subjects. No consistent pupillary dilation or constriction could be observed in response to marihuana smoking. Likewise, no change in accommodation to light or convergence was noted in any of the subjects. All subjects experienced increased tearing associated with marihuana smoking, but this did not persist when subjects were not smoking. Conjunctival injection occurred in all subjects during marihuana smoking, and was generally more marked in subjects who smoked more heavily. One subject (2C), who smoked very little marihuana, developed only mild and transient conjunctival injection. Three subjects (5H, 8H, and 10H) had conjunctival injection on the first examination, no doubt related to recent marihuana smoking before entering the research ward. In five of the heavy users and nine of the casual users there was a lag of several days between onset of marihuana smoking and the development of conjunctival injection. In all subjects, conjunctival injection persisted for at least 24 hours after discontinuing marihuana use, while several subjects maintained conjunctival injection throughout the five-day post-drug period. The persistence of this finding correlated with the quantity of marihuana smoked.

2.7. Neurological

Each physical examination included a complete neurological examination. Cranial nerve function was unchanged throughout the examinations. Cerebellar function, evaluated by finger to nose, heel to shin, gait, and speech testing, was not impaired at any time in any of the subjects. No sensory changes were noted for the following modalities: touch, pin prick, vibration, and position; no numbness or paresthesias were noted.

Autonomic function as assessed by degree of sweating and piloerection was unchanged; tachycardia and blood pressure changes are discussed in the following chapter. Deep tendon reflexes (biceps, triceps, supinator, patellar, and achilles tendon) varied in most subjects throughout the study, but this variation could not be correlated with marihuana smoking. Plantar reflexes were downward in all cases. No motor weakness was found. One subject, 8H, had a fine lateral tremor of his head, throughout all examinations, made worse by concentrating on a fixed object.

Eighteen of the 20 subjects had fine finger tremors noted on one or more examinations during the marihuana smoking period. One additional subject (1C) showed a fine tremor of the fingers only once, on the second post-drug day, and one subject (10H) never had finger tremor on any examination.

Five subjects (2C, 9C, 10C, 6H, and 8H) had fine tremors of the fingers at the start of the study. Finger tremors disappeared by the fifth post-drug day in all but four subjects (2C, 6C, 8C, and 7II).

All subjects except 2C, who smoked very little marihuana, were noted to have lateral gaze nystagmus on several occasions during the period of observation. Only one casual user (10C) had nystagmus on the initial pre-drug examination, while seven heavy users (3H, 4H, 5H, 6H, 8H, 9H, and 10H) had lateral gaze nystagmus on the initial examination. Five casual users (5C, 6C, 7C, 9C, and 10C) and six heavy users (3H, 5H, 6H, 8H, 9H, and 10H) had persistent nystagmus on the fifth post-drug day.

3. DISCUSSION

Based on our initial medical histories and physical examinations, it was clear that the general state of health and nutrition in all of our subjects, both casual and heavy marihuana users, was quite good. There was no preponderance of any particular medical complaint which could be linked to their prior use of the drug. The initial physical examinations were all essentially normal except for findings which will be discussed below, and which may well be related to use of marihuana within a few days prior to entry into the research ward.

Despite use of marihuana for 2 to 17 years, there were no abnormalities present on the chest X-ray in any subject.

Urine examinations and blood urea nitrogen determinations done during all study periods failed to reveal any evidence of renal disease.

A small decrease in blood urea nitrogen generally noted after the second week of marihuana smoking may well be related to minor degrees of fluid retention, which could possibly partly account for the weight gains noted. Indeed, at the end of the study, after five drug-free days, the blood urea nitrogen levels returned to the pre-smoking levels and the subjects generally lost much of the weight gained during marihuana smoking.

The urine specific gravity in the casual users was identical in the two drug-free periods. The specific gravity variation between the five determinations for a given subject tended to be rather small, except for the final measurements after five drug-free days in the heavy users. In this latter group each subject had higher urine specific gravity measurements than in any previous determination. The mean of the final post-drug period specific gravities for the heavy users was 1.028, as compared to a mean of 1.018 in the initial pre-drug period. This increase in urine specific gravity could have been a compensatory reaction to diuresis which may have occurred in these subjects within the first few post-drug days.

Blood cell counts and cell morphology showed no change during the course of these investigations. Modest increases in mononuclear cells and eosinophiles were frequently encountered during the course of marihuana smoking; increases in the latter correlate generally with allergic reactions, although the magnitude of the increments were such that these observations are probably without major clinical significance.

The blood chemistry determinations were within normal limits, except for a few sporadic abnormalities. As previously noted, these did not correlate with marihuana use and are not felt to be clinically significant. Although fasting blood glucose determinations were all within the normal range, the mean presmoking fasting glucose was somewhat higher (93 mg percent) in the heavy users than in the casual users (79 mg percent). In the casual users the plasma glucose rose slightly following marihuana smoking, though this did not occur in the heavy users. These data are consistent with the modest blood sugar elevations reported by Allentuck (1944).

All of our subjects, except casual user 7C, gained weight during the course of the marihuana smoking period, the maximum weight being generally achieved toward the end of the smoking period. During the post-drug periods, the subjects generally lost weight, but most showed a net increase over their initial weights. The final net gains were generally greater in the heavy than in the casual users. The weight gains noted in our subjects during marihuana smoking agree with the data reported by Williams *et al.* (1946). Our findings of increased appetite, particularly for sweets and carbohydrate-containing fruit juices, are consistent with previous reports by Hollister (1971) and Allentuck (1944).

Our finding of lowered body temperature during marihuana smoking, although apparently not dosage related, confirms the work of Waskow (1970).

Previous studies by Ames (1958) and others have reported dryness of the mouth and throat associated with marihuana smoking. Our work confirms these findings. In addition, we frequently noted objective evidence of pharyngeal inflammation on physical examination during the smoking phase of the study.

Wheezing has not been previously associated with marihuana smoking in otherwise asymptomatic subjects. However, we encountered high-pitched wheezes throughout all lung fields on one or more occasions in four of our subjects. One of the subjects had a history of bronchial asthma in childhood, and another had previously experienced wheezing with heavy cigarette smoking. Although in no case was specific bronchondilator therapy required, these findings suggest that patients with asthmatic histories should probably be advised to avoid marihuana smoking. The clinical studies by Tennant (1971), Henderson (1972), and co-workers have shown an association between hashish smoking and asthma, bronchitis, and related respiratory tract abnormalities. In Chapter 12 we will discuss our pulmonary function test results which have bearing on these clinical findings.

In discovering no change in visual acuity, we are in agreement with the findings of Caldwell *et al.* (1969). Although Allentuck (1944) reported enlarged, sluggishly reacting pupils associated with marihuana use, we found no change in pupil size or reaction to light or accommodation, and are thus in agreement with the more recent report by Weil *et al.* (1968).

Most previous investigators, including Allentuck (1942), Ames (1958), and Weil *et al.* (1968) have reported conjunctival injection associated with marihuana use. Our work confirms this finding, in that conjunctival injection occurred in all 20 of our subjects. There was a dosage correlation, in that one subject who smoked very little marihuana developed only mild and transient conjunctival injection, while in other subjects the severity and persistence of this condition was generally related to the quantity of marihuana smoked. A time lag of several days from onset of marihuana smoking to appearance of conjunctival injection was usually noted and tended to be inversely proportional to the quantity of marihuana smoked.

There was also a time lag between discontinuance of smoking and disappearance of conjunctival injection; this finding persisted into the post-drug period in all subjects. Seven heavy users and four casual users had persistent conjunctival injection on the fifth post-drug day. The duration of this finding appeared to directly parallel the quantity of marihuana smoked. In considering the appearance of the conjunctivae and the time lags that preceded and followed this finding, the reaction may represent an inflammatory process rather than simply vasodilation. Sterne and Ducastaing (1960) have described a vasculitis of the large arteries of the legs in young Moroccan males who smoke cannabis indica. Unfortunately, that report failed to describe the gross or microscopic appearance of small blood vessels; yet their findings may well have some bearing on the conjunctival injection that we and others have observed: Perhaps even a similar mechanism is operative.

The absence of major neurological changes associated with marihuana has previously been reported by Allentuck (1944) and by Rodin (1970) and our findings concur with these authors.

Nineteen of our twenty subjects developed a fine tremor of the fingers during the study. This finding has been previously reported by Ames (1958), Allentuck (1944), and other authors. In all of our subjects who developed tremors, the tremors persisted into the post-drug period, and four subjects had persistent tremor even on the fifth post-drug day. The amplitude and frequency of the tremor did not appear to vary with the quantity of marihuana smoked.

Nineteen of our twenty subjects had lateral gaze nystagmus at some time during the period of observation. This finding appeared to correlate positively with the amount of marihuana consumed. Casual user 2C, who smoked next to the least marihuana, was the only subject who did not develop nystagmus. Nystagmus generally persisted into the post-drug period. Five casual users and six heavy users had persistent nystagmus on the fifth post-drug day. Allentuck (1942) has previously reported the appearance of nystagmus associated with marihuana use. Lateral gaze nystagmus is a well-recognized physical sign associated with intoxication by alcohol, barbiturates, and other drugs acting on the central nervous system.

None of our subjects showed any objective physical or physiological evidence of a drug withdrawal syndrome during the five days of observation after the discontinuance of marihuana smoking.

4. SUMMARY

1. All of our subjects were in good general health. Physical examinations failed to show any adverse effects of their prior 2 to 17 year histories of marihuana use.

2.   Laboratory studies of urine and blood failed to reveal any pathological abnormalities, although some minor variations in urine specific gravity, plasma glucose, blood urea nitrogen, and eosinophile and monocyte counts were noted during marihuana smoking.

3.   There was a significant weight gain in 19 of 20 subjects during marihuana smoking. Although they lost weight when marihuana smoking was discontinued, the final weight was generally somewhat greater than the weight on entrance into the study.

4.   Body temperature was decreased somewhat during the period of marihuana smoking.

5.   Dryness of the mouth and pharyngeal irritation were frequently seen, and pulmonary wheezing was occasionally encountered.

6.   Conjunctival injection was present in all subjects and appeared to correlate with the quantity of marihuana smoked. There was a time lag between onset of smoking and appearance of conjunctival injection, and between discontinuance of smoking and disappearance of conjunctival injection.

7.   Although major neurological changes did not occur, fine tremors of the fingers and lateral gaze nystagmus were present in 19 of 20 subjects. The latter seemed to correlate with marihuana dose and both findings persisted into the post-drug period.

8.   There was no evidence of withdrawal signs or symptoms during the post-drug period.

12
Physiological Assessments: Cardiopulmonary Function

Jerrold G. Bernstein, David Becker, Thomas F. Babor, and Jack H. Mendelson

The usual method of cannabis use involves inhalation of smoke, most frequently from marihuana cigarettes and less often from a pipe. Through this means, pharmacologically active and inert materials present in marihuana are volatilized, come into contact with the pulmonary alveoli, and are absorbed into the circulation. Knowledge of these facts immediately raises the questions of whether there is any local effect of marihuana smoke on the respiratory tract and lungs, in addition to any systemic effects caused by absorption of pharmacologically active substances from the inhaled smoke.

One cannot help but consider the analogy to tobacco smoking, where much clinical and scientific evidence has incriminated tobacco smoke as either a causative or accessory factor in the development of irritative, inflammatory, and neoplastic bronchopulmonary disease. Although it is true that the tobacco smoker generally consumes larger numbers of cigarettes than does the marihuana smoker, making the frequency of exposure greater for the former than the latter, qualitative aspects of exposure must also be given serious consideration. The marihuana smoker generally inhales much more deeply in order to maximize his intake of the drug, since he must do so in order to get the desired effect, while many people smoke tobacco compulsively, with limited inhalation of the smoke. Another relevant difference between marihuana and tobacco smoking is that virtually all users of the former leave a very tiny butt ("roach") at the completion of smoking, while most tobacco smokers leave a one to one and one-half inch butt when they finish a cigarette. This difference in butt length suggests that at least a portion of the smoke delivered toward the end of a marihuana cigarette is hotter and subjected to less filtering than smoke which might be inhaled from a tobacco cigarette. The almost ubiquitous occurrence of throat discomfort and irritation associated with marihuana smoking, compared to less frequent throat irritation seen in tobacco smokers, is another reason to suspect a potentially deleterious effect of marihuana smoking on the lungs.

Virtually all previous studies of marihuana have called attention to the tachycardia produced by the drug. Yet there is considerable disagreement regarding the blood pressure response to marihuana; hypotension, hypertension, and no effect have all been variably reported. Perhaps some of the discrepancies in blood pressure data may be related to dosage, time, and subject position variables. Despite the striking tachycardia reported with marihuana, there have been only limited electrocardiographic studies reported. Since marihuana is known to have some effect on cardiopulmonary function, it is likely to have an influence on capacity to perform strenuous physical work, yet marihuana has not previously been studied from this standpoint.

1. METHODS

Pulmonary function tests were performed using a nine-liter Collins Vitalometer (recording spirometer) equipped with an electromagnetic timing mechanism. Vital capacity and one-second timed forced expiratory volume ($FEV_{1.0}$) measurements were done on all subjects upon arising and at bedtime daily throughout the entire study period. Subjects performed these tests while standing erect, and all subjects had been instructed in the proper manner of blowing into the spirometer prior to initiating the study. At the completion of the entire study, we calculated predicted normals for each subject. We derived the predicted normal values from the nomogram published by Kory *et al.* (1961) based on the Veterans Administration–Army Cooperative Study of pulmonary function in normal men. We selected these normals because we felt that Kory's population was more comparable to our own study population than the subjects used for deriving other normal pulmonary function data in the literature. We compared our control measurements, random measurements during the smoking period, and measurements done within one hour of marihuana smoking with these predicted normals.

Blood pressure and pulse measurements were recorded three times daily: on arising, at 5:00 p.m., and at bedtime in all subjects. The radial pulse was counted by palpation for 15 seconds and multiplied by four to give a rate per minute; care was taken to note any irregularity in rhythm during palpation of the pulse. Blood pressure was recorded by the standard auscultatory method with the sphygmomanometer cuff applied always to the right arm. All blood pressure and pulse measurements were first done in the sitting position; the subject was then told to stand and the measurements were repeated 30 seconds later. These determinations were done in this manner in order to learn whether marihuana smoking had any effect on postural tachycardia and whether the drug could induce postural hypotension.

In the heavy user group we attempted to correlate tachycardia with estimates of the subjective "high" induced by the drug. For this purpose we asked the subjects to rate how "high" they felt before and after each marihuana cigarette smoked on alternate days throughout the smoking phase of the study. Subjects were asked to provide this information by making a check mark on a printed rating scale.

The categories of high were listed in order of increasing "high" from (0) "No effect, not high at all," to (10) "Highest ever," as previously described in Chapter 10. The pulse was counted and the rate recorded immediately before smoking and after completing the marihuana cigarette. This was done in order to correlate the pulse rate change with the change in the feeling state of being "high." We could therefore ascertain whether or not tolerance developed to tachycardic and subjective marihuana effects over a period of repeated drug use.

Conventional 12-lead electrocardiograms were taken along with a longer segment of lead II for assessments of rhythm disturbances. The chest (V) leads were in all cases recorded with the aid of a template for lead placement, so that the electrodes were in exactly the same position each time that a tracing was taken on a given subject. An initial control electrocardiogram was taken on all subjects at the time of admission to the study. Subsequently, electrocardiograms were done on arising and at bedtime on all subjects every second day throughout the pre-smoking, smoking, and post-smoking periods of the study. Electrocardiograms were taken twice daily because it was felt that if there was an effect of marihuana on this parameter it would be best to be able to compare a pre-drug tracing taken on arising with a later tracing the same day following marihuana smoking. On the morning of the last day of marihuana smoking an electrocardiogram was taken immediately after each subject smoked a single marihuana cigarette.

All subjects were tested for exercise endurance using a modified Harvard Step-Up Test (AMA Committee 1967). This test was administered five times to each subject: at the end of the pre-drug period, at the end of each week of the marihuana smoking period, and at the end of the post-drug period. The test was always done at least three hours after lunch in the afternoon. We did not, however, limit smoking of either tobacco or marihuana prior to testing. For this test, the subjects were required to step up and down on a bench (16 inches high) at a rate of 30 times a minute for four minutes. At the end of the exercise period, the pulse was counted for 30 seconds on three occasions, beginning at one, two, and three minutes following exercise. From these pulse measurements a recovery index (R.I.) was calculated:

$$R.I. = \frac{\text{duration of exercise in seconds} \times 100}{\text{sum of 30-second pulse counts in recovery} \times 2}$$

Response to the test is graded excellent (R.I. $\geq$ 91); very good (R.I. = 81–90); good (R.I. = 71–80); fair (R.I. = 61–70); or poor (R.I. $\leq$ 60). This test and modified versions of it have been evaluated and standardized in numerous studies of healthy and convalescing young men (Brouha et al., 1943; Karpovich 1959). Since little oxygen debt is incurred in this moderately intense, short duration exercise, it is chiefly a measure of anerobic metabolism. This test procedure is of greater value in assessing the level of physical fitness in a given individual and comparing the performance over time than it is in comparing one individual's performance to that of another individual (AMA Committee 1967).

2.   RESULTS

2.1.   Pulmonary Function Testing

We compared the mean of morning vital capacity and one-second forced expiratory volume ($FEV_{1.0}$) measurements over the initial five-day pre-

Table 12.1

Lung Vital Capacity (VC) and One-Second Forced Expiratory Volume (FEV_{1.0}):
Casual Users

Subject	Predicted[a] VC SEE = 0.58	Predicted[a] FEV_{1.0} SEE = 0.52	Observed[b] VC ± SE	Observed[b] FEV_{1.0} ± SE	Percent deviation from predicted[c] VC	Percent deviation from predicted[c] FEV_{1.0}
1C	4.86	4.00	3.42 ± 0.08[e]	3.28 ± 0.11	30	18
2C	5.44	4.50	5.12 ± 0.08	3.60 ± 0.14[e]	6	20
3C[d]	4.84	4.00	4.44 ± 0.25	3.46 ± 0.56	8	14
4C	5.28	4.40	4.24 ± 0.21[e]	3.12 ± 0.30[e]	19	29
5C	5.18	4.30	4.15 + 0.21[e]	3.80 + 0.08	19	12
6C	4.94	4.10	4.00 ± 0.12	3.96 ± 0.11	18	3
7C	5.10	4.25	4.34 ± 0.15	4.08 ± 0.13	15	4
8C[d]	5.10	4.30	3.80 ± 0.42[e]	3.58 ± 0.26	26	17
9C[d]	5.44	4.50	4.28 ± 0.46[e]	3.76 ± 0.18	21	16
10C[d]	5.04	4.30	4.00 ± 0.20[e]	3.34 ± 0.13[e]	21	21

[a] Predicted VC and FEV_{1.0} based on Veterans Administration–Army Cooperative Study (Kory et al. 1961).
[b] Observed VC and FEV_{1.0} mean of five measurements on successive mornings during the pre-drug period.
[c] Percent deviation represents decrement from mean unless noted (+) increment.
[d] Subject has a history of tobacco smoking or smokes tobacco currently.
[e] Deviation of at least 2 SEE from the predicted value.

smoking period with predicted values in each of the ten casual and ten heavy marihuana users. According to the technique mentioned in the methods section, we accepted a decrement of twice the standard error of the estimate to be evidence of significant impairment. These data are presented in Tables 12.1 and 12.2.

Four casual users (1C, 5C, 8C, and 9C) and four heavy users (1H, 2H, 4H, and 10H) all had significant impairments of vital capacity alone; of these, only casual subjects 8C and 9C had a prior history of tobacco smoking. Subject 2C in the casual group, and 3H, who was also a tobacco smoker, in the heavy group, had significant impairments of FEV_{1.0} only. Significant reductions in both vital capacity and FEV_{1.0} were noted in casual users 4C and 10C and in heavy users 8H and 9H; they were all to-bacco smokers with the exception of subject 4C, who had a history of bron-chial asthma in childhood.

Minor changes in either vital capacity or FEV_{1.0} were noted occa-sionally during the 21 days of marihuana smoking. When subjects had

Table 12.2

Lung Vital Capacity (VC) and One-Second Forced Expiratory Volume ($FEV_{1.0}$): Heavy Users

Subject	Predicted[a] VC SEE = 0.58	Predicted[a] $FEV_{1.0}$ SEE = 0.52	Observed[b] VC ± SE	Observed[b] $FEV_{1.0}$ ± SE	Percent deviation from predicted[c] VC	Percent deviation from predicted[c] $FEV_{1.0}$
1H	5.64	4.60	4.29 ± 0.23[e]	4.22 ± 0.19	24	8
2H	5.00	4.20	3.90 ± 0.33[e]	3.53 ± 0.26	22	16
3H[d]	5.78	4.75	6.06 ± 0.31	3.26 ± 0.70[e]	+5	31
4H	5.02	4.20	3.58 ± 0.08[e]	3.54 ± 0.05	29	16
5H[d]	4.88	4.10	4.66 ± 0.09	4.30 ± 0.06	5	+5
6H[d]	5.02	4.20	4.75 ± 0.44	3.83 ± 0.39	5	9
7H[d]	5.30	4.40	5.19 ± 0.19	4.33 ± 0.11	2	2
8H[d]	4.98	4.20	3.72 ± 0.22[e]	2.84 ± 0.42[e]	25	32
9H[d]	4.92	4.20	3.70 ± 0.63[e]	2.30 ± 0.16[e]	25	45
10H	5.56	4.60	4.34 ± 0.12[e]	4.02 ± 0.18	22	13

[a] Predicted VC and $FEV_{1.0}$ based on Veterans Administration–Army Cooperative Study (Kory *et yl.* 1961).
[b] Observed VC and $FEV_{1.0}$ mean of five measurements on successive mornings during the pre-drug period.
[c] Percent deviation represents decrement from mean unless noted (+) increment.
[d] Subject has a history of tobacco smoking or smokes tobacco currently.
[e] Deviation of at least 2 SEE from the predicted value.

smoked marihuana within an hour prior to pulmonary function testing, minor further reduction in both vital capacity and $FEV_{1.0}$ were seen in four casual users (2C, 3C, 5C, and 6C) and three heavy users (1H, 2H, and 4H). Some reduction in $FEV_{1.0}$ was seen in heavy user 7H following consumption of a marihuana cigarette. In two heavy users, 2H and 4H, the reduction in $FEV_{1.0}$ reached statistical significance within an hour after smoking a marihuana cigarette.

2.2. Blood Pressure and Pulse Data

Most subjects had slightly lower systolic and diastolic pressures during the marihuana smoking period than in the pre- and post-drug periods. These changes were generally most marked when measurements were taken within one hour of previous marihuana smoking. Postural decreases in systolic pressure of at least 20 millimeters were seen on several occasions in casual users 6C and 8C, and heavy users 1C, 3C, 5C, 7C, 8C, and 10C within one hour of marihuana consumption. Lesser degrees of postural change in systolic blood pressure were encountered frequently. Significant postural changes in diastolic blood pressure were not encountered. In no case did subjects experience symptoms of postural hypotension. Three casual users, 2C, 5C, and 9C, were noted to have some increase in systolic blood pressure occasionally following marihuana smoking. There was no set pattern of blood pressure variation between morning, 5:00 p.m., and bedtime determinations.

The pulse rates were generally more rapid during marihuana smoking than during the pre- and post-drug periods. The pulse rate increases were inversely related to the time interval between marihuana smoking and pulse rate determination. Smaller increases in pulse rate occurred if the pre-drug pulse rate was more rapid. There were also lesser pulse rate increments noted with succeeding marihuana cigarettes if they were smoked within a short time span, suggesting that tachyphylaxis to the drug may occur. Some degree of tolerance was likewise suggested by the fact that tachycardic responses to marihuana were frequently less pronounced in the latter portion of the 21-day marihuana smoking period than at the beginning of this phase of the study.

The standing pulses were particularly accelerated, and most subjects encountered their most rapid pulse rate when standing, within a short interval following marihuana consumption. There were generally greater pulse rate increases between the sitting and standing positions in subjects during the marihuana smoking phase of the study than during either pre- or post-drug phases, and the difference was particularly marked if the measurement was made within one hour of smoking marihuana.

2.3. Relationship of Pulse Rate Change and Subjective Marihuana Effect

For each heavy user, difference scores were computed from "before" and "after" measures of both pulse rate and subjective level of intoxication. These difference scores were then correlated with each other to learn whether pulse rate varied consistently with self-reports of subjective intoxication. Since some subjects smoked marihuana cigarettes in rapid succession, both pulse changes and subjective intoxication might have been influenced by this variability in dosage scheduling. In order to control for the uneven time intervals at which subjects smoked, the statistical method of partialing was employed. By means of this method, it is possible to correlate two variables of interest while at the same time controlling for the effect of a third "extraneous" variable. In the present instance, correlations were computed between the pulse changes and changes in subjective high while partialing out the variance attributable to the elapsed time since the previous smoking occasion. The resulting average partial Pearson r representing the mean correlation in the ten heavy users was found to be 0.14 (t = 7.67, p. < 0.001). This correlation indicates a significant but low positive relationship between pulse increase and subjective high. The statistical methods and computations of Pearson r are described in detail in Chapter 5.

The difference measures of pulse rate change after smoking were also used to explore the possibility that heavy user subjects would develop tolerance to the tachycardic effect as they continued to smoke marihuana. Pulse difference scores were therefore correlated with the rank order of the "joint" (marihuana cigarette) at which the readings were taken. Since baseline pulse rates were quite variable during the marihuana smoking period, and since the initial pulse rate is an important determinant of the pharmacological effect on this parameter, we partialed out the pre-drug pulse rate in computing these correlations. The average Pearson r summarizing the relationship between the cumulative rank of the marihuana cigarette smoked and the corresponding pulse rate change was found to be -0.21 (t = -3.00, p. < 0.001), thus indicating that, as individuals continued to consume the drug, the increments in pulse rate diminished, suggesting tolerance to the tachycardic effect of marihuana. Other correlates of the ratings of subjective high are discussed in detail in Chapter 11.

2.4.   Electrocardiograms

The initial electrocardiograms were normal in all subjects, except for the following minor abnormalities which were noted.

Casual user 1C had nonspecific ST-T wave abnormalities in his initial as well as all subsequent tracings. Subject 3C had an indeterminate frontal plane axis with a persistent S wave through lead V6 in all of his electrocardiograms. PR and QRS durations were normal in all subjects throughout the study, except for heavy user 1H, who had incomplete right bundle branch block which was stable throughout all of his tracings. Five of the casual users and four of the heavy users had slight increases in PR intervals, not exceeding 0.04 second, during marihuana smoking; the PR intervals never exceeded normal limits however. No abnormalities in P, QRS, or T configurations or changes in their respective vectors were noted at any time during marihuana smoking, except for diminution in T wave amplitude in the limb leads of casual user 4C immediately following a marihuana cigarette on study day 26, and the previously noted ST-T changes in casual user 1C.

Prominent sinus arrythmias were frequently encountered in all subjects prior to, during, and following the marihuana smoking phase of the study.

Although marihuana smoking was generally followed by sinus tachycardia, a bradycardic response was often seen, and, in some cases, marihuana seemed to accentuate the sinus arrythmia in the electrocardiograms. Casual user 4C had two premature atrial contractions noted on study day 17 and a single premature atrial contraction on study day 19. Two premature ventricular contractions were noted on study day 6 in casual user 9C. No other disturbances of cardiac rhythm were encountered.

2.5.   Physical Fitness and Exercise Endurance

Utilizing a modification of the Harvard Step-Up test, we found the physical performance level of our subjects to be generally below what one would expect normally for healthy young men. Performance on this test was rated as "Excellent," "Very good," "Good," "Fair," or "Poor" according to standardized criteria.

Casual users 1C and 3C were unable at any time to keep up the pace necessary for this task, and on each of the five trials their performance was inadequate for rating. Subject 3H in the heavy user group was unable to perform on the initial trial adequately for rating, and attained "poor" ratings in subsequent testing. The initial control performance ratings prior to marihuana smoking were either "fair" or "poor" in five of the casual users and six of the heavy users. Interestingly, two heavy users (1H, 2H) with initial "fair" ratings improved to "very good" during marihuana smoking, while the other nine subjects remained unchanged. Two heavy users (4H, 8H) with initial "good" ratings and two casual users (7C, 10C) with initial "very good" ratings showed impaired exercise endurance during marihuana smoking. One casual (2C) and one heavy user (6H) each with "good" ratings in the pre-drug phase showed no change during the marihuana phase of the study.

Since this test was physically demanding, it should be noted that at no time did any of the subjects refuse to undergo the rather arduous procedure, whether or not he had been smoking marihuana. Also, it should be pointed out that all subjects performed the test each time to the best of their capability. As described in the methods section, the performance ratings are based on post-exercise pulse rate recovery and not on any parameter within the subjects' voluntary control.

3.   DISCUSSION

3.1.   Pulmonary Function

Considering the depth of inhalation usually encountered in marihuana smoking, the apparent local irritative effects of the acrid smoke, and what is known of the relationship between tobacco smoking and lung disease, we felt it imperative to examine pulmonary function in marihuana smokers. Although the earlier studies of Allentuck (1944) reported no significant effect of marihuana on vital capacity, there was some decrease in vital capacity in 41 of their 66 subjects. Unfortunately, Allentuck's report fails to give enough details about the measurement of this parameter for us to make any comparison of their data with ours.

Tennant *et al.* (1971) and Henderson *et al.* (1972) reported on abnormalities of respiratory function in a group of American servicemen stationed in Germany who consumed large quantities of hashish. These studies were the result of their clinical examination of these young men who presented with various medical and respiratory complaints and who were examined and subsequently studied. In the initial publication (Tennant *et al.* 1971) they reported on the appearance of a high incidence of bronchitis associated with productive cough, dyspnea, and wheezing. They noted that a number of the affected individuals were disabled to the point that they could not function in their normal working capacity. Four of their initial series of 31 required hospitalization for treatment. Five patients in their initial study underwent pulmonary function testing and revealed mild obstructive pulmonary defects. These defects were partially corrected during a period of reduced hashish intake. Their second publication (Henderson *et al.* 1972) reports on 200 hashish smokers who were studied under similar circumstances. In this group, 20 patients presented with bronchitis, four with asthma, 150 with pharyngitis, and 26 with rhinitis. In the 20 patients presenting with chronic bronchitis, symptoms included dyspnea, productive cough, and decreased exercise tolerance. Rhonchi, wheezes, and rales were found at physical examination. Chest X-rays were generally normal except for some increase in bronchopulmonary markings. In this group of 20 subjects, vital capacity was decreased from 15 to 40% below normal predicted values. Two clinical studies appeared in the literature subsequent to the completion of our own studies and at least initially appeared to conflict with our data and the data of Tennant and Henderson. The first of these studies, reported by Vachon *et al.* (1973), indicated that airway resistance, measured by body plethysmography, fell by 38% and that specific airway conductance increased by 44% in a group of 17 healthy college students 20 minutes after smoking marihuana. It must be remembered, however, that this study was searching for acute effects of marihuana on pulmonary function and that this group of investigators clearly stated that they screened their subjects specifically to include subjects only with initially normal pulmonary function tests. In another recent investigation, Tashkin and co-workers (1973) reported on acute pulmonary physiological effects of marihuana and Δ^9-tetrahydrocannabinol in a group of 32 healthy, experienced male marihuana smokers. They noted that with acute administration of either smoked marihuana or Δ^9-tetrahydrocannabinol there was a significant increase in specific airway conductance. It must be noted, however, that in this study, as well as in the previous study, the subjects were pre-screened so that all subjects admitted to the study had normal pulmonary function tests prior to their participation in the investigation.

The design of our study, employing free choice marihuana smoking, did not allow for as extensive or sensitive measurements of *acute* effects of marihuana on pulmonary function as did the studies of Vachon *et al.* (1973) and Tashkin *et al.* (1973). However, since we did not measure pulmonary function prior to selecting our experimental subjects, we had the unique opportunity to measure vital capacity and timed vital capacity repeatedly in 20 otherwise healthy young men with considerable marihuana smoking experience. The major question that our pulmonary function data answers is that of the potential of adverse pulmonary effects of chronic marihuana use in asymptomatic subjects. In this respect, it is important to note the study of Peters and Ferris (1967), where there was no impairment of vital capacity or one-second timed vital capacity in a group of asymptomatic young men who were chronic smokers of tobacco cigarettes.

Measurements of pulmonary function each morning during the initial five marihuana-free days of our study revealed significant reductions in vital capacity in six of ten casual users and six of ten heavy users. Two subjects in each group had significantly reduced $FEV_{1.0}$ in addition to the vital capacity abnormality. One casual and one heavy user each had subnormal $FEV_{1.0}$ values in the presence of normal vital capacity. Thus 14 of our 20 experienced marihuana users had significant abnormalities of pulmonary function at the outset of our study, presumably related to their prior marihuana use. Only six of these 14 subjects had a prior history of tobacco use, while eight of the 14 had never smoked tobacco, and four subjects who smoked both tobacco and marihuana had normal pulmonary function. Eight of our subjects showed further reductions in either vital capacity, one-second timed vital capacity, or both when these parameters were measured within one hour following marihuana smoking, during the drug phase of the study.

Mann and co-workers (1971) studied alveolar macrophages from the lungs of health nonsmokers, marihuana smokers, and tobacco smokers who had no history of lung disease and who had normal pulmonary function tests. Although these investigators found no functional difference in macrophages taken from the three groups of subjects, they did note that cells taken from the marihuana smokers had certain needle-shaped structures and cytoplasmic inclusions which were absent in cells from nonsmokers examined in a similar manner electron microscopically. They also noted that, on the average, fewer macrophages could be recovered from marihuana smokers than nonsmokers.

The work of Sterne and Ducastaing (1960), which described a vasculitis of large arteries in marihuana smokers, as mentioned previously in Chapter 11, may also have some bearing on the abnormal pulmonary functions revealed in our present studies. Although these authors do not describe changes in smaller blood vessels, certainly a similar inflammatory or low-grade vasculitic process can produce restrictive lung disease.

Our pulmonary function abnormalities encompassed both restrictive and obstructive changes. The restrictive changes may well be related to a local inflammatory response to marihuana smoke. The finding of wheezing in several of our subjects after marihuana smoking, as mentioned in the previous chapter, is consistent with the possible production of bronchospasm by marihuana, which could account for the obstructive elements noted in our pulmonary function tests.

3.2. Blood Pressure and Pulse

Although, generally, marihuana lowered blood pressure slightly in our subjects, as previously reported by Waskow *et al.* (1970), in a few cases hypertensive responses were noted, which is consistent with the findings of Allentuck (1944). Generally, when hypertensive responses were noted in our subjects, they occurred when the individual smoked marihuana after a period of abstinence, and were usually associated with a pronounced tachycardia. It is reasonable to assume that in these cases, cardiac output increased due to the tachycardia, to exceed the fall in peripheral resistance produced by the vasodilator action of marihuana. We also encountered some degree of postural hypotension in several subjects, again probably due to the vasodilator action of the drug, not adequately compensated for by increased heart rate.

Our finding of increased pulse rate associated with marihuana agrees with the previous work of Allentuck (1944), Meyer *et al.* (1971), and others. Although we are in agreement with the quantitative relationship of dose to magnitude of heart rate increase, as reported by Meyer *et al.* (1971), we noted that the pre-smoking heart rate and time interval since the previous marihuana use were highly important determinants of this quantitative relationship. These factors also suggest the possibility of some tachyphylaxis or even tolerance to the tachycardic response to marihuana. We found the tachycardia to be enhanced if the subject was standing, which we feel is due to the pooling of blood in the presence of drug-induced vasodilation.

3.3.   Pulse Rate Changes and Their Correlation with Subjective Effects

The previous study by Isbell *et al.* (1967a) has demonstrated a quantitative relationship between pulse rate increase and subjective effects of orally administered and smoked delta 9 THC, although we are unaware of any prior scientific investigation demonstrating this correlation for natural marihuana. Our studies do indicate a statistically significant positive relationship between marihuana-induced tachycardia and subjective effects. The imperfect dose response correlation of this finding is reflected, however, by the rather low (0.14) Pearson *r* which we found. Although the dose response relationship of marihuana to pulse rate change has been previously reported (Meyer *et al.* 1971; Renault *et al.* 1971) and confirmed by our own work, we also noted that the stability of this relationship deteriorated during the course of continued marihuana smoking. Our statistical analysis revealed that as individuals continued to consume marihuana, the pulse rate increments diminished, thus supporting our previous subjective impression regarding the development of tachyphylaxis and particularly tolerance to the tachycardic effects of the drug.

3.4.   Electrocardiograms

We found only minimal electrocardiographic effects following marihuana smoking. These effects included minor repolarization changes in two subjects and slight prolongation of PR intervals in nine subjects; in no cases were the latter prolongations beyond the normal range. Sinus arrythmias were prominent in many of the electrocardiograms taken and were present on more than one occasion in all subjects during marihuana smoking. One subject had premature ventricular contractions, and another had premature atrial contractions associated with marihuana smoking; in both cases they were transient, single abnormal events. Our electrocardiographic findings are in agreement with previous work by Allentuck (1944) and Johnson and Domino (1971), studying acute electrocardiographic effects of marihuana.

3.5.   Physical Fitness and Exercise Endurance

We found that our subjects were generally in rather poor physical condition from the standpoint of a standardized test of physical fitness (AMA Committee 1967). In fact, five of the casual users and six of the heavy users were rated as fair or poor on the initial control testing, while two of the casual users and one of the heavy users could not perform well enough on the initial testing to even achieve a rating. There was no consistent effect of marihuana on performance ratings in the fitness test. It is significant to note, however, that despite·the hard work demanded of subjects in performing this task, and despite their own awareness of difficulties that they encountered performing the test, on no occasion did any subject refuse to attempt exercise testing. In this particular task there was no observable effect of marihuana on motivation or willingness to expend physical energy.

4. SUMMARY

1. We found statistically significant impairments in pulmonary function tests, vital capacity, $FEV_{1.0}$, or both, in 14 of our subjects at the outset of these studies, suggesting the possibility that their prior marihuana smoking may have adversely affected their lungs.

2. Eight of the subjects showed some further reduction in pulmonary function test results when tested within an hour of marihuana smoking, again lending credence to the apparent effect of marihuana on the respiratory tract.

3. Marihuana generally produced rather mild hypotensive effects, particularly on standing systolic blood pressure. Occasionally, hypertensive responses were seen associated with marihuana.

4. Marihuana smoking appeared to produce postural hypotension in several of our subjects, although they never experienced subjective symptoms associated with this finding.

5. Sinus tachycardia was generally seen after marihuana smoking, being particularly pronounced when subjects were standing.

6. The tachycardic response showed some relation to marihuana dosage, but there appeared to be some degree of tachyphylaxis and tolerance to the effect of the drug.

7. We found a low but statistically significant positive correlation between the tachycardic and subjective effects of marihuana. Our data also provide statistically significant evidence of tolerance to the chronotropic effect of marihuana.

8. No major electrocardiographic abnormalities were encountered at any time. Minor prolongation of PR intervals was occasionally encountered, and only two subjects showed any repolarization changes.

9. Electrocardiographic evidence of pronounced sinus arrythmia was noted on multiple occasions in all subjects. One subject had premature ventricular contractions on one occasion, and another subject had premature atrial contraction on two occasions.

10. The subjects were generally in poor condition, based on a step test of physical fitness, though there was no consistent effect of marihuana smoking on this test procedure.

13
Sleep–Wakefulness Behavior

A. Michael Rossi, Jerrold G. Bernstein, and Jack H. Mendelson

The results of accumulated animal research investigating the pharmacologic action of tetrahydrocannabinols have been summarized and interpreted as evidence that the drug is both a stimulant and depressant (Gershon 1970; Braude *et al*. 1971). Many authors have noted that marihuana has soporific properties in humans (Allentuck and Bowman 1942; Bloomquist 1968; Bromberg 1934; Cohen 1968; Gaskill 1945; R. D. Johnson 1968; Jaffe 1965; Walton 1938; Weil *et al*. 1968), and 20% of the respondents in a questionnaire survey of marihuana users reported that they occasionally use the drug "to go to sleep" (Haines and Green 1970). The use of marihuana as a sedative was discussed by several nineteenth century advocates of marihuana as a medicinal substance (M'Meens 1860; Birch 1889; Mattison 1891; Reynolds 1890).

Despite the wide agreement that marihuana has sleep-producing properties, empirical evidence of the nature of this effect in humans is relatively rare. Apparently, the ready acceptance of the existence of this effect is based on its almost universal inclusion in anecdotal descriptions by users of the drug. In one of the few research studies that produced objective data on this subject, observers used the Clyde Mood Scale to describe subjects' behavior, and the results showed that "The THC subjects (compared to placebo subjects) appeared more sleepy (p. < 0.01) . . ." (Waskow *et al.* 1970, p. 100). In the reports of two previous long-term studies of marihuana, the methods for recording sleep behavior were not described, but the reports reach the conclusion that marihuana increased sleep behavior. In one of these studies it was reported that: "Physiological effects observed in addition to intoxication were a marked increase in pulse and in appetite and the induction of sleep." and "there were no other distinctive physiological changes observed other than a tendency to sleep, in which some indulged for a short while an hour or two after smoking" (Siler *et al.* 1933, p. 278). In another long-term study, it was reported that when marihuana cigarettes were used, "The patients slept more during the period of smoking than during either the preliminary or post-smoking observation period," and "Sleep was increased during pyrahexyl administration, particularly during the early part. During the latter part it became progressively less" (Williams *et al.* 1946, p. 1063). In discussing the results of a recent study of the effects of THC and synhexyl on EEG sleep patterns, the authors state: "The decrease in time spent awake after sleep onset and the increase in Stage 4 sleep, however, could be interpreted as indicating, respectively, less disturbed and 'deeper' sleep, thereby empirically supporting the attribution of sedative properties to THC" (Pivak *et al.* 1972, p. 433).

Anecdotal and research literature presently available strongly support the view that marihuana has sleep-inducing properties. However, sleep is not an uncomplicated behavior or state, and it has been demonstrated repeatedly that drug-induced sleep often differs in important ways from natural sleep (Oswald *et al.* 1963; Kales *et al.* 1969). For example, research on the effects of alcohol on sleep have shown that ethanol leads to a decrease in Stage I REM sleep (Greenberg and Pearlman 1967; Gross and Goodenough 1968; L. C. Johnson 1969; Gresham *et al.* 1963; Knowles *et al.* 1968). This decrease is one of the conditions characterizing 'poor' sleep, and thus, research results contradict the commonly held belief that alcohol improves sleep. In a series of studies of phenomenological sleep patterns of alcoholic subjects during prolonged periods of experimental intoxication, further research evidence was accumulated demonstrating that while alcohol may be soporific, chronic ingestion of the drug may disrupt normal sleep patterns with potentially undesirable consequences (Mello and Mendelson 1970*b*). The implications of the foregoing for marihuana research is that much more needs to be known about the effect of marihuana on sleep than the simple fact that it is soporific. In the present research systematic records of sleep behavior were made in order to provide an empirical description of sleep patterns of marihuana users before, during, and after an extended period of marihuana smoking.

1. METHOD

The general design of this study and subject selection have been described in Chapters 1 and 2. Two groups of experienced marihuana users were employed as subjects in two separate but identical studies. One group of ten subjects, defined as casual users, had at least a one-year history of marihuana use and were currently averaging eight smoking sessions per month. The other group of ten subjects, defined as heavy users, had a two-to-nine-year history of marihuana use and were currently averaging 33 smoking sessions per month.

Each group of subjects lived on a closed hospital research ward for 31 days, and living conditions were made as comfortable as possible, consistent with security and experimental requirements. From the sixth through the twenty-sixth day of each study, subjects were permitted to purchase and smoke *ad lib* one-gram marihuana cigarettes with approximately 2.0% delta 9 THC content. The method by which subjects could purchase marihuana and the amount and temporal distribution of their marihuana consumption are described in Chapter 3.

Sleep ratings based on phenomenological observations were made hourly on all subjects every day during the study. These ratings were completed by members of the research staff who made a judgment as to whether or not a subject had been sleeping most of the preceding hour. For the most part, subjects tended to sleep in their individual bedrooms. Some subjects also slept on chairs in the lounge.

Data were analyzed to indicate the total *amount* of sleep for a 24-hour-period; the number of discrete *episodes* of sleep within a 24-hour period; and the *distribution* of consecutive hours of sleep during the pre-drug, drug, and post-drug periods.

Discrete episodes of sleep indicate how many times the subject was asleep, as defined by an intervening awake time. A discrete sleep episode lasted for at least one hour, but could be of any length of time. For example, if a subject slept a total of ten hours with three discrete sleep episodes, these episodes could be of any length if their sum equaled ten.

The actual duration of discrete sleep episodes is reflected in the distribution of consecutive hours of sleep. Sleep distributions were calculated by summing the total hours of sleep during an experimental period (e.g., the entire five-day pre-drug period) and determining what percentage of the total sleep time was accounted for by discrete episodes of sleep lasting one hour, two hours, etc. This analysis yielded a distribution of the percentage of total sleep accounted for by blocks of consecutive hours of sleep from one to twelve hours.

In these studies, each subject is used as his own control and the effects of marihuana smoking are evaluated by comparing each subject's sleep pattern during the pre-drug, drug, and post-drug periods.

2. RESULTS

Data describing the amount of sleep (Table 13.1), number of discrete episodes of sleep (Table 13.2), and frequency distribution of consecutive hours of sleep (Table 13.3) were not similar for both casual and heavy users.

Table 13.1

Hours of Sleep per Day: Means and Ranges (in parentheses)

		Marihuana smoking period				
	Pre-drug 5 days	1st 5 days	2nd 5 days	3rd 5 days	4th 6 days	Post-drug 5 days
Casual users						
1C	6.0(5–7)	10.8(8–12)	8.4(7–10)	9.2(7–11)	10.3(9–13)	6.2(1–10)
2C	8.2(6–10)	9.8(7–12)	9.8(9–12)	8.6(7–10)	9.2(8–10)	9.8(9–11)
3C	7.5(7–9)	9.4(7–14)	8.6(5–11)	8.4(6–10)	8.2(8–9)	9.4(8–10)
4C	7.5(6–8)	8.4(6–12)	9.4(8–11)	8.0(7–12)	9.7(8–11)	10.6(9–12)
5C	7.2(6–8)	10.2(9–13)	10.6(8–13)	8.4(7–12)	9.5(7 11)	8.8(7 11)
6C	6.2(5–7)	7.8(7–10)	9.8(8–13)	8.2(7–9)	8.8(7–10)	8.2(6–10)
7C	6.7(6–8)	8.6(6–11)	8.2(6–11)	7.8(6–9)	8.7(7–10)	8.2(7–10)
8C	6.7(6–8)	8.2(7–10)	7.4(6–9)	7.6(6–12)	7.0(4–10)	4.4(2–10)
9C	7.2(6–9)	8.4(6–11)	9.2(7–11)	8.2(7–10)	9.0(8–11)	8.6(6–11)
10C	6.2(6–7)	7.0(5–8)	7.8(7–9)	7.0(5–10)	8.2(7–9)	8.2(6–10)
Group	7.0	8.9	8.9	8.1	8.9	8.2
Heavy users						
1H	5.8(5–7)	7.0(5–11)	7.4(6–9)	7.0(6–8)	8.1(6–13)	7.0(5–10)
2H	7.6(7–9)	9.0(6–12)	8.6(6–10)	9.8(8–12)	9.2(7–11)	10.6(8–12)
3H	8.0(7–9)	9.6(7–12)	8.6(8–10)	10.0(8–13)	9.0(7–11)	7.6(5–11)
4H	8.0(6–10)	8.4(8–10)	7.6(6–9)	7.8(6–10)	7.7(4–10)	7.8(6–10)
5H	8.6(7–10)	8.6(6–10)	8.0(6–10)	9.0(8–10)	8.0(5–10)	7.0(6–8)
6H	6.8(4–8)	8.2(7–12)	8.2(5–11)	8.4(7–10)	8.0(7–10)	6.0(5–7)
7H	8.2(7–9)	8.8(6–12)	8.0(5–10)	8.2(5–13)	7.5(3–9)	7.4(5–9)
8H	6.0(4–9)	7.6(6–10)	5.2(5–7)	6.2(5–8)	6.5(3–12)	4.6(2–6)
9H	8.4(6–11)	9.4(8–11)	8.0(5–11)	7.4(4–10)	10.2(8–13)	6.6(3–11)
10H	8.2(7–10)	10.6(8–14)	10.2(8–12)	10.2(9–13)	10.3(8–15)	8.8(6–11)
Group	7.5	8.7	8.0	8.4	8.4	7.3

Table 13.2

Number of Discrete Episodes of Sleep: Total Numbers

Consecutive hours	Pre-drug 5 days	Marihuana smoking period				Post-drug 5 days
		1st 5 days	2nd 5 days	3rd 5 days	4th 6 days	
Casual users						
1	12	33	11	8	21	19
2	—	13	8	6	10	11
3	—	1	7	1	7	9
4	—	3	—	4	4	1
5	2	2	1	2	2	2
6	25	11	7	6	6	8
7	15	19	11	17	12	9
8	6	8	15	14	18	17
9	1	—	11	6	7	7
10	—	4	5	4	1	2
11	—	3	—	—	—	—
12	—	2	—	—	—	—
Heavy users						
1	9	22	6	6	10	16
2	2	5	2	1	16	15
3	—	5	2	5	6	1
4	4	4	1	8	3	3
5	4	11	7	2	7	6
6	8	5	5	8	8	19
7	8	10	8	7	10	5
8	12	13	12	9	16	7
9	13	4	10	9	1	5
10	—	2	5	8	1	2
11	1	3	1	—	1	—
12	—	2	1	2	2	—

2.1.   Baseline Sleep Patterns

During the five-day baseline period, subjects in both groups displayed normal, stable sleep patterns. The casual users averaged seven hours of sleep per day during this period (Table 13.1) and 90% of the total amount of sleep occurred in blocks of six to nine consecutive hours of sleep (Table 13.3). The heavy users averaged 7.5 hours of sleep per day, and 84% of the sleep occurred in blocks of six to nine hours. Although the sleep patterns of both groups were within normal ranges, there was more variability in daily amounts for the heavy user subjects; while their 5-day averages were within

Table 13.3

Frequency Distribution of Consecutive Hours of Sleep: Percentage of Total Sleep

Consecutive hours	Pre-drug 5 days	Marihuana smoking period				Post-drug 5 days
		1st 5 days	2nd 5 days	3rd 5 days	4th 6 days	
Casual users						
1	0.04	0.07	0.02	0.02	0.05	0.05
2	0	0.06	0.04	0.03	0.04	0.05
3	0	0.01	0.05	0.01	0.04	0.07
4	0	0.03	0	0.04	0.04	0.01
5	0.04	0.02	0.01	0.02	0.03	0.02
6	0.43	0.15	0.09	0.09	0.08	0.12
7	0.30	0.30	0.17	0.28	0.20	0.15
8	0.14	0.15	0.27	0.27	0.33	0.33
9	0.03	0	0.22	0.13	0.15	0.15
10	0	0.09	0.11	0.10	0.04	0.04
11	0	0.07	0	0	0	0
12	0	0.05	0	0	0	0
Heavy users						
1	0.02	0.05	0.01	0.01	0.02	0.04
2	0.01	0.02	0.01	0.01	0.07	0.08
3	0	0.03	0.01	0.04	0.04	0.01
4	0.04	0.04	0.01	0.08	0.03	0.03
5	0.05	0.13	0.09	0.02	0.09	0.08
6	0.13	0.07	0.07	0.11	0.12	0.31
7	0.15	0.16	0.14	0.12	0.16	0.09
8	0.25	0.24	0.24	0.17	0.30	0.15
9	0.31	0.08	0.22	0.19	0.03	0.12
10	0	0.05	0.12	0.19	0.02	0.05
11	0.03	0.08	0.03	0	0.02	0
12	0	0.06	0.03	0.06	0.07	0

the normal range (six to nine hours), three subjects slept less than six hours on some days, and four other subjects slept more than nine hours on some days. This variability in range contrasts with the casual user group, in which two subjects slept less than six hours and only one subject slept more than nine hours on some days.

2.2.   Increase in Amount of Sleep during Drug Period

During the first five days of the drug period, there was an increase in both the amount and variability of sleep in both groups of subjects. During this period the casual users averaged 8.9 hours of sleep per day, compared to their seven hour per day pre-drug average, and the heavy users averaged 8.7 hours per day compared to their 7.5 pre-drug average. It was mentioned that only one casual user subject and four heavy user subjects slept more than nine hours in any one day during the pre-drug period. In the first five days of the drug period, nine of the casual users and all ten of the heavy users had at least one day of ten or more hours of sleep.

Total daily amounts of sleep remained elevated throughout the remainder of the study for the casual users (Table 13.1). The slight decrease to an 8.2 hours per day average that occurred during the postdrug period can be attributed to the fact that two subjects (1C and 8C) had only two hours of sleep on the last day and night of the study. In contrast, total daily amounts of sleep for the heavy users remained elevated only during the drug period and returned to pre-drug levels during the post-drug period. However, while the total daily amount of sleep returned to pre-drug levels for the heavy users, the patterns of sleep remained disrupted during the post-drug period for both groups (Tables 13.2, 13.3).

2.3.   Other Changes in Sleep Patterns

During the first five days of the drug period, only 60% of the sleep for casual users occurred in blocks of six to nine consecutive hours (compared to 90% during the pre-drug period), and the remainder of the sleep occurred about equally often in blocks of less than six hours or more than nine hours (Table 13.3). Associated with this bidirectional shift from the modal pre-drug sleep pattern, these also was an increase in number of discrete episodes of sleep (periods of at least one hour of sleep separated by at least one hour of wakefulness) with the peak number of such episodes consisting of short (one to three hour) segments of sleep (Table 13.2). The *flattening* (bidirectional shift in frequency distribution of sleep segments) and *fragmentation* (increased number of discrete episodes of sleep per day) that occurred in the sleep patterns of the casual users during the first five days of the drug period were attenuated slightly during the remainder of the drug period. However, some indications of flattening and fragmentation were still apparent in sleep patterns occurring during the post-drug period.

The sleep patterns of heavy users showed similar disruptions with the onset of the drug period. The percent of sleep occurring in blocks of six to nine hours dropped from 84% during the pre-drug period to 55% during the first five days of the drug period. At the same time, the number of discrete episodes of sleep increased, with the peak episodes consisting of one or two hours of sleep (i.e., short naps). Similar to the casual users, the fragmentation and flattening of sleep patterns of the heavy users abated somewhat during the remainder of the drug period, but continued on into the post-drug period. Thus, although the total amount of daily sleep by the heavy users during the post-drug period returned to pre-drug levels, other aspects of their sleep patterns remained changed.

Graphic displays of each subject's sleep–wakefulness behavior are presented in Figures 13.1 and 13.2. The temporal relationship between the beginnings of both the marihuana smoking and the disrupted sleep patterns which are clearly evident in these graphs leaves little doubt that the changes in sleep patterns were marihuana-related. It may appear in these graphs that the disruption of sleep patterns, in general, was more pronounced at the beginning and ending of the drug period. However, this appearance is due to the fact that the occurrence of short episodes of sleep is more noticeable in the graphs than the occurrence of longer than normal episodes of sleep. The data in Table 13.2 make it clear that fragmentations of sleep patterns related to increased number of short episodes of sleep were most pronounced during the first and last five days of the drug period, while fragmentations related to increased length of sleep remained unchanged during the drug period. It is noteworthy that the frequency of napping did not remain constant during the drug period, but rather appeared to be cyclical in occurrence.

2.4. Variance in the Relation between Marihuana and Changed Sleep Patterns

The relationship between marihuana smoking and fragmentation or flattening of sleep patterns was not invariant. Some subjects who smoked very heavily either had almost no changes (e.g., 1H) or only minimal changes in sleep patterns (e.g., 7C). Further, there appeared to be no strong linear relationship between amount of marihuana smoking and amount of disruption of sleep patterns. For example, although subjects smoked approximately 40% more marihuana during the last five days of the drug period than during the first five days, there appeared to be no corresponding increase in disrupted sleep patterns. Again, some subjects who smoked the most among the heavy users (e.g., 5H) displayed no greater disruption in sleep patterns than subjects who smoked much less (e.g., 2H). However, while the relationship between marihuana smoking and disrupted sleep patterns was not invariant, the existence of the relationship was evident in the temporal relation in the occurrence of both phenomena, and by such observations as the fact that the heaviest smokers in the casual user group (1C, 3C, 8C) displayed the greatest amount of change in sleep patterns. It is unfortunate that the sleep patterns of two casual user subjects (5C, 2C) who smoked comparatively few marihuana cigarettes during the study

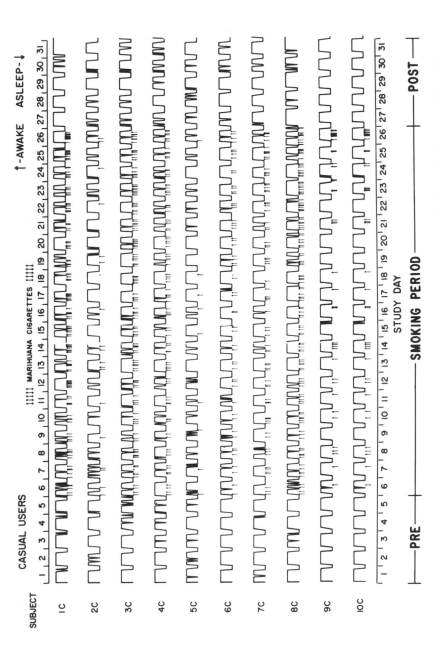

Figure 13.1. Casual users: Continuous record of sleep–wakefulness behavior before, during, and after extended marihuana smoking period.

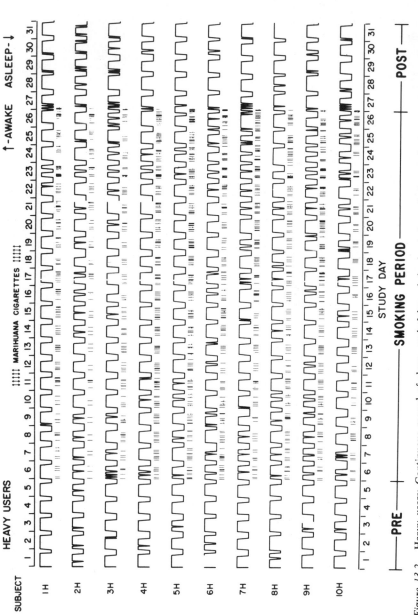

Figure 13.2. Heavy users: Continuous record of sleep—wakefulness behavior before, during, and after extended marihuana smoking period.

could not be used as controls, because their sleep patterns during the pre-drug period were atypical. These two subjects were roommates before entering the study and they engaged in minimal social interactions with other subjects. The high incidence of napping in their sleep records during the pre- and post-drug periods apparently was related to their preference for relative social isolation.

2.5. Acute Effect of Marihuana on Sleep Induction

While the data indicate that a tendency toward fragmentation and flattening of sleep patterns occurs over an extended period of marihuana smoking, the data were inconsistent in indicating a direct acute effect of the drug in inducing sleep. An acute effect was suggested both by the abrupt appearance of napping on the first smoking day for many subjects, and the temporal relation between napping and marihuana smoking that frequently occurred (Figures 13.1 and 13.2). Indeed, some subjects more often slept following marihuana use than not (e.g., 9C, 10C). However, it is readily apparent in the graphs that most smoking was not followed by sleep within a few hours, and most subjects had occasions when they would smoke several marihuana cigarettes over the course of a day without going to sleep until their regular bedtimes.

3. DISCUSSION

The data in this study represent the first systematic measurement of the sleep–wakefulness behavior of subjects during an extended period of marihuana smoking. These measurements were based on phenomenological observations rather than psychophysiological recordings. Although no correlation was found between observational ratings and EEG criteria of sleep *onset* (Synder and Scott 1970), a 93% concordance has been reported between observational ratings and EEG criteria of *sleep* alone (Erwin and Zung 1970). That is, while the observational technique may be unreliable in making the fine discrimination of when a person passes from wakefulness to sleep, the technique is reliable in making the gross discrimination between ongoing sleep and wakefulness. Other investigators have found the observational technique to be a reliable measure as used in this study (Feinberg *et al.* 1965; Mello and Mendelson 1970*b*).

One of the clear findings of this study was that amount of sleep increased during the drug period. The abrupt appearance of the increase with the onset of the drug period and its disappearance during the post-drug period for the heavy users were among the factors that suggested that the increased amounts of sleep were related to the marihuana use and not some other situational factor. For example, if the increased amount of sleep had been related to growing boredom, it would be expected that the increased sleep would have continued through the post-drug period for the heavy users. This finding of a marihuana-related increase in sleep confirms reports from other long-term marihuana studies which were based on less systematic observations of sleep.

More interesting than the mere occurrence of increased amounts of sleep was the finding that sleep patterns became fragmented and flattened with marihuana use. The results of sleep research have suggested that a certain amount of REM activity normally occurs during sleep, and REM activity is associated with dream production (Hartmann 1967). (REM activity is characterized by low-voltage, mixed-frequency electroencephalograms and rapid eye movements customarily measured with an electroculogram.) When this normal amount is decreased ("REM deprivation"), a corresponding increase occurs in subsequent sleep ("REM rebound") (Dement *et al.* 1967). Interest in this phenomenon is associated with early results and speculations that dreaming is necessary to maintain emotional equilibrium (Dement 1960). Subsequent research has not produced consistent results regarding the behavioral effects of REM deprivation (Webb 1969), but the possibility of a link between dream (i.e., wish-fulfilling fantasy) reduction and the occurrence of hallucinations or delusions in the waking state continues to be explored in the search for an understanding of the mechanisms underlying each (cf. Feinberg and Evarts 1969). For example, the relation between insomnia and hallucinosis has been studied in alcoholics (Gross *et al.* 1966) and several investigations have been undertaken on the effects of addictive drugs such as morphine and alcohol on REM activity (Kay *et al.* 1969; Greenberg and Pearlman 1967; Gross and Goodenough 1968).

In a study on the effect of delta 9 THC on sleep patterns, Pivak *et al.* (1972) found that the drug led to a slight but consistent reduction of REM activity. The significance of this finding was strengthened by simultaneous findings of increased sleep on the drug night, an REM rebound on the first post-drug night, and a decreased latency from sleep onset to the first REM activity on the first post-drug night (the last taken as an indication of internal pressures for the expression of REM sleep). It is noteworthy that these authors found that the reduction in REM activity occurred during the second half of the drug night and not the first half. The drug was administered orally prior to sleep, and it has been determined that peak effects of oral administration sometimes require up to four hours to occur (Isbell *et al.* 1967*a*).

In the present study napping increased during the drug period, and a high percentage of REM activity is reported to occur during naps (Snyder and Scott 1970). Together, these findings suggest that the increased napping may have occurred in response to a buildup in internal pressure for REM activity. Decreased latency between sleep onset and the occurrence of REM activity is another index of the presence of this pressure. Hollister (1971) observed that subjects reported frequent bursts of disconnected dreams while napping between clinical trials with THC, and this suggests that the drug does reduce latency since 90 minutes ordinarily is required for the onset of dreams in normal sleep (Dement 1965).

Thus, an integration of the results obtained by Hollister (1971), Pivak et al. (1972), and the present study suggests the possibility that marihuana has an acute depressant effect on neurophysiologic systems underlying REM production which leads to a buildup in internal pressure for REM activity, which, in turn, is relieved by both increased amounts and episodes of sleep. Confirmation of this sequence in subsequent research could lead to interesting lines of inquiry based on the conjecture that the same neurophysiologic systems are involved in both dreams (REM activity) and hallucinations (cf. Evarts 1962).

The variability that was found in the present study between marihuana use and napping (i.e., most daytime marihuana use did not lead to a subsequent nap) would not necessarily contradict the suggested relation between marihuana and REM activity. It is possible that marihuana-induced pressure for REM activity could be relieved in the longer periods of sleep (i.e., more than nine hours) that occurred with increasing frequency during the smoking period. In addition, there is much variability both between individuals and within the same individual at different times in regard to REM disrupting influences. For example, in the study by Pivak et al. (1972), one subject's REM responses to two identical doses of THC were in opposite directions, and another subject had a more marked REM reduction at the lowest dosage level rather than at the higher.

The fragmentation and flattening of sleep patterns which appeared during the drug period were present, in a lesser degree, during the post-drug period. The continuation of the disrupted sleep patterns past the drug period is consistent with recent results regarding the metabolism of THC. Metabolites of the drug have been found to be present in plasma and urine for several days after ingestion (Lemberger et al. 1970; Galanter et al. 1972). The slow disappearance of this drug from the body may make it possible for sleep patterns to gradually change to normal without the occurrence of insomnia that has been found with alcohol-induced fragmentation of sleep (Isbell et al. 1955; Mendelson 1964).

The results of this study disclosed no consistent temporal relation between marihuana use and onset of sleep. The implication of this finding is that marihuana may not have direct pharmacologic sleep-inducing properties. This suggestion is supported by the results (but not the conclusion) of the investigation by Pivak *et al.* (1972), in which marihuana (THC) related sleep was inspected for the presence of three variables commonly associated with sleep-inducing drugs: latency to sleep onset, time awake after sleep onset, and body movements of at least 15 seconds duration during sleep. Their results indicated that two of these three indices were absent in marihuana-related sleep.

The anecdotal-based belief that marihuana does have direct sleep-inducing properties may be a reflection both of its sleep-fragmenting effects and of the time of day that marihuana is customarily used. The sleep fragmentation, as discussed above, may be produced through the effects of marihuana on other neurophysiologic systems than those involved with the induction of sleep. This study and surveys by others (Haines and Green 1970) have found that marihuana is customarily used during evening hours. The occurrence of sleep following this customary usage would be otherwise naturally occurring sleep, but it is possible that it is attributed to the marihuana because sleep is more pleasant due to fatigue, release of pressure for REM activity, or some other effect that was more directly related to marihuana use. Thus, marihuana may contribute to sleep through its effects on intermediary processes rather than being directly sleep inducing.

14
Conclusions and
Implications

Jack H. Mendelson, Roger E. Meyer,
and A. Michael Rossi

A number of specific questions were posed at the outset of this research. The findings of our study are summarized within the context of these questions.

1. QUESTIONS POSED FOR RESEARCH

1.1. Does Chronic Use of Marihuana Systematically Affect Motivation to Engage in a Variety of Social and Goal-Directed Activities?

Both the casual and heavy users displayed similar work contingent operant acquisition behavior. The most significant feature of this behavior was that, almost without exception, every subject earned the maximum number of reinforcement points every day during both studies. This finding is in marked contrast to results obtained in alcohol-related research, in which alcoholics have periodic, complete cessation of work output when they are consuming alcohol (Mello and Mendelson 1972). Subjects in the present study not only earned the maximum number of reinforcement points throughout the drug period, but there was also no consistent change in the pattern of work contingent operant acquisition that could be related to marihuana use. Subjects often showed very high work output while they were smoking marihuana and when they were experiencing the maximum effects of the drug. Thus, our data disclosed no indication of a relationship between decrease in motivation to work at an operant task and acute or repeat dose effects of marihuana.

Several other significant findings related to motivation and marihuana smoking observed in this study should be emphasized. First, all subjects completed the study. This is again in marked contrast to similar studies carried out with alcoholic subjects. Alcoholics frequently attempted to terminate participation by overt or covert aggressive behavior, particularly when intoxicated. All subjects in the present study expressed a strong desire to complete the study and rarely tried to impede the research. Second, subjects maintained interest and participation in a variety of personal activities, such as writing and reading literature, interest in and knowledge of current world events, participation in both athletic and aesthetic endeavors.

1.2.   Are There Consistent Relationships between Free-Choice Marihuana Intake and Antecedent and Consequent Mood States?

There were a number of findings in the present research which indicate that the effects of marihuana on mood are complex and not invariably euphorogenic. Different results were obtained when subjects were and were not aware that their mood ratings would be related directly to the acute effects of marihuana smoking. The "aware" mood ratings obtained following marihuana use reflected a pattern of euphoria consistent with anecdotal accounts of the effect of the drug. The "unaware" mood ratings obtained following marihuana use reflected a simple rise in all prevailing mood states (with a slightly greater increase in pleasant moods). Various interpretations of these findings have been discussed in Chapter 10.

Depression increased during both "aware" and "unaware" marihuana-related assessments. This finding raises a question about the interpretation of marihuana-induced euphoria. In a study of the psychological effects of synhexyl (a THC homologue), Pond (1948) concluded that to employ the term "euphoria" to describe the effect of the drug is to change the meaning of the word "from its original sense of normal bodily well-being to a sense of abnormal intoxication" (p. 278). The somewhat paradoxical finding of increased dysphoria and depression following chronic marihuana use in this study is similar to the findings obtained in studies of chronic ethanol intoxication (Mendelson and Mello 1966; Nathan *et al*. 1970).

There were no major differences in the mood ratings of casual and heavy users that would suggest a differential mood response to marihuana between the two groups. The failure to find the differences related to previous marihuana use histories that have been described by others (Weil *et al*. 1968; Grinspoon 1971; Mirin *et al*. 1971) may be a function of either subject selection procedures employed in the present study or the fact that both groups of subjects engaged in relatively heavy marihuana smoking during this study. The history of marihuana use of the casual users indicated that they smoked less marihuana than the heavy users in the present study but more than casual user groups employed in other studies (see Chapter 2). Perhaps differences in mood reactions would have been found if the casual users had less previous experience with the drug. Marihuana consumption during the study for both groups of subjects was higher than their self-reported habitual consumption (see Chapter 3), and this relatively heavy smoking may have obliterated mood reaction differences that may occur outside the laboratory.

Mood ratings that were obtained during the post-drug period were almost the obverse of those obtained during special marihuana-related assessments. If the latter ratings can be accepted as a valid indication of the pharmacological action of the drug on mood states, the reciprocal relation would suggest that possibly a rebound reaction occurred during the post-drug period. It is also possible that the negative mood state patterns were a compensatory reaction following an extended period of marihuana-induced positive mood states. This interpretation is consistent with hypotheses regarding the pharmacological alterations of normal central nervous system functional states (Cannon and Rosenblueth 1949).

The mood ratings obtained from subjects just prior to smoking marihuana failed to disclose any unique mood patterns related to the initiation of marihuana smoking; were all elevated compared with their usual ratings, but ratings from the casual users tended to be lowered rather than elevated just prior to smoking. However, the exception to this trend for the casual users was a slight rise in ratings of friendliness. This exception, and the fact that ratings of friendliness were higher than ratings of other moods just prior to smoking, suggest that the feeling of "friendliness" may be the most predominant mood state existing at the initiation of marihuana smoking. This would be consistent with other results in the present study which indicate that most occasions of marihuana smoking occurred with two or more participants, and subjects often solicited or waited for other participants rather than smoke alone (see Chapter 4). Numerous surveys have yielded results indicating that marihuana smoking is primarily a social activity in this country (cf. Haines and Green 1970, etc.), and this corroborates the findings of the present study which suggest that feelings of "friendliness" may be the best mood predictor for initiation of marihuana smoking.

1.3.   What Are the Relationships between Free-Choice Marihuana Intake and Patterns of Verbal Interaction?

Patterns of verbal interaction were studied during and after episodes of marihuana smoking, in both structured and unstructured situations. The results indicate very strongly that marihuana smoking in informal situations (in addition to providing a subjective drug experience) is a social activity around which verbal interaction and other types of social behavior are centered. Marihuana was smoked almost exclusively in small group settings. Subjects rarely chose to smoke alone. More than 94% of all marihuana consumed by both casual and heavy users was smoked in a place where other subjects were present. Typically, one or two subjects would actively organize a group smoking session by asking the researcher to initiate distribution of marihuana cigarettes, and by actively soliciting other subjects to join the group.

Although the data indicate that both types of users tended to smoke in groups, the results also suggest that heavy users were more inclined to join their comrades once the smoking occasion had been initiated. This readiness to indulge, but not necessarily to initiate, might indicate that the heavy users were more susceptible to group influences than the casual users. For the former, marihuana use is pivotal activity around which much of their lives revolve. It would seem likely that the norm for heavy smoking would be a stronger for the heavy users, not only because smoking was a primary means of reinforcing group solidarity, but also because each heavy user shared expectations of how other heavy users were supposed to act in that type of situation.

Social influence and social reinforcement were important factors in determining frequency of smoking. The social affiliation behavior of both the casual and heavy user groups appeared to be strongly determined by patterns of marihuana use. These subjects seemed to mutually support one another's smoking behavior, as well as offering reciprocal role support for the lighter smokers. Praise, attention, and the assurance of frequent association with other "heads" may have been just a few of the social reinforcements contingent on the smoking response.

Even though marihuana smoking tended to be a group centered

activity, subjects did not always engage in verbal interaction while smoking. It was not uncommon to observe some or all of the subjects withdrawing from verbal interaction during the smoking occasion. Heavy users tended to be more withdrawn than the casual users at such times, as indicated by their lower frequency of verbal communication. Heavy users appeared to be more inclined to seek the personal subjective effects of the drug, while the casual users were more inclined to emphasize the social effects. These results are consistent with results on the Subjective Drug Effects Questionnaire (Katz *et al.* 1968), where heavy users reported subjective states that suggested hallucinogenic drug activity.

Group interaction patterns in formal discussion groups also indicated a general tendency for subjects to withdraw from verbal interaction after smoking. When marihuana-intoxicated subjects did engage in verbal interaction, their responses were likely to be less task-oriented but more positive than when they were not "high." Subjects varied the amount and quality of their conversation when high, but they remained quite capable of engaging in intelligible, goal-directed interaction.

The present findings indicate that marihuana is highly "sociogenic" in the sociological sense of the term (Goode 1969*a*). That is, initiation of marihuana use draws people together in a common bond of friendship. However, pharmacologically, marihuana may have quite the opposite psychosocial effect once the drug is ingested. Thus, *after* the act of "turning on," individuals may tend to withdraw from verbal interaction, both in formal and informal situations.

1.4.   What Are the Relationships between Free-Choice Chronic Marihuana Intake and Performance on Psychological Tasks Which Assess Functions such as Problem Solving, Memory, Time Estimation, and Cognitive Function?

1.4.1.   *Problem Solving Behavior.*   Assessments of group problem solving behavior in the Twenty Questions game showed that marihuana did not interfere with the smoker's ability to formulate a conceptual strategy and to efficiently employ new information to solve problems. Group performance was actually better during sessions when marihuana was available to group members. Contrary to some previous findings (Melges *et al.* 1970*a,b*), no evidence of "temporal disintegration" was found. This may have been due to the relatively uncomplicated nature of the Twenty Questions task, or to the similarity of this task to real-life problem solving situations.

1.4.2. *Cognitive Function.* Acute and repeat dose effects of marihuana on cognitive function were studied with a battery of psychological tests known to be sensitive as detectors of organic brain dysfunction.

No impairment of performance on tests of cognitive and motor function was observed prior to, during, or following marihuana smoking. Two of the subjects in each group performed less well than would have been predicted on the basis of their I.Q. scores and educational background. It cannot be determined if this inferred impairment of performance was related to a history of prior drug use.

1.4.3. *Memory.* Heavy and casual users both performed better at a memory task during nonmarihuana assessments than during marihuana-related assessments. In addition, there was a slight, but statistically significant, correlation between time elapsed since smoking and performance. These results indicate that marihuana has an acute, slight, decremental effect on ability to perform on a memory task. The magnitude of this effect remained unchanged within the 21-day period of marihuana smoking, indicating that tolerance for this acute effect did not develop within the time span of this study.

A unique aspect of the design of this study made it possible to obtain marihuana-related assessments of short-term memory both when experienced subjects were and were not aware that their performance would be directly related to acute marihuana use. A comparison of "aware" and "unaware" marihuana-related assessments indicated that subjects displayed less impairment when they were aware that their performance would be related to marihuana use. In fact, a few subjects obtained higher memory performance scores during the "aware" assessments than during non-marihuana-related assessments, although these same subjects obtained their lowest memory performance scores during "unaware" marihuana-related assessments. These results indicate that the acute deleterious effect of marihuana on ability to perform on a memory task may not be a reflection of direct impairment of neuronal systems subserving memory, but rather a reflection of what a person chooses to attend to while under the influence of the drug. Evidence that attention can be maintained under the influence of marihuana is provided by the results of other studies which showed that marihuana does not affect a test of sustained attention (Weil *et al.* 1968; Meyer *et al.* 1971).

There were no indications in the present study that the repeated use of marihuana significantly interfered with the ability of subjects to improve their performance with practice.

1.4.4. *Time Estimation.* Both casual and heavy users made significantly shorter estimates of time while under the influence of marihuana than at other times. Also, a correlation was found between time estimate scores and time elapsed since marihuana was smoked. This result suggests that an acute effect of the drug induces a speeding up of the hypothetical "internal clock" so that real time appears to pass more slowly.

There was a small but statistically significant trend toward an attenuation of this acute effect with repeated use of marihuana. There were no significant differences between the heavy and casual users for this trend. These results indicate that tolerance for the acute effect of marihuana on time perception was beginning to develop during the 21-day drug period.

A finding in the present study that has not been previously reported is that time estimations progressively increase over an extended period of marihuana smoking. This trend is in the opposite direction from the acute effect of the drug, suggesting that the increase represents a compensating or rebound reaction to the acute effect. This, in turn, suggests that the acute effect of marihuana on time perception is produced by direct action of delta 9 THC within the central nervous system.

In contrast to results obtained in assessments of short-term memory, there were no consistent differences in time estimations made during "aware" and "unaware" marihuana-related assessments. The similarity in performance under both conditions provides a further indication that the acute effect of the drug on time perception is brought about by direct action on neuronal systems, thereby making it less susceptible to either volitional control of subjects or other influences. Finally, the indication that tolerance for this acute effect was beginning to develop during the 21-day drug period also is consistent with a direct pharmacological action of the drug.

1.5.   Are There Characteristic Differences in Marihuana Smoking Patterns between Casual and Heavy Users, and Are There Identifiable Parameters Related to the Different Patterns?

Approximately twice as much marihuana was consumed by the heavy users than by the casual users, and this higher rate of consumption was expected from subject selection criteria. However, three casual user subjects had higher rates of marihuana consumption than three heavy user subjects. The ranges of average daily marihuana cigarette consumption were 0.8–6.2 for the casual users and 3.6–8.7 for the heavy users.

In post-study interviews subjects were asked how typical they felt their smoking behavior had been during the study compared to their usual smoking behavior, particularly in regard to quantity of marihuana cigarettes smoked. From their responses, it appears that the quantity of marihuana smoked by most of the heavy users during the study was consistent with their previous real-life smoking behavior. Two heavy users smoked more and two less than usual. The quantity of marihuana use by the casual users during the study was reported as more than usual for all but two, or possibly three, subjects. Five of the casual users attributed their higher rate of marihuana consumption during the study to experimental conditions (including boredom and "expectation"), and two attributed the increase to availability (i.e., they would normally smoke more marihuana "outside" if it were as available as in the study). It is of interest that these latter two subjects had the highest rates of marihuana consumption among the casual users during the study.

The high rates of marihuana consumption by subjects in the present study are consistent with findings in other long-term studies of marihuana (Siler *et al.* 1933; Mayor's Committee on Marihuana 1944; Williams *et al.* 1946). The consistency in the results regarding marihuana use in all four long-term studies supports the conclusion that despite the high importance attributed to "setting" by many marihuana users, subjects will consume large amounts of marihuana on a free choice basis within research environments. This finding increases the prospects of developing a scientific body of knowledge concerning marihuana use through the conduct of laboratory research with human subjects.

There was a definite trend toward increased use of marihuana during the course of the study. For the casual users, a 46% increase in use of marihuana occurred during the fourth quarter of the drug period as compared to the first quarter. This increase in marihuana use occurred for both the number of new initiations of smoking (cigarettes purchased) and the total amount of marihuana actually smoked (cigarettes purchased minus marihuana returned). An examination of consumption patterns for individual subjects in the casual user group showed that the trend toward increased use was greater in those subjects who initially were the heaviest users of the drug. Subjects in this group who initially were the least frequent users of the drug did not show an increase in use during the study.

A similar trend toward increased marihuana consumption was observed in the heavy user group. There was an average 37% increase in smoking in the fourth quarter of the drug period as compared to the first quarter. However, in direct contrast to the casual user group, the heavy users who initially smoked the least during the first quarter showed a greater increase in smoking (74%) during the fourth quarter.

Combining the data for both casual and heavy users, the increase in marihuana smoking was least among subjects who initially had comparatively very low or very high marihuana consumption rates, and the increase in smoking was greatest among subjects who initially had comparatively moderate marihuana consumption rates.

The increase in marihuana consumption that was observed during the present study is open to several interpretations. Some subjects attributed the increase to boredom. Others said they increased their marihuana purchases after they had accumulated enough reinforcement points to assure them of a desired amount of money at the end of the study. Global measures of "highness" for the heavy users showed no correlation between subjective level of highness and smoking day. These data suggest that the increase in consumption was not due to a growing tolerance to subjective effects. However, many subjects complained of decreasing potency of the marihuana as the studies progressed. All the marihuana cigarettes came from a standard lot with the same delta 9 THC content, and deterioration in potency could not have occurred as rapidly as subjects complained. Thus, the increase in marihuana use during both studies may have been at least partially due to growing tolerances for the drug. There are many reports in the literature that marihuana is unique among psychoactive drugs in that habitual users develop a reverse tolerance for the drug. That is, the more the drug is used (up to a point) the less is needed to achieve a standard effect. There was no evidence of reverse tolerance occurring within the period of the present study, at least as it relates to quantity of marihuana consumption; and, as noted above, there are some indications of usual patterns of tolerance.

Personality factors were found to be poor predictors of smoking frequency, but a significant relation was found between smoking of tobacco and marihuana for both casual and heavy users. This tobacco cigarette smoking habit may facilitate the acquisition and maintenance of marihuana smoking behavior.

1.6. Are Physiological and Biochemical Changes Associated with Repeated Doses of Marihuana?

Nineteen of the twenty subjects gained weight during the study. The maximum weight gain occurred during the period of marihuana smoking, and subjects lost weight during the post-drug period. For casual users, the mean weight gain during the drug period was 7.8 pounds, and for the heavy users it was 10.4 pounds. The mean net weight gain during the entire study was 1.3 pounds for the casual users and 4.8 pounds for the heavy users.

Subjects had body temperatures at the low end of the normal range throughout the study, with no apparent temperature change related to marihuana smoking.

Fourteen of the twenty subjects had significant decreases in pulmonary function at the outset of the study; only six of these fourteen subjects were cigarette smokers, and one had a history of asthma in childhood. Four of the six subjects with normal pulmonary function tests were tobacco smokers. It is not known if the abnormalities are related to prior marihuana smoking. Eight subjects showed some further decrement in pulmonary function when tested within one hour of marihuana smoking. Four subjects were found to have respiratory wheezes occasionally on physical examination during the marihuana smoking phase of the study.

Variable blood pressure changes, both increases and decreases, were observed during the period of marihuana smoking. The most commonly observed change was a decrease in the systolic pressure upon standing. Pulse rate changes in relation to marihuana smoking were also variable, although an increase in pulse rate was most frequently observed and was most marked when subjects were standing. Occasionally, marihuana smoking was associated with either no change or a decrease in pulse rate. Tachycardia following marihuana smoking was more pronounced during the initial phase of the drug period. This finding suggests that tolerance may occur with respect to marihuana-induced changes of cardiac rate. A positive correlation was also noted between tachycardia and subjective effects of marihuana.

No significant electrocardiographic changes were observed in any subject during the period of marihuana smoking. Two subjects showed minor repolarization changes in their EKGs; one subject had a few premature ventricular contractions.

There was no apparent effect of marihuana smoking on exercise-related cardiac performance testing, or upon such function following recovery from exercise. The initial exercise tests carried out during the pre-drug period revealed that seven casual users and seven heavy users performed in the fair to poor range.

No significant abnormalities of urine specific gravity or acidity were found. There was no proteinurea, glycosuria, ketonuria, or hematuria. There was no abnormality in blood cell morphology, white blood count, or hemoglobin. All subjects had slightly increased monocyte counts, and eight of the twenty subjects had very slight eosinophilia. There were no significant abnormalities in blood chemistry determinations for calcium, phosphorus, albumin, total bilirubin, alkaline phosphatase, lactic dehydrogenase, or serum glutamic oxalocetic transaminase. Although plasma glucose measurements remained within the normal range in both casual and heavy users throughout the study, the mean pre-drug period plasma glucose was slightly higher (93 mg percent) in the heavy user group than in the casual user group (79 mg percent). There was also a trend for the plasma glucose to increase slightly during the drug period in the casual users; this was not noted for the heavy users.

1.6.1. *Physical Examination Findings.* All twenty subjects developed conjunctival injection during the period of marihuana smoking, which tended to persist following cessation of marihuana use. Four casual and seven heavy users showed conjunctival injection throughout the last examination on the fifth post-drug day.

Nineteen of the twenty subjects developed nystagmus during the drug period which persisted beyond it. Five casual users and six heavy users showed nystagmus as late as the fifth post-drug day.

Eighteen of the twenty subjects developed fine tremors of the fingers during the drug period. These subjects also had tremors following cessation of marihuana smoking. One subject who did not have a tremor during marihuana smoking developed a transient tremor 24 hours after marihuana smoking was discontinued. Only one subject did not have tremors at any time during the study. Tremors remitted in all but three subjects on the fifth post-drug day. There were no significant changes in deep tendon reflexes during the study.

No physical signs of a drug withdrawal syndrome were encountered in any of the subjects upon cessation of marihuana smoking.

1.6.2. *Sleep Patterns.* An increased amount of sleep occurring in both shorter and longer blocks of consecutive hours of sleep was observed during the period of marihuana smoking. Associated with this bidirectional shift from normal sleep patterns was an increase in the number of discrete episodes of sleep (periods of at least one hour of sleep separated by at least one hour of wakefulness), with the peak number of such periods consisting of short (one to three hours) segments of sleep. The *fragmentation* (increased number of discrete episodes of sleep per day) and *flattening* (bidirectional shift in distribution of episodes) were most likely marihuana induced. This inference is supported by the abrupt appearance of these changes in sleep patterns following the onset of marihuana smoking and their gradual disappearance during the post-drug period. The gradual disappearance of the disrupted sleep patterns after cessation of smoking is consistent with recent results regarding the metabolism of delta 9 THC. Metabolites of the drug have been found to be present in plasma and urine for several days after ingestion. (Lemberger *et al.* 1970; Galanter *et al.* 1972). The slow disappearance of this drug from the body may make it possible for sleep patterns to gradually change to normal without the occurrence of insomnia that has been found with alcohol-induced fragmentation of sleep (Isbell *et al.* 1955; Mendelson 1964).

The results of this study were variable in indicating a direct acute effect of the drug in inducing sleep. The existence of an acute effect was suggested both by the abrupt appearance of napping on the first drug day for many subjects, and the close temporal relation between napping and marihuana smoking that frequently occurred during the course of the study. However, most smoking occasions were not followed by sleep within a few hours, and most subjects had occasions when they would smoke several marihuana cigarettes over the course of a day without going to sleep until their regular bedtime. The anecdotal-based relief that marihuana does have direct sleep inducing properties may be a reflection both of its sleep fragmenting effects and of the fact that marihuana is customarily used during evening hours.

2. CONCLUSIONS

This research was carried out following a request by the National Commission on Marihuana and Drug Abuse for data on the chronic use of marihuana by casual and heavy users of the drug. The Marihuana Commission was acting on a mandate established by the President and Congress (National Commission on Marihuana and Drug Abuse 1972a, 1972b).

Mandates of such commissions generally contain the requirement that conclusive statements be made about subjects of public interest and/or concern. In contrast, scientific research such as we have carried out often results in the generation of a new (and, hopefully, more sophisticated) range of questions rather than provides definitive answers. For a subject as controversial and complex as marihuana, the public's demand for some definition of risk cannot be met by the findings of a single research study. Risk can be best defined by comparing data obtained on individuals with widely differing use patterns, and by assessing biological and behavioral functions in a variety of settings, by a number of research scientists and clinicians.

The assessments of psychological performance, acute and subacute physiological effects, and operant work output in the present study are similar to assessments made in studies of alcohol-intoxicated individuals and/or in other experimental work with human subjects. While the research design obviously did not permit direct comparisons of types of intoxication (alcohol versus marihuana) in the same individuals, interesting differences did emerge when one compared the acute and repeat dose effects of marihuana in persons who normally use it every day (heavy users) with repeat and acute dose effects of alcohol in problem drinkers. In this study, heavy marihuana users were arbitrarily defined as persons with a two-to-nine year history of marihuana use, who were currently averaging 33 smoking sessions per month. Does this constitute a problem marihuana user?

McGlothlin (1972) has observed that the daily intake of tetrahydrocannabinol among heavy hashish smokers may be ten times the daily dose of the average American marihuana user. The latter may smoke one or two marihuana cigarettes a day (average weight 0.5 gram, average delta 9 THC content less than 1%), and accumulate a maximum daily dose of 10–15 mg of delta 9 THC. It is of significant interest, therefore, that some of the heavy users in the present study smoked as many as ten one-gram cigarettes per day (mean delta 9 THC content 0.2%), and apparently accumulated a maximal daily dose of 200 mg of delta 9 THC without significant ill effects. They did not become psychotic, although lower doses of delta 9 THC have caused hallucinatory states in acute administration studies (Isbell et al. 1967a; Hollister et al. 1970). The data suggest that subjects who self-administered such high doses were tolerant to many of the hallucinogenic effects of the drug. The only subjective report suggesting hallucinogenic effects was the high "ambivalence" score on the Subjective Drug Effects Questionnaire; but from reports in the literature one would have expected a more dramatic response to such a high daily dose of delta 9 THC. The absence of such dramatic effects was best illustrated by one subject who smoked 20 one-gram cigarettes on the last day of the drug period, including ten during the final six hours of this 24-hour day. Two hours after smoking his last marihuana cigarette, his performance on tests of recent memory, time estimation, and psychomotor function were within his normal range, and his general behavior disclosed no discernible effects from having ingested such a massive dose of delta 9 THC.

Subjects in this study, under conditions of ready availability and little alternative recreation, self-administered doses of delta 9 THC at an atypically high rate. Apparently, a rapid buildup of tolerance (a characteristic of hallucinogenic drugs which occurs under conditions of daily usage) permitted the daily self-administration of a large concentration of delta 9 THC. The absence of disruptive psychological, behavioral, or physiological effects does not mean that these doses are not potentially harmful. In the nontolerant individual they would be likely to result in a hallucinogenic state.

The medical question that can be asked is what the effects of chronic self-administration of high doses of delta 9 THC would be upon physical and mental functioning. The American experience is not extensive enough to suggest an answer to this question. It will be necessary to follow heavy users in this country over many years in order to determine whether they develop patterns of high dose marihuana intake analogous to the patterns of alcohol intake of our alcoholics (and similar to the patterns of hashish administration in the Middle East and North Africa). In the repeat dose study reported here, subjects did not alter their daily pattern of activities, nor did they demonstrate impaired performance related to repeated high dose self-administration.

The reader may ask whether the relatively high rate of smoking which developed on the research ward indicates that the subjects had made a gross underestimation of their usual intake on the pre-study questionnaire. This is a legitimate question for which we can offer no definitive answer. Nevertheless, subjects could gain no advantage for understanding marihuana use on the questionnaire since they had no information whatsoever of the criteria used for subject selection in regard to past marihuana use. In addition, all subjects reaffirmed the accuracy of their answers on the drug use questionnaire during interviews held on the last nights of both studies (i.e., at a time when subjects had nothing to gain or lose by being truthful).

There was no single reason for the high frequency of marihuana use during the study compared to subjects' usual patterns of use. A few subjects said that they smoked during the study to test the limits of their own endurance while in a safe environment (i.e., they were conducting personal studies of their own). Other subjects said that they smoked large quantities in order to demonstrate this harmlessness to the research staff. Still other subjects said their increased smoking was related to the restrictions of the research ward (i.e., "there was little else to do").

From the results relating to smoking and verbal interaction, it is likely that the increased smoking by some subjects (motivated by a need to "prove" something either to themselves or to the research staff) served as a stimulus for increased smoking by other subjects.

Tolerance to drug effects occurs over time with a variety of pharmacologic agents, not all of which are drugs of abuse. Tolerance to the effects of delta 9 THC in the pigeon has been described by McMillan et al. (1970). Tolerance to the physiological and psychomotor effects of delta 9 THC in man can only be verified by the administration of fixed doses over time, or by the administration of a dose of THC just prior to an extended smoking period and at the end of a smoking period.

Nevertheless, the results of the present study strongly suggest that there is tolerance to the cardiovascular (pulse rate) effects, as well as to the effects which impair time estimation. The absence of active hallucinatory states associated with daily doses of delta 9 THC as high as 200 mg per day suggests tolerance also to the hallucinogenic effects of this drug. Moreover, the tendency of subjects to increase their daily intake by shortening the interval between smoking occasions suggests that the duration of the intoxication is reduced with frequent use. Confirmatory studies using fixed doses of tetrahydrocannabinol with careful monitoring of metabolic turnover (as well as specific effect upon biogenic amines and steroid metabolism) are essential to clarify the nature of this phenomenon.

Throughout the study, a number of physiological and biochemical parameters were monitored. In addition, subjects underwent repeated physical examinations. Of interest was an apparently diminished vital capacity in both groups of users which was present prior to their smoking marihuana during the study. These data suggest that chronic marihuana use may impose some risk of chronic lung disease. However, large-scale population surveys with a variety of pulmonary function studies are essential to any definition of risk. Such studies must include detailed smoking, occupational, and residential histories in order to sort out the specific effects of marihuana smoking from the effects of air pollution and tobacco smoking.

The minor effects of marihuana smoking over a 21-day period on vital capacity and timed vital capacity imply that smoking involved no major acute or subacute impairment of respiratory function.

The presence of lateral gaze nystagmus and hand tremor associated with marihuana smoking merely confirms that this substance is causing nonspecific acute effects within the central nervous system (a characteristic of most centrally acting drugs). The persistence of some of these findings beyond the drug period warrants further investigation, which must include some estimate of the persistence of delta 9 THC and its metabolites in tissues. In the absence of a measure of duration of metabolic activity, it is impossible to assess the significance of this finding.

The effects of marihuana upon group and individual behavior failed to confirm the reports of those who most strongly advocate for or against its use. While both groups of users preferred to smoke in groups, there was no observable facilitation of verbal interaction, and subjects tended to remain as aggressive while marihuana intoxicated as when not intoxicated.

On the basis of past history and ward behavior, it appeared that recruitment into marihuana smoking was not a function of aberrant personality pattern, but was rather a function of group norms. This was dramatically demonstrated in the casual user group, where the two subjects who smoked the least had been roommates prior to the study, and the maintenance of their previous relationship shielded them from any subtle or overt group pressures to engage in heavier smoking. Similarly, the heaviest smokers tended to recruit each other into smoking activity, with solitary smoking being an unusual occurrence.

The data obtained in this study indicated that acute and repeat dose marihuana administration did not alter the recreational, physical, and operant work patterns of subjects. These results differ sharply from those found in alcohol research employing the same research paradigm as used in the present study. In alcohol studies, alcohol intoxication reduces work output to zero (as in "real life"). Chronic, habitual alcohol use results in job loss and deterioration of self-care. In contrast to alcohol, acute marihuana intoxication over a period of three weeks did not noticeably affect the motivational patterns of any subject, and may therefore not have a direct effect on motivation in "real life." This does not mean that heavy use is not a factor in "dropping out" by some young people. Motivation is obviously a complex phenomenon related to early life experiences, peer and adult approval, and stability of identity and role models. How marihuana use interacts with and affects this complex phenomenon may never be determined even within the context of long-term studies of chronic heavy use of marihuana.

References

E. Abel, Marijuana and memory, *Nature* **227**:1151–1152 (1970).

E. Abel, Marijuana and memory: Acquisition or retrieval?, *Science* **173**:1038–1040 (1971*a*).

E. Abel, Effects of marijuana on the solution of anagrams, memory, and appetite, *Nature* **231**:260–261 (1971*b*).

H. Abelson, R. Cohen, and D. Schrayer, *Public Attitudes Toward Marihuana, Part I*, Response Analysis Corporation, Princeton, New Jersey (1972).

J. R. Allen and L. J. West, Flight from violence: Hippies and the green rebellion, *Am. J. Psychiat.* **125**:364–370 (1968).

S. Allentuck, Organic and systemic functions, in *Mayor's Committee on Marihuana, The Marihuana Problem in the City of New York: Sociological, Medical, Psychological, and Pharmacological Studies*, Cattell Press, Lancaster, Pennsylvania (1944).

S. Allentuck and K. M. Bowman, The psychiatric aspects of marihuana intoxication, *Am. J. Psychiat.* **99**:248–251 (1942).

AMA Committee on Exercise and Physical Fitness, Is your patient fit? *J.A.M.A.* **201**:131–132 (1967).

American Institute of Public Opinion (Gallup), *Gallup Opinion Index: Results of 1971 Survey of College Students*, Princeton, New Jersey Library (1972).

F. Ames, A clinical and metabolic study of acute intoxication with cannabis sativa and its role in the model psychoses, *J. Ment. Sci.* **104**(437):972–999 (1958).

R. F. Bales, *Interaction Process Analysis, A Method for the Study of Small Groups*, Addison-Wesley, Reading, Massachusetts (1950).

H. Barry and R. Kubena, Acclimation to laboratory alters response of rats to delta-one tetrahydrocannabinol, in *Proceedings of the 77th Annual Convention*, American Psychological Association (1969), Vol. 4, pp. 865–866.

C. Baudelaire, De L'Ideal Artificiel, *La Revue Contemporaine*, Paris (1858).

H. S. Becker, *Outsiders: Studies in the Sociology of Deviance*, Macmillan, New York (1963).

H. S. Becker, History, culture and subjective experience: An exploration of the social bases of drug-induced experiences, *J. Health Soc. Behav.* **8**:163–176 (1967).

D. E. Bennett, Marihuana Use among College Students and Street People: It Just Brings Out What's There, unpublished senior honors thesis, Harvard University (1971).

L. Berkowitz, *Aggression: A Social Psychological Analysis*, McGraw-Hill, New York (!962).

E. A. Birch, The use of indian hemp in the treatment of chronic chloral and chronic opium poisoning, *Lancet* **1**:625 (1889).

E. R. Bloomquist, Marijuana: Social benefit or social detrement?, *Calif. Med.* **106**:346–353 (1967).

E. R. Bloomquist, *Marijuana*, Glencoe Press, Beverly Hills, California (1968).

R. H. Blum *et al.*, *Drugs I, Society and Drugs*, Jossey Bass, San Francisco (1969).

R. A. Bogg, R. G. Smith, and S. D. Russell, Drugs and Michigan high school students, *Final Report, Special Committee on Narcotics,* Michigan Department of Public Health (1969).

E. S. Boyd, E. D. Hutchinson, L. C. Gardner, and D. A. Merritt, Effects of tetrahydrocannabinols and other drugs on operant behavior in rats, *Arch. Int. Pharmacodyn.* **144**:533 (1963).

M. C. Braude, R. Monsaert, and E. B. Truitt, Jr., Some pharmacological correlates to marihuana use, *Seminars in Drug Therapy I* (1971).

W. Bromberg, Marihuana intoxication: A clinical study of cannabis sativa intoxication, *Am. J. Psychiat.* **91**:303–330 (1934).

L. Brouha, C. W. Heath, and A. Graybiel, Step test: Simple method of measuring physical fitness for hard muscular work in adult men (1943).

W. S. Burroughs, Points of distinction between sedative and consciousness-expanding drugs in *The Marihuana Papers* (D. Solomon, ed.) pp. 440–446, New American Library, New York (1966).

A. Buss and A. Durkee, An inventory for assessing different kinds of hostility, *J. Consult. Psychol.* **21**:343–349 (1957).

D. F. Caldwell, S. A. Myers, E. F. Domino, and P. E. Merriam, Auditory and visual threshold effects of marihuana in man, *Percept. and Motor Skills* **29**:755–759 (1969).

W. B. Cannon and A. Rosenblueth, *The Sensitivity of Denervated Structures,* Macmillan, New York (1949).

E. A. Carlini, Tolerance to chronic administration of Cannabis sativa (marihuana) in rats, *Psychopharmacology* **1**:135–142 (1968).

E. A. Carlini and C. Kramer, Effects of cannabis sativa (marihuana) on maze performance of the rat, *Psychopharmacologia* **7**:175–181 (1965).

I. C. Chopra and R. N. Chopra, The use of cannabis drugs in India, *U.N. Bull. Narc.* **9**:4–29 (1957).

L. D. Clark and E. N. Nakashima, Experimental studies of marihuana, *Am. J. Psychiat.* **125**:379–384 (1968).

L. D. Clark, R. Hughes, and E. N. Nakashima, Behavioral effects of marihuana: experimental studies, *Arch. Gen. Psychiat.* **23**:193–198 (1970).

S. Cohen, Pot, acid, speed, *Med. Sci.* **19**:30–35 (1968).

R. Dagirmanjian and E. S. Boyd, Some pharmacological effects of two tetrahydrocannabinols, *J. Pharm. Exp. Therap.* **135**:25 (1962).

P. Dally, Undesirable effects of marihuana, *Brit. Med. J.* **3**:367 (1967).

W. Dement, The effect of dream deprivation, *Science* **131**:1705–1707 (1960).

W. Dement, An essay on dreams: The role of physiology in understanding their nature, in *New Directions in Psychology* (T. M. Newcomb, ed.), Vol. II, pp. 135–257, Holt, Rinehart, and Winston Inc., New York (1965).

W. Dement, P. Henry, H. Cohen, and J. Ferguson, Studies on the effect of REM deprivation in humans and in animals, in *Sleep and Altered States of Consciousness* (S. Kety, E. Evarts, and H. Williams, eds.), pp. 456–468, The Williams and Wilkins Company, Baltimore, Maryland (1967).

R. L. Dornbush, M. Fink, and A. M. Freedman, Marihuana, memory, and perception, *Am. J. Psychiat.* **128**:194–197 (1971).

M. G. Eggleton, The effect of alcohol on the central nervous system, *Brit. J. Psychol.* **32**:52–61 (1941).

C. W. Erwin and W. W. K. Zung, Comparison of behavioral and EEG criteria of sleep in humans, Paper read at 10th Annual Meeting of the Association for the Psychophysiological Study of Sleep at Santa Fe, New Mexico (1970).

E. V. Evarts, A neurophysiologic theory of hallucinations, *in Hallucinations* (L. J. West, ed.), pp. 1–13, Grune and Stratton, New York (1962).

D. L. Farnsworth, The drug problem among young people, *W. Va. Med. J.* **63**:433–437 (1967).

I. Feinberg and E. V. Evarts, Some implications of sleep research for psychiatry, in *Neurobiological Aspects of Psychopathology* (Proc. of 58th Annual Meeting of the American Psychopathological Association; J. Zubin and C. Shagass, eds.), Vol. XXV, pp. 334–393, Grune and Stratton, New York (1969).

I. Feinberg, N. Heller, H. R. Steinberg, and V. Stoffler, The relationship of sleep disturbance to behavior pathology in a group of schizophrenic patients, *Compr. Psychiat.* **6**:374–380 (1965).

S. Feshbach, The function of aggression and the regulation of aggressive drive, *Psychol. Rev.* **71**:257–272 (1964).

H. L. Freedman and M. J. Rockmore, Marihuana: A factor in personality evaluation and army maladjustment, *J. Clin. Psychopathol.* **7**:765–782 (Part I); **8**:221–236 (Part II) (1946).

M. Galanter, R. J. Wyatt, L. Lemberger, H. Weingartner, T. B. Vaughn, and W. J. Roth, Effects on humans of delta 9 tetrahydrocannabinol administered by smoking, *Science* **176**:934–936 (1972).

S. Garattini, Effects of a cannabis extract on gross behavior, in *Hashish: Its Chemistry and Pharmacology*, Ciba Foundation Study Group No. 21 (G. E. W. Wolstenholme and J. Knight, eds.), pp. 70–78, Little Brown and Company, Boston (1965).

J. C. Garriott, L. J. King, R. B. Forney, and F. W. Hughes, Effects of some tetrahydrocannabinols on hexobarbital sleeping time and amphetamine-induced hyperactivity in mice, *Life Sciences* **6**:2119–2128 (1967).

H. S. Gaskill, Marihuana, an intoxicant, *Am. J. Psychiat.* **102**:202–204 (1945).

S. Gershon, On the pharmacology of marihuana, *Behav. Neuropsychiat.* **1**:9–18 (1970).

A. Ginsberg, First manifesto to end the bringdown, in *The Marihuana Papers* (D. Solomon, ed.), New American Library, New York (1966), pp. 230–238.

J. W. Goldstein, J. H. Korn, W. H. Abel, and R. M. Morgan, The social psychology and epidemiology of student drug usage, report on Phase I, Report No. 70-18, Department of Psychology, Carnegie-Mellon University, Pittsburgh, Pennsylvania (1970).

E. Goode, Multiple drug use among marihuana smokers, *Soc. Prob.* **17**:48–64 (1969*a*).

E. Goode, Marihuana and the politics of reality, *J. Health Soc. Behav.* **10**:83–94 (1969*b*).

E. Goode, ed., *Marihuana*, Atherton Press, New York (1969*c*).

E. Goode, *The Marihuana Smokers*, Basic Books, New York (1970).

R. Greenberg and C. Pearlman, Delirium tremens and dreaming, *Am. J. Psychiat.* **124**:133–142 (1967).

S. C. Gresham, W. B. Webb, and R. L. Williams, Alcohol and caffeine: Effect on inferred visual dreaming, *Science* **140**:1226–1227 (1963).

L. Grinspoon, Marihuana, *Scientific American* **221**:17–25 (1969).

L. Grinspoon, *Marihuana Reconsidered*, Harvard University Press, Cambridge, Massachusetts (1971).

M. M. Gross and D. Goodenough, Sleep disturbances in the acute alcoholic psychoses, in *Clinical Research in Alcoholism*, Psychiatric Res. Report No. 24 (J. O. Cole, ed.), pp. 132–147, A.P.A., Washington, D.C. (1965).

M. M. Gross, D. Goodenough, M. Tobin, E. Halpert, D. Lepore, A. Perlstein, M. Serota, J. DeBeanco, R. Fuller, and I. Kishner, Sleep disturbance and hallucinations in the acute alcoholic psychoses, *J. Nerv. Ment. Dis.* **142**:493–514 (1966).

L. Haines and W. Green, Marihuana use patterns, *Brit. J. of Addict.* **65**:347–362 (1970).

E. Hartmann, *The Biology of Dreaming*, Charles C. Thomas, Springfield, Massachusetts (1967).

J. L. Hekimian and S. Gershon, Characteristics of drug abusers admitted to a psychiatric hospital, *J.A.M.A.* **205**:125–130 (1968).

R. L. Henderson, F. S. Tennant, and R. Guerry, Respiratory manifestations of hashish smoking, *Arch. Otolaryng.* **95**:248–251 (1972).

L. E. Hollister, Marihuana in man: Three years later, *Science* **172**:21–29 (1971).

L. E. Hollister and H. K. Gillespie, Marihuana, ethanol, and dextroamphetamine: Mood and mental function alterations, *Arch. Gen. Psychiat.* **23**:199–203 (1970).

L. E. Hollister, R. K. Richards, and H. K. Gillespie, Comparison of tetrahydrocannabinol and synhexyl in man, *Clin. Pharm. Therap.* **9**:783–791 (1968).

L. E. Hollister, F. Moore, S. Kanter, and E. Noble, Delta-1-tetrahydrocannabinol, synhexyl, and marihuana extract administered orally in man: Catecholamine excretion, plasma cortisol levels, and platelet serotonin content, *Psychopharmacologia* (Berlin) **17**:354–360 (1970).

H. Isbell, H. F. Fraser, A. Wikler, R. E. Belleville, and A. Eisenman, An experimental study of the etiology of 'rum fits' and delirium tremens, *Quart. J. Stud. Alc.* **16**:1–33 (1955).

H. Isbell, C. W. Gorodetzky, D. Jasinski, U. Claussen, F. von Spulak, and F. Korte, Effects of $(-) \Delta^9$-Trans-tetrahydrocannabinol in man, *Psychopharmocologia* **11**:184–188 (1967*a*).

H. Isbell, D. R. Jasinski, C. W. Dorodetzky, F. Korte, U. Claussen, M. Haage, H. Sieper, and F. von Spulak, Studies on tetrahydrocannabinol, *Bulletin: Problems of Drug Dependence,* pp. 4832–4846 (1967*b*).

J. H. Jaffe, Cannabis (marihuana), in *The Pharmacological Basis of Therapeutics* (L. S. Goodman and A. Gilman, eds.), 3rd ed., Macmillan, New York (1965).

L. C. Johnson, Physiological and psychological changes following total sleep deprivation, in *Sleep: Physiology and Pathology* (A. Kales, ed.), pp. 206–220, J. B. Lippincott Company, Philadelphia, Pennsylvania (1969).

R. D. Johnson, Medico-social aspects of marijuana, *R. I. Med. J.* **51**:171–178 (1968).

S. Johnson and E. F. Domino, Some cardiovascular effects of marihuana smoking in normal volunteers, *Clin. Pharm. Therap.* **12**:762–768 (1971).

R. T. Jones and G. C. Stone, Psychological studies of marihuana and alcohol in man, Paper read at 125th Annual Meeting of the American Psychiatric Association, Bal Harbour, Florida (1969).

E. Josephson, P. Haberman, A. Zares, and J. Ellinson, Adolescent marihuana use: Report on a national survey, Paper read at 1st International Conference on Student Drug Surveys, New Jersey College of Medicine and Dentistry, Newark, New Jersey (1971).

A. Kales, E. J. Malmstrom. M. B. Scharf, and R. T. Rubin, Psychophysiological and biochemical changes following use and withdrawal of hypnotics, in *Sleep: Physiology and Pathology* (A. Kales, ed.), pp. 331–343, J. B. Lippincott Company, Philadelphia, Pennsylvania (1969).

F. Kant, Uber reaktionsformen im giftrausch: Mit einem beitrag zum halluzinationsproblem, *Archive fur Psychiatrie und Nervenkrankheiten* **91**:694–721 (1930).

J. Kaplan, *Marijuana—The New Prohibition,* World Publishing Company, New York (1969).

P. V. Karpovich, *Physiology of Muscular Activity,* W. B. Saunders Company, Philadelphia, Pennsylvania (1959).

M. M. Katz, I. E. Waskow, and J. Olsson, Characterizing the psychological state produced by LSD, *J. Abnorm. Psychol.* **73**:1–14 (1968).

H. Kaufman, Definitions and methodology in the study of aggression, *Psychol. Bull.* **64**:351–364 (1965).

D. C. Kay, R. B. Eisenstein, and D. R. Jaskinski, Morphine effects on human REM state, waking state, and NREM sleep, *Psychopharmacologia* **14**:404–416 (1969).

M. H. Keeler, Motivation for marihuana use: A correlate of adverse reaction. *Am. J. Psychiat.* **125**:386–393 (1968).

F. W. King, Marihuana and LSD usage among male college students: Prevalence rate, frequency and self-estimates of future use, *Psychiatry* **32**:265–276 (1969).

J. B. Knowles, S. G. Laverty, and H. A. Kuechler, Effects of alcohol on REM sleep, *Quart. J. Stud. Alc.* **29**:342–349 (1968).

R. C. Kory, R. Callahan, H. G. Boren, and J. C. Snyder, The Veterans Administration–Army cooperative study of pulmonary function, *Am. J. Med.* **30**:243–258 (1961).

M. Lavenhar, A survey of drug abuse in six suburban New Jersey high schools, Paper read at 1st International Conference on Student Drug Surveys, New Jersey College of Medicine and Dentistry, Newark, New Jersey (1971).

L. Lemberger, R. B. Silberstein, J. Axelrod, and I. J. Kopin, Marihuana: Studies on the disposition and metabolism of delta 9 tetrahydrocannabinol in man, *Science* **170**:1320–1322 (1970).

M. R. Lipp, Marihuana use by medical students, *Am. J. Psychiat.* **128**:207–212 (1971).

G. Mandler, Emotion, in *New Directions in Psychology* (R. Brown, E. Galanter, E. H. Hess, and G. Mandler, eds.), pp. 267–343, Holt, Rinehart, and Winston, Inc., New York (1962).

D. F. Manheimer, G. D. Mellinger, and M. B. Bolter, Marihuana use among urban adults, *Science* **166**:1544–1545 (1969).

P. E. G. Mann, A. B. Cohen, T. N. Finley, and A. J. Ladman, Alveolar macrophages: Structural and functional differences between non-smokers and smokers of marihuana and tobacco, *Lab. Invest.* **25**:111–120 (1971).

J. B. Mattison, Cannabis indica as an anodyne and hypnotic, *St. Louis Med. Surg. J.* **61**:265–271 (1891).

Mayor's Committee on Marihuana, *The Marihuana Problem in the City of New York*, Jacques Cattell Press, Lancaster, Pennsylvania (1944).

W. H. McGlothlin, The use of cannabis: East and west, in *Biochemical and Pharmacological Aspects of Dependence and Reports on Marihuana Research* (H. M. Van Praag, ed.), pp. 167–193, DeGruen F. Bohn, N.V., Haarlem, Netherlands (1972).

W. H. McGlothlin and L. J. West, The marihuana problem: An overview. *Am. J. Psychiat.* **125**:126–134, 370–378 (1968).

W. H. McGlothlin, D. O. Arnold, and P. K. Rowan, Marihuana use among adults, *Psychiatry* **33**:433–443 (1970).

W. M. McIsaac, G. E. Fritchie, H. Idanpaam, J. E. Heikkila, and L. F. Engler, Distribution of marihuana in monkey brain and concomitant behavioral effects, *Nature* **230**:593–594 (1971).

D. E. McMillan, L. S. Harris, J. M. Frankenheim, and J. S. Kennedy, Delta-9-trans-tetrahydrocannabinol in pigeons: Tolerance to the behavioral effects, *Science* **169**:501–503 (1970).

A. M. Meerlo, Variable tolerance for alcohol, *J. Nerv. Ment. Dis.* **105**:59–598 (1947).

F. T. Melges, J. R. Tinklenberg, L. E. Hollister, and H. K. Gillespie, Temporal disintegration and depersonalization during marihuana intoxication, *Arch. Gen. Psychiat.* **23**:204–210 (1970*a*).

F. T. Melges, J. R. Tinklenberg, L. E. Hollister, and H. K. Gillespie, Marihuana and temporal disintegration, *Science* **168**:1118–1120 (1970*b*).

N. K. Mello and J. H. Mendelson, Experimentally induced intoxication in alcoholics: A comparison between programmed and spontaneous drinking, *J. Pharm. Exp. Therap.* **173**:101–116 (1970*a*).

N. K. Mello and J. H. Mendelson, Behavioral studies of sleep patterns in alcoholics during intoxication and withdrawal, *J. Pharm. Exp. Therap.* **175**:94–112 (1970*b*).

N. K. Mello and J. H. Mendelson, Drinking patterns during work-contingent and non-contingent alcohol acquisition, *Psychosom. Med.* **34**:139–164 (1972).

J. H. Mendelson, ed., Experimentally induced chronic intoxication and withdrawal in alcoholics, *Quart. J. Stud. Alc.*, suppl. 2 (1964).

J. H. Mendelson and N. K. Mello, Experimental analysis of drinking behavior of chronic alcoholics, *Ann. N.Y. Acad. Sci.* **133**:828–845 (1966).

J. H. Mendelson and S. Stein, Serum cortisol levels in alcoholic and nonalcoholic subjects during experimentally induced ethanol intoxication, *Psychosom. Med.* **27**:616–626 (1966).

R. E. Meyer, R. C. Pillard, L. M. Shapiro, and S. M. Mirin, Administration of marihuana to heavy and casual marihuana users, *Am. J. Psychiat.* **128**:198–204 (1971).

S. M. Mirin, L. M. Shapiro, R. E. Meyer, R. C. Pillard, and S. Fisher, Casual versus heavy use marihuana: A redefinition of the marihuana problem, *Am. J. Psychiat.* **127**:1134–1140 (1971).

G. L. Mizner, J. T. Barter, and P. H. Werme, Patterns of drug use among college students, *Am. J. Psychiat.* **127**:55–64 (1970).

R. R. M'Meens, Report of the committee on cannabis indica, in *Transactions of the Fifteenth Annual Meeting of the Ohio State Medical Society* Vol. 15 pp. 75–100 (1860).

C. Morris and L. V. Jones, Value scales and dimensions, *J. Abnorm. Soc. Psychol.* **51**:523–535 (1955).

F. A. Mosher and J. R. Hornsby, On asking questions, in *Studies in Cognitive Growth* (J. S. Bruner, R. R. Oliver, P. M. Greenfield *et al.*, eds.), pp. 86–102, John Wiley and Sons, New York (1956).

H. B. M. Murphy, The cannabis habit: A review of the recent literature, *Addictions* **13**:3–25 (1966).

P. E. Nathan, N. A. Titler, L. M. Lowenstein, P. Solomon, and A. M. Rossi, Behavioral analysis of chronic alcoholism, *Arch. Gen. Psychiat.* **22**:419–430 (1970).

National Commission on Marihuana and Drug Abuse, *Marihuana: A Signal of Misunderstanding*, U. S. Government Printing Office, Washington, D.C. (1972*a*).

National Commission on Marihuana and Drug Abuse, *Marihuana: A Signal of Misunderstanding*, Appendix Vol. 1: *The Technical Papers*, pp. 311–329, U.S. Government Printing Office, Washington, D.C. (1972*b*).

M. T. Orne, On the social psychology of the psychological experiment with particular reference to demand characteristics and their implications, *Am. Psychologist* **17**:776–783 (1962).

I. Oswald, R. J. Berger, R. A. Jaramillo, K. G. M. Keddie, P. C. Olley, and G. M. Plunkett, Melancholia and barbiturates: A controlled EEG, body and eye movement study of sleep, *Brit. J. Psychiat.* **109**:66–78 (1963).

W. Oursler, *Marihuana: The Facts, the Truth*, Paul S. Eriksson, New York (1968).

J. M. Peters and B. G. Ferris, Smoking, pulmonary function, and respiratory symptoms in a college-age group, *Amer. Rev. Resp. Dis.* **95**:774–782 (1967).

R. C. Pillard, Marihuana, *N.E.J.M.* **283**:294–303 (1970).

R. T. Pivak, V. Zarcone, W. C. Dement, and L. E. Hollister, Delta-9 tetrahydrocannabinol and synhexyl: Effects on human sleep patterns. *Clin. Pharm. Therap.* **3**:426–435 (1972).

D. A. Pond, Psychological effects in depressive patients of the marihuana homologue synhexyl, *J. Neurol. Neurosurg. Psychiat.* **11**:271–279 (1948).

A. Raskin, J. Schulterbrandt, and Reatig, Factors of psychopathology in interview, ward behavior, and self-report ratings of hospitalized depressives, *J. Consult. Psychol.* **31**:270–278 (1967).

P. F. Renault, C. R. Schuster, R. Heinrich, and D. X. Freedman, Marihuana: Standardized smoke administration and dose effect curves on heart rate in humans, *Science* **174**:589–591 (1971).

J. R. Reynolds, Therapeutic uses and toxic effects of cannabis indica, *Lancet* **1**:637–638 (1890).

E. S. Robbins, W. Robbins, A. Frosch, and M. Stern, College student drug use, *Am. J. Psychiat.* **126**:1743–1751 (1970).

E. Rodin and E. F. Domino, Effects of acute marihuana smoking in the electroencephalogram, *Electroencephalography and Clinical Neurophysiology* **29**:321 (1970).

R. Rosenthal, *Experimenter Effects in Behavioral Research*, Appleton-Century Crofts, New York (1966).

S. Schachter, Deviation, rejection, and communication, *J. Abnorm. Soc. Psychol.* **46**:190–207 (1951).

S. Schacter and J. E. Singer, Cognitive, social, and physiological determinants of emotional state, *Psych. Rev.* **69**:379–399 (1962).

C. J. Schwartz, Toward a medical understanding of marihuana, *Canad. Psychiat. Assoc. J.* **14**:591–600 (1969).

W. A. Scott, Reliability of content analysis: The case of nominal scale coding, *Pub. Opin. Quart.* **19**:321–325 (1955).

S. K. Sharpless, Reorganization of function in the nervous system—Use and disuse, *Physiology* **26**:357–388 (1964).

J. F. Siler, W. L. Sheep, L. B. Bates, G. F. Clark, G. W. Cook, and W. A. Smith, Marihuana smoking in Panama, *Milit. Surg.* **73**:269–280 (1933).

R. G. Smart, Relationships between parental and adolescent drug use, Paper read at Annual Meeting of the Eastern Psychological Association, New York, New York (1970).

D. E. Smith and C. Mehl, An analysis of marijuana toxicity, in *The New Social Drug: Cultural, Medical, and Legal Perspectives on Marijuana* (D. E. Smith, ed.), pp. 63–77, Prentice-Hall, Englewood Cliffs, New Jersey (1970).

G. M. Smith, Personal communication (1970).

F. Snyder and J. Scott, Psychophysiology of sleep, in *Psychophysiology* (N. Greenfield and R. Sternbach, eds.), Holt, Rinehart and Winston, Inc., New York (1970).

S. H. Snyder, *Uses of Marijuana*, Oxford University Press, New York (1971)

J. Sterne and C. Ducastaing, Les arterites du cannabis indica, *Arch. des Mal. Coeur* **53**:143–147 (1960).

S. A. Stouffer and J. Toby, Role conflict and personality, in *Toward a General Theory of Action* (T. Parsons and E. A. Shils, eds.), pp. 481–494, Harvard University Press, Cambridge, Massachusetts (1951).

E. A. Suchman, The hang-loose ethic and the spirit of drug use, *J. Health Soc. Behav.* **9**:146–155 (1968).

J. S. Tamerin, S. Weiner, and J. H. Mendelson, Alcoholics' expectancies recall of experiences during intoxication, *Am. J. Psychiat.* **126**:1697–1704 (1970).

C. Tart, *On Being Stoned: A Psychological Study of Marijuana Intoxication*, Science and Behavior Books, Palo Alto, California (1971).

D. P. Tashkin, B. J. Shapiro, and I. M. Frank, Acute pulmonary physiologic effects of smoked marihuana and oral delta-9-tetrahydrocannabinol in healthy young men, *N.E.J.M.* **289**:336–341 (1973).

F. S. Tennant, Jr., M. Preble, T. J. Prendergast, and P. Ventry, Medical manifestations associated with hashish, *J.A.M.A.* **216**:1965–1969 (1971).

J. R. Tinklenberg, F. T. Melges, L. E. Hollister, and H. K. Gillespie, Marihuana and immediate memory, *Nature* **226**:1171–1172 (1970).

L. Vachon, M. X. Fitzgerald, N. H. Solliday, I. A. Gould, and E. A. Gaensler, Single dose effect of marihuana smoke—Bronchial dynamics and respiratory center sensitivity in normal subjects, *N.E.J.M.* **288**:985–989 (1973).

J. R. Valle, J. A. Souza, and N. Hyppolito, Rabbit reactivity to cannabis preparations, pyrahexyl, and tetrahydrocannabinol, *J. Pharm. Pharmac.* **18**:476 (1966).

G. B. Wallace, Summary, in *The Marihuana Problem in the City of New York 1944*, Mayor's Committee on Marihuana, as quoted in *The Marihuana Papers* (D. Solomon, ed.), pp. 354–360, Bobbs-Merrill Company, New York (1966).

P. A. Walters, G. W. Goethals, and H. G. Pope, Drug use and life style among 500 college undergraduates, *Arch. Gen. Psychiat.* **26**:92–96 (1972).

R. P. Walton, *Marihuana, American's New Drug Problem*, J. B. Lippincott, Philadelphia (1938).

I. E. Waskow, J. E. Olsson, C. Satzman, and M. Katz, Psychological effects of tetrahydrocannabinol, *Arch. Gen. Psychiat.* **22**:97–107 (1970).

W. B. Webb, Partial and differential sleep deprivation, in *Sleep: Physiology and Pathology* (A. Kales, ed.), pp. 221–231, J. B. Lippincott Company, Philadelphia (1969).

A. Weil and N. E. Zinberg, Acute effects of marihuana on speech, *Nature* **222**:434–437 (1969).

A. Weil, N. E. Zinberg, and J. M. Nelson, Clinical and psychological effects of marihuana use in man, *Science* **162**:1234–1242 (1968).

E. G. Williams, C. K. Himmelsbach, A. Wikler, D. C. Ruble, and B. J. Lloyd, Studies on marihuana and pyrahexyl compound, *Pub. Health Rep.* **61**:1059–1083 (1946).

J. R. Young, Blood alcohol concentration and reaction time, *Quart. J. Stud. Alc.* **31**:828–831 (1970).

Index

63256